BLOOD

Famed for its nationw... ... and punishment, *Court TV* ... source for the most up-to-date, in-depth, on-the-scene true crime reporting. Now, for the millions of fans of the acclaimed series, *Crime Stories*, comes the shocking facts about today's most sensational trials.

VAMPIRE MURDERER—Eustis, Florida, teenager Rod Ferrell fancied himself a vampire. The brutal bludgeoning to death of his girlfriend's parents made him the youngest inmate on Death Row.

TOMATO PATCH MURDER—Ludowici, Georgia, residents agreed Thurman Martin was a hard man, but did he deserve to die? Grandson Billy Crowder shot him, claiming Martin had raped his own daughter and abused him.

FATAL PASSION—Wilmington, Deleware, attorney Thomas Capano had it all, money, social position, loving family, and several mistresses. He murdered one of them, Anne Marie Fahey, and used his brother's boat to dump her body at sea. His 1998 trial scandalized the town.

With 16 pages of exclusive photos
provided by *Court TV!*

BOOK YOUR PLACE ON OUR WEBSITE AND MAKE THE READING CONNECTION!

We've created a customized website just for our very special readers, where you can get the inside scoop on everything that's going on with Zebra, Pinnacle and Kensington books.

When you come online, you'll have the exciting opportunity to:

- View covers of upcoming books
- Read sample chapters
- Learn about our future publishing schedule (listed by publication month *and author*)
- Find out when your favorite authors will be visiting a city near you
- Search for and order backlist books from our online catalog
- Check out author bios and background information
- Send e-mail to your favorite authors
- Meet the Kensington staff online
- Join us in weekly chats with authors, readers and other guests
- Get writing guidelines
- AND MUCH MORE!

**Visit our website at
http://www.pinnaclebooks.com**

CRIME STORIES:
THE BEST OF *COURT TV*

BLOOD
AND LUST

David Jacobs

PINNACLE BOOKS
Kensington Publishing Corp.
http://www.pinnaclebooks.com

CONTENTS

Florida v. *Ferrell:* "THE BLOOD IS THE LIFE"

THE CRIME

On the night of Monday, November 25, 1996, the Lake County Florida Sheriff's Office received a desperate 911 call for help. After giving her address, a young female caller said in a rush, "My mother and father have just been killed. I don't know what's happened. I walked in the door and they are dead. I can't go in there. I'm their daughter."

The dispatcher taking the call asked, "What makes you think they're dead?"

"There is blood everywhere."

"We have a car on its way."

Riding alone on patrol, Deputy Jeff Taylor drove to the address on Greentree Lane in Eustis, a quasi-rural town about 35 miles northwest of Orlando.

Taylor was the first to respond to the crime

scene. It was a handsome piece of property, a five-acre ranchette. He pulled up on the lawn, to avoid damaging any evidence that might be on the dirt driveway. A lush green lawn led to a handsome ranch-style house, low and spacious.

He was met by the young woman who had made the call, 17-year-old Jennifer Wendorf. She seemed to be in a state of hysteria.

Taylor began an armed felony search of the residence, beginning with the garage, whose door gaped open. He searched the garage for suspects or victims, finding neither. An unlocked door provided entry into the house.

Taylor moved through the space, an adrenaline-pumping experience even for an armed and trained, professional law enforcement officer. In a kind of family room or den, he found the first victim, an adult male lying on the couch. This was Richard Wendorf, 49. As Taylor would later recall on the witness stand, "His glasses were smashed and his face looked like a hamburger."

In the hallway, the phone cord had been torn out of the wall, disabling it. Jennifer Wendorf had made the emergency call with her cell phone.

Continuing the search, Taylor next checked the bedrooms. In the master bedroom, drawers were pulled out and overturned, their contents dumped on the floor, where scattered pieces of jewelry also lay. Robbery? As for intruders or bodies, the bedrooms and bathroom were all clear.

The kitchen was not. Here he found the second victim, an adult female lying sprawled on the floor in a pool of blood. This was Naoma Ruth Wendorf, 53. In the back of her head was a hole through which her brain could be seen.

There could be no doubt both victims were dead. No one could sustain that kind of damage and live. Taylor did not touch either of them, nor did he step on areas of tile and carpet that might contain valuable traces of evidence. From the moment he had first arrived on the scene, he'd been careful to avoid contaminating it.

He searched quickly, then got out quickly.

A veteran Florida law enforcement officer since 1993, this was his first homicide. The way the victims had been slaughtered was beyond overkill. It was a scene out of a horror movie, a bloodbath.

Jennifer Wendorf was able to ID at least two items that were definitely missing from the house: the Wendorfs' blue Ford Explorer; and their 15-year-old daughter (and Jennifer's sister), Heather.

EMS paramedics arrived. Although certain that the victims were dead, Taylor had the paramedics enter and verify that they were indeed deceased. All were careful to avoid contaminating the scene.

Other law enforcement officers began arriving, many of them.

Taylor then put out a BOLO (Be On the Look Out) advisory regarding the blue Ford Explorer and Heather Wendorf, stating that the juvenile was possibly endangered.

Not long afterward, Jennifer Wendorf was interviewed by Lake County Detective Al Gussler, who asked her about her missing sister's friends and associates. That was the first time Gussler ever heard the name "Rod Ferrell."

Further information was provided by Suzanne LeClaire, a Eustis High School teacher and the mother of two teenage daughters, one of whom, Jeanine, had been Heather Wendorf's best friend on and off through the years. Suzanne herself was acquainted with the Wendorfs.

Earlier that night, Jeanine had told Suzanne that Heather was talking about running away. Suzanne had phoned the Wendorfs to warn them, but the operator said that their phone was out of service. She got in her car and drove to the Wendorfs', only to see flashing lights, police cars, uniformed and plainclothes officers, an EMS ambulance, and a gathering crowd of the curious.

She communicated her information to a police officer, who told her that he'd like to speak to her daughter. Suzanne went home to get Jeanine. It wasn't until later that she learned that the Wendorfs had been murdered.

Once again, Rod Ferrell's name came up. He was Jeanine LeClaire's ex-boyfriend. The now 16-year-old Ferrell had formerly lived in Eustis, moving away a year ago with his guardian and mother, single parent Sondra Gibson, relocating in Murray, Kentucky. Only a day or two ago, Ferrell and three of his Murray friends had resurfaced in Eustis, driving a red car. The others were one male and two females: Scott Anderson, 16; Charity Keesee; and Dana Cooper.

The foursome said they were just passing through on their way to New Orleans. Jeanine LeClaire and Heather Wendorf were thinking of possibly running away with them. It was something the two Eustis teens had talked about, both with each other and the charismatic Rod Ferrell, with whom Heather especially had racked up endless hours of phone chats between home and Murray. The plans had been in the talking stage for a long time, but Rod Ferrell and company had suddenly shown up without warning, Ferrell telling them that if they wanted to go, it had to be now.

Suzanne knew Rod Ferrell and didn't like him. She hadn't known he was in town. Trying to piece together a profile of Ferrell, detectives got a picture of a "spooky" individual with dyed-black long hair, black fingernails, and all-black clothes. His persona seemed to possess more than a whiff of the dark side: occultism, satanism, who knew what else. Just the sort to warm the hearts of the parents of a teenage daughter.

With this information, the Lake County sleuths contacted the Calloway County, Kentucky, Sheriff's Department, in whose jurisdiction Murray lay. Rod Ferrell was no stranger to them. He'd had some minor scrapes with the law before. In fact he was due in court that very day to face charges that were not so minor, namely that he had broken into an animal shelter and sadistically tortured and killed some puppies.

It was early in the investigation, but more and more Rod Ferrell and company were looking like a pretty good fit for prime suspects. But this was more than an investigation—it was an active, ongoing manhunt. What had happened to Heather Wendorf? Was she dead, too, her body stuffed in a culvert or hidden in a thicket of roadside brush? Or was she still alive? If so, was she a kidnapping victim, held against her will? Or had she actually conspired in the death of her parents, even taking part in the killings?

With at least two humans that the police knew of sadistically slaughtered, how soon before the perps would kill again? Would they target strangers, or one of their own?

No possibility was too macabre, too far-fetched to consider, not with a gruesome double homicide on their hands. And not with what they were learning about the elusive, eccentric Mr. Ferrell.

After consulting with the sheriff in Murray, Lake County police had reason to believe that Rod Ferrell and his friends might try to return to that town. Detective Al Gussler pointed a car toward Murray and started driving northward.

But the next lead came from a different direction.

Deputy Sheriff Charles Frazier of Seminole County, Florida, came in contact with an abandoned red vehicle on the evening of November 26. It was called in, and he went out and saw it, an abandoned Buick Skyhawk with no keys and Florida plates. Frazier called in the plate number and it matched the Wendorfs' Ford Explorer, not the red car. When he ran the vehicle ID number (VIN), he learned that it belonged to a car from Kentucky. On the radio he got the BOLO for a red car from Kentucky. He called Lake County police, who took the vehicle back with them.

It was an old car-theft trick, Car Theft 101, switching license plates to create confusion and lay down a smokescreen. In this case, however, even the switched plates pointed a finger at the perps, trailing right back to their doorstep.

On November 27, the Lake County Sheriff's Office investigators quickly learned that the red Buick was registered to Howard Anderson of Kentucky, but driven by his wife, the mother of Scott Anderson, the other male in the Murray clique.

There was more. A few days earlier in Murray, when he supposed to pick up his brothers and give them a ride home, Scott Anderson, accompanied by Rod Ferrell and the two females, had told his brothers to say that they had been kidnapped by Jaden Steven Murphy.

Jaden Steven Murphy was another personality well known to Calloway County law enforcement. Murphy, age 18, was the leader of a local "vampire clan," a mixed group of local black-clad outcasts who favored body-piercing, self-mutilation, blood-drinking, and nocturnal get-togethers in the cemetery. Baptizing himself in blood, he had christened himself with the vampire name "Jaden." His few brushes with the law had been minor infractions, but given his colorful public persona in a dry (i.e., no liquor) church-ridden town, he made a memorable impression.

Rod Ferrell, another member of the clan, was Jaden's onetime best friend. It was Jaden who, by sharing blood with Rod in a graveyard at night, had "crossed him over" into vampirism. In the argot of the blood-drinkers, Jaden was Rod's "sire," christening him with the vampire name "Vesago."

But the two had had a falling-out, caused in no small part by Rod's having picked up a cat and brained it against a tree. The hostilities culminated in a brawl between the two in which Jaden, the over-18 adult, had been arrested and put in jail. Since then, there had been "bad blood" between Ferrell and his "sire." Murphy had been in jail when the animal shelter atrocities had taken place.

The night before leaving Murray, Ferrell and Scott Anderson, also known by his vampire name "Nosferatu," his friend since second grade and slavish follower, had had a public beef with Jaden Murphy and his clique at a fast-food joint.

The next lead came courtesy of a stolen Discover card, which was used on Tuesday, November 26, at a Wal-Mart and a gas station. The name signed on the Wal-Mart receipt was "Richard Wendorf."

The net spread, reaching out across the South, from the border state of Kentucky to the Gulf Coast.

Then came the break that busted the case wide open.

On Thanksgiving Day, Florida police received a phone call from the grandmother of one of the suspects, saying that the kids would be staying at a Baton Rouge motel, but she didn't know which one.

Baton Rouge Police Department Detective Dennis Moran was on duty at headquarters when he got a call from Florida regarding the BOLO on the missing vehicle and suspects. Uniformed officers were sent to local hotels and motels to look for a 1993 blue Ford Explorer.

Baton Rouge police officer James Welbourne was on uniformed patrol when he received the BOLO on a blue Ford Explorer with out-of-state plates, wanted in connection with a Florida double homicide. Five Caucasians were believed to be in the vehicle.

Welbourne and three other officers met outside a downtown hotel, formerly a Howard Johnson's but now called the All-Around Suites, to discuss a plan of action. Other police officers had already patrolled the parking lot of the hotel, but not found anything yet. They split up and other officers went to the front of the building, checking that area, leaving Welbourne alone.

At that point, while the other officers were gone, Welbourne saw a vehicle pull into the parking lot. It stood out because of its color, a kind of bright blue or aqua. Confirming the spotting via the radio mike on his shoulder, he said there were five Caucasians in the blue Explorer.

The vehicle backed into the north parking lot. As Welbourne pulled up alongside it, two females got out and walked to the front of the hotel where the other police officers were. There were two males, toward the driver's side, and a female in the car, whose door was open.

It was a ticklish situation. Welbourne was in a marked unit in full uniform. Calling for backup, he approached the suspects. They definitely saw his car—there were only two vehicles in the area.

Bracing the suspects, Welbourne stood facing them, firm, yet not menacing. They were

Rod Ferrell, Scott Anderson, and Heather Wendorf.

Welbourne was familiar with the demeanor of people under the influence of alcohol or other substances. Rod Ferrell did not appear to be under the influence of any substance, but seemed to be in control. The other male and female seemed nervous. Heather was standing by the vehicle. She'd been the one driving when the Explorer had rolled in.

Welbourne would later testify: "From my observations, Ferrell appeared to be the one in control, the one the others looked to for guidance because they were scared. In fact, Rod Ferrell was intimidating—that was one reason I called for backup."

Welbourne had the three of them come around in front of the vehicle. Meanwhile, his backup had arrived. Welbourne asked the youths where they came from. Their answers were not satisfactory. He asked Heather, "Aren't your parents worried about you?" She became still more nervous. It was a warm night, but she was almost hysterical, shaking uncontrollably.

A search for weapons yielded only a knife in the possession of Scott Anderson, who was relieved of it. The suspects were taken into custody.

They were cooperative. There was no back talk, no need to use force. Rod Ferrell and Scott Anderson were put in the back of Welbourne's car. That was when he caught Ferrell doing his Svengali number, as he later testified:

"The two males were put in the backseat of my car. Heather Wendorf, the female, she kept looking towards the vehicle, I couldn't figure out what she was doing. I saw Ferrell staring at her, so I stepped between them so there wouldn't be any contact, even eye contact."

Welbourne was one smart cop.

Baton Rouge Police Department Sergeant Ben Odom, a 22-year veteran on the force, was now assigned to the Robbery/Homicide Division, where he commanded a squad of six officers. He was working the "dog shift" on Thanksgiving Day eve, five P.M. to three A.M. Notified by Detective Moran of the arrests, Odom went to the hotel.

At the scene, he ordered a canine unit to do an article search—that is, a weapons search on the Ford Explorer. Then he verbally advised each of the suspects of their rights, Mirandaizing them.

Detective Thomas Dewey, a member of Odom's squad, arrived at the hotel at approximately nine P.M., where he drew the assignment of transporting the two males back to the station. Detective Coulter was delegated to transport the girls.

In Dewey's car, Ferrell said he was glad he was caught because he had been on the road for several days. Dewey had not done anything to prompt the conversation, even advising Ferrell not to talk, because he was a juvenile. Saying he had no information on the case, the officer reminded him of his rights, which had been read to him by Odom in the parking lot of the motel.

For Dewey, it was a rough ride, as the suspects reeked with rank body odor, a fact he'd eventually testify to in court.

Odom had the Explorer towed to the evidence building, then went back to the station. Ironically, the structure had formerly housed a high school. The main squad room was a large, high-ceilinged space with lots of desks. The suspects were brought in and seated at desks, an unintentionally macabre parody of after-school detention.

As per departmental procedure, all five suspects were kept apart from each other. The girls were scattered throughout the squad room, two of them in the main office, the third in an inner room. Scott Anderson was placed in a supervisor's office, while Rod Ferrell was secured in an interior room by Detective Dewey, who took the shoestrings out of Ferrell's boots, so he couldn't hang himself with them.

Posted at a large desk in the squad room, Moran's job was to oversee the suspects, making sure that they were secure and that their needs (water, bathroom) were met.

Ferrell said that Charity Keesee, "Che" (pronounced *shay*), was his girlfriend and was two months pregnant with their child. He really wanted to be with her here, if only for a little while. He was told that could be arranged.

Dewey said Ferrell wanted to talk. Sergeant Odom worked the phones, contacting other law enforcement agencies. The problem was that four of the suspects were juveniles, and Louisiana law prohibited interviewing juveniles without their parents or guardians being present. Florida law was different, permitting the interview of juveniles. Odom needed to sort things out with Florida authorities before talking to the suspects.

Things got sorted out. On November 29, at a few minutes past midnight, two hours after he had been brought in, Ferrell began to be interviewed by Odom. The interview was videotaped, starting with Odom once again reading Rod his Miranda rights.

Rod Ferrell talked. The story would become a twice-told tale, as developed by Ferrell in the course of his two videotaped confessions, with certain variations and hazy areas emerging:

On November 22–23, 1996 (late Friday/early Saturday), Rod Ferrell, Charity Keesee, Scott Anderson, and Dana Cooper left Murray in Anderson's red Buick Skyhawk. They drove to Florida to get Jeanine LeClaire and Heather Wendorf as Ferrell had discussed with them

numerous times on the phone over the course
of the previous year.

Arriving in Eustis on Sunday, Ferrell looked
up several old friends, visiting Audrey Presson,
Jeanine LeClaire, and Shannon Yohe. That
evening, Rod had a phone conversation with
Heather.

On Monday, Ferrell met Wendorf at Eustis
High School. The gang of five went to a local
Wal-Mart and bought some razor blades. Then
they went to the cemetery near the school
where Rod initiated the crossing over of
Heather. He cut her arm with a razor blade
and drank her blood. He was bladed and she
drank his blood. All five suspects were found
to have razor-blade cuts on their forearms,
some fresh, some not so fresh. These were
photographed by the Baton Rouge police.

Again, that brought in the whole vampire
element. In Kentucky, Murphy had been Ferrell's sire. Now, in Eustis, Ferrell had become
the sire of Wendorf, or "Zoey," the clique
name she preferred to go by.

Later that same day, Ferrell and the others
from Murray were questioned by police briefly
after the car got a flat tire. Ferrell, spooked,
decided to push his schedule ahead, leaving
town on Monday night. The Murray foursome
returned to Shannon Yohe's home to phone
Jeanine LeClaire and Heather Wendorf to tell
them of the change in plans.

At this time, Rod Ferrell allegedly discussed
with the group, in Shannon Yohe's presence,

a plan to kill the Wendorfs and take their Ford
Explorer.

Ferrell said that he spoke to Heather by
phone, drew a map to her house from her directions, and exited Shannon Yohe's residence.

The group arrived at the area of the Wendorf residence and met Heather down the
road from her home. Ferrell sent the three
girls away, to visit Heather's boyfriend and pick
up Jeanine LeClaire. Rod Ferrell and Scott Anderson stayed behind to burglarize the home,
take money and the vehicle, and to kill the
Wendorfs. Ferrell said that the girls were unaware of their plans.

Now carrying clubs, Ferrell and Anderson
looked for access to the property. They entered the home via an unlocked garage entry-
way door and searched the garage to find
better weapons. Ferrell armed himself with a
crowbar. They entered the house and Ferrell
ripped the phone cord from the wall.

Richard Wendorf, sleeping on the family
room sofa, was the first victim. Beaten by Rod
Ferrell in the head multiple times with the
crowbar, he sustained extensive wounds, some
of which fractured his skull, causing his death.
He also suffered multiple chest wounds with
fractured ribs on his right side.

Naoma Wendorf came from the bathroom
to the kitchen, where she confronted Ferrell.
He had blood on his clothes and was carrying
the bloody crowbar. She threw hot coffee on
him, scratched his face, and put up a hell of

a fight until she was knocked down to the floor and her head was beaten in.

Afterward, Ferrell and Anderson searched the house for valuables, money, and keys. A Discover card was taken from Richard Wendorf's corpse, and the duo exited the scene in the Wendorfs' Ford Explorer.

They met up with Dana Cooper, Charity Keesee, and Heather Wendorf in the Buick Skyhawk as the girls returned to Heather's home. Rod Ferrell maintained that the girls knew nothing of the murder plans.

The group left Eustis in both vehicles, traveling in a two-car caravan to Sanford, Florida, east of Eustis, where they abandoned the Buick. The license plates were switched so the Buick had Florida plates and the Ford Explorer had Kentucky plates.

The Explorer drove west, its ultimate destination New Orleans. Somewhere, a couple hundred miles down the road, Heather learned of her parents' death. The blue Ford SUV rolled along I-10 through Tallahassee and Crestview, Florida, where the Discover card was used to buy gas and a knife from Wal-Mart.

When they finally reached New Orleans, all was not paradise. According to Ferrell, the sight of "blacks walking around in their back-yards with AK-47s [assault rifles]" so freaked out Charity Keesee, unused to the big city, that the group moved on to Baton Rouge. However, the group did not follow through on their half-baked plan to seek out best-selling author Anne Rice of *Interview with a Vampire* fame.

In Baton Rouge, Rod, against his "better judgment," had allowed Charity Keesee to make a phone call to her grandmother, during which she said that the group would be staying in one of the city's motels.

The woman in turn had notified Eustis law enforcement, who passed on the information to the BRPD, with the result that all five had been collared in the hotel parking lot.

Rod Ferrell was nonchalant about how he had gone about committing these murders. He bragged about how he was the strongest one and how the others looked up to him.

During this time, Thanksgiving Day and the morning after, the detectives observed Ferrell's behavior both inside and outside the interview room. They allowed him to see his girlfriend in one of the inner rooms while they watched from a videotape monitor outside. Ferrell and Charity Keesee made out, hugging and kissing during their hour together. The interlude was videotaped by the cops.

The teens breakfasted on fast food from McDonald's, where the police had an account. In the afternoon, they were transferred to the juvenile detention center. Moran and Odom transferred Ferrell and Anderson, while another pair transported the girls. They checked in the prisoners and confiscated their clothes, placing them in plastic bags.

Meanwhile, the roundabout odyssey of LCSD Detective Al Gussler had finally brought him within reach of his quarry. The well-intentioned but wrong-way lead which had sent him toward Murray had taken him as far as Atlanta, Georgia, before he was beeped by his own department and advised that the suspects had been spotted in Baton Rouge. Leaving Atlanta on November 28 in late afternoon, he arrived in Baton Rouge at 6:30 the next morning. He checked into a hotel, showered and, still sleepless, made his way to the BRPD.

In an interview room, Gussler and his Lake County colleague Sergeant Wayne Longo interrogated Rod Ferrell for his second videotaped confession. The session began at 5:30 P.M., with Gussler Mirandaizing Ferrell yet again, reading him his rights off a card. Rod cockily recited them along with the detective, who had to tell him to be quiet.

Ferrell retold his tale with some variations, the session ending about an hour after it had started. He was in shackles and asked why he had to be in restraints, when he was cooperating. The Lake County detectives told him that it was standard Baton Rouge police procedure and they had to play by the local rules. Ferrell seemed to accept that.

Later, he and the others were transported back to Florida, to Tavares in Lake County. Rod Ferrell, Dana Cooper, Scott Anderson, and Heather Wendorf were arrested and charged with murder for the deaths of the Wendorfs. Charity Keesee was charged with being an accessory to murder after the fact.

Detective Al Gussler was present to preserve the integrity of the unbroken chain of evidence when blood samples were taken from Ferrell upon his return.

From the time of his arrest, Rad Ferrell maintained a plea of not guilty. He tried out a couple of alternate versions of his story, at one time saying that his lifelong buddy Scott Anderson was the real killer, and that he had taken the rap out of misplaced loyalty to "his people." Another variant was that the killings had been done by a "rival vampire gang" that wanted to frame him.

More and more, though, he was trying to hang it on Heather Wendorf, claiming that during their countless hours of phone calls between Murray and Eustis, she had constantly complained of parental abuse, expressing the wish time and again that her parents would die. Ferrell maintained that while she had never actually come out and solicited him to kill them, she had hinted around it, planting "subliminal" clues and signposts that would naturally induce a chivalrous lad such as himself to rush to help a damsel in distress.

Heather Wendorf said that not only had she known nothing of the murder plans, but that she didn't even know about the planned car theft until Rod and Scott had pulled up to the meeting place in the Ford Explorer.

Meanwhile, Ferrell remained in the lockup. Even if bail money could have been raised, the question was academic. There was no bail in this capital murder case. For a year, Ferrell was held in the Marion Juvenile Detention Facility in Ocala, Florida.

That was where he first met his court-appointed lawyer, Assistant Public Defender Candace Hawthorne. She and her associates, Assistant Public Defenders Bill Lackay and David Norris, would try to save Rod's life. The State was going to demand the death penalty.

On December 17, 1996, Rod Ferrell and Scott Anderson were indicted by a grand jury.

Though the State did indeed present a case against her, on January 28, 1997 the grand jury declined to indict Heather Wendorf, issuing this statement:

"While she certainly acted inappropriately in planning to leave home and arguably so in remaining with the others after learning what had been done, we acknowledge that these acts are not crimes. We also wish to unequivocally state that these actions were wrong. Heather Wendorf, her sister, and the families of both Richard Wendorf and Naoma Ruth Wendorf will live the rest of their lives with the consequences of Heather's choice of associates and activities. Nothing that anyone can say or do will change the loss they have suf-

fered. We wish them God's mercy and grace
in the recovery that must follow."

Brad King, the elected state attorney for the
Fifth Judicial Circuit of the State of Florida,
was in charge of the prosecution. In early
1997, he was approached by Rod Ferrell's attorneys with a plea bargain for a sentence of
four consecutive life sentences, to run consecutively. That offer was not accepted by the State.

THE TRIAL

Change of Plea

The trial was scheduled to be held on February 12, 1998, at Lake County Courthouse,
Tavares, Florida, presided over by the Honorable Judge Jerry T. Lockett. Prosecuting the
case were Brad King and Assistant State Attorney Jim McCune, while the defense consisted
of Assistant Public Defenders Candace Hawthorne, Bill Lackay, and David Norris.

The charges against Rod Ferrell were one
count of armed burglary, one count of armed
robbery, and two counts of first-degree murder. Hanging over the proceedings was the
shadow of the ultimate penalty, death by execution in the electric chair.

According to Florida law, there are twelve
jurors on a capital case; a vote of six for life
and six for death was an automatic life sentence.

The insanity defense was out. Florida law stated that for the insanity defense to apply, the "person had to not know what was transpiring at the time—had a total inability to function in the environment around them and know what was going on."

That wouldn't play here, and besides, Florida juries had proven notably unsympathetic to the insanity defense in recent years. Still, the defense would try to argue a kind of temporary insanity, brought on by LSD and Ferrell's flashing back to alleged satanic ritual sex abuse which he had suffered at age five when molested by his grandfather and others.

The defense was concentrating on beating the death penalty due to mitigating factors, which they listed as the defendant's age at the time of the crime (16); use of drugs, especially LSD; and his dysfunctional family background. To this end, they had lined up three mental-health professionals as expert witnesses to establish their case: Drs. Elizabeth McMahon, Harry Krop, and Wade Meyers.

The trial would be divided into two phases—the guilt phase and the penalty phase. During the three days of jury selection and motions to suppress evidence, Rod Ferrell maintained his plea of not guilty.

Candace Hawthorne later recalled, "When we began, we entered pleas of not guilty to the charges, because we have to do the investigation—background investigation, interview witnesses, look at evidence, independently test

the evidence. . . . We knew we had significant
problems in the guilt phase. . . . Mr. Norris
and Mr. Lackay, who was co-counsel with me
and co-chaired the case, had seen Rod over
the last two weeks before trial to discuss
whether he was going to waive [the] first phase
and go straight to penalty phase."

The jury selection completed, the judge
gave the jurors preliminary instructions and
the prosecution began its opening statements.

Brad King had no sooner gotten into the
first paragraph of his opening, introducing
himself to the jurors, when the unpredictable
Rod Ferrell threw a curve ball at his own attorneys, telling them that he wanted to plead
guilty.

Candace Hawthorne commented, "I did not
know—none of us really knew—if Rod wanted
or was going to enter a plea and not go
through the guilt phase, and then I was notified. I asked him. . . . Then we stopped the
proceedings. . . . We were surprised."

Defense Attorney Bill Lackay stood up and
said, "Your Honor, Mr. Ferrell has asked us to
do something that may affect some things, so
we're asking you to excuse the jury and let us
approach the bench."

Upon clearing the courtroom of jurors, and
spectators, too, Judge Lockett was apprised
that the defendant wished to change his plea.
That being so, the first order of business was
to determine outside the presence of the jury
the factual basis for the plea.

Brad King outlined the prosecution's case. "Had we proceeded in this matter, the State would have asserted that on November 25, 1996 . . . Mr. Ferrell and Scott Anderson armed themselves with a crowbar and once inside [the house] found Richard Wendorf on the sofa and Ferrell proceeded to beat Mr. Wendorf in the head with a crowbar, inflicting twenty separate wounds to the head and face. . . .

"That after that beating, Rod Ferrell confronted Naoma Ruth Wendorf in the breakfast area of the kitchen and began to beat her. She turned and retreated through the kitchen. She fell, and he continued to beat her until he literally shattered her skull and fractured her brain stem.

"The State of Florida will show those acts were done inside the Wendorf home. Entry was made without their consent with the intent of committing murder . . . and part of that intent was to obtain keys for the Explorer, credit cards, and money. Rod Ferrell and Scott Anderson left that home in the Explorer. . . . He entered that home without their consent with the intent to perform the crime therein—which was murder.

"I believe it also proves beyond any doubt that Wendorfs' deaths occurred through the criminal acts of Rod Ferrell, which include first-degree murder and felony murder during burglary."

The judge called for Ferrell to be brought to

the podium. The Rod Ferrell who now stood before the bar was quite different from the one who had been nabbed by the Baton Rouge police in the hotel parking lot on Thanksgiving Day, 1996. Gone was the shoulder-length, black-dyed hair, black fingernails, all-black clothes, and the sneering, smirking reveling in his own badness. Now the hair had been trimmed to collar length, reverting to its natural color, a kind of brick red. He wore a dark jacket and slacks and a white dress shirt, buttoned up to the neck. His demeanor was respectful enough, his face guarded, watchful.

Bill Lackay said, "Your Honor, please the court, this is Roderick Justin Ferrell." He repeated the charges of the four-count indictment, saying that Rod had been fully informed of the possible penalties, but still wanted to withdraw his not-guilty plea on all four counts.

Lackay said, "He wishes to enter the plea set forth because he is guilty of the charges and for no other reason, is that correct?"

Ferrell said, "Yes."

"He acknowledges that no one has made any promises about possible sentences he may get as a result of this plea. . . . He has not been promised nor has it been suggested that he will be rewarded in any manner or that he will be given leniency," the judge continued.

Again, "Yes."

"He understands he is waiving the right to assert an affirmative defense; he understands counts 3 and 4 [the murder counts] will have a trial regarding the death penalty versus life without parole," Lackay said.

The judge then questioned the defendant. Had he fully discussed the case with his attorney? Did he fully understand his plea? Was he pleading guilty without reservation to robbery and murder one of Richard Wendorf and Naoma Wendorf? The pleas were being entered without duress? Did he understand the constitutional rights he was giving up?

To all of these questions, Rod Ferrell answered, "Yes."

The judge asked if he was under the influence of any drugs.

"No."

Counsel affirmed that Ferrell's attorneys felt that their client was competent and understood the plea.

The court accepted Ferrell's change of plea on all four charges, duly ajudging him guilty of one count of armed burglary, one count of armed robbery, and two counts of first-degree murder. Sentencing was deferred on all counts and the jury which had been impaneled and sworn would hear evidence regarding the penalty: specifically, whether Rod Ferrell should receive life in prison without parole or be sentenced to death in Florida's electric chair.

That settled the guilt phase of the trial, which now moved directly into the penalty phase.

* * *

In Florida, the penalty phase requires a sentencing proceeding. The jury listens to testimony regarding aggravating and mitigating circumstances and makes a recommendation to the judge on what penalty should be imposed, either death or life imprisonment. The proceeding is conducted like any other jury trial, with almost exactly the same rules of evidence. The difference is that the jury recommends a sentence as opposed to finding the defendant guilty or not guilty.

Trial Judge Jerry T. Lockett would then consider the jury's proposal and make his own determination as to Rod Ferrell's fate. He was not bound by the jury. If they voted for death, the punishment lay within his discretion, and he could conceivably hand down a life sentence instead.

It's interesting to speculate on Ferrell's motivation as regards the last-minute change of plea. In many capital cases, defendants plead guilty to receive a sentence of life without parole in unofficial return for saving the State the cost of a trial. Ferrell's lawyers had tried to plead him guilty in return for a life sentence, but the State wasn't buying. The prosecution wasn't making any deals, not with what they thought they had on Rod. Perhaps Ferrell's eleventh-hour plea change was prompted by the thought that it would buy him some small measure of goodwill from the judge or jurors or maybe both.

THE TRIAL: PENALTY PHASE

Day One

It was "All rise" when the judge entered the courtroom and took the bench. The jurors were sworn and the penalty phase began.

The judge instructed the jury. "The defendant has already pled guilty. Do not concern yourself with the issue of guilt, only sentencing. Final judgment rests with the court. You are to issue an advisory sentence, the court gives great weight to your recommendation. You will consider aggravating versus mitigating factors."

The prosecution began its opening statement. Brad King said, "Our case to you will be narrow, concise and it will focus on the circumstances surrounding the deaths of the victims. We will not focus on the vampire cult . . . but on the fact that choices were made, responsibility was taken, and decisions were made.

"You can consider that Rod Ferrell committed two separate murders, during the course of an armed robbery, for financial gain, that they were especially heinous and atrocious, they were cold, calculated, and premeditated.

"Evidence will show you that at the Wendorf home, on the eve of November 25, 1996, daughter Jennifer came home and found something startling."

He went on. "There was a 911 call to the

scene, an officer arrives. He determines that the victims were dead. The next afternoon, the medical examiner [ME] goes to the house to examine the bodies where they lay. You'll hear the ME describe the beatings that the Wendorfs sustained, and it's not going to be pretty.

"You'll also hear that in Baton Rouge, that Ferrell made two statements, to the Baton Rouge police and the Lake County sheriffs."

Brad King continued. "He details going in, finding a crowbar, then going into the house to beat sleeping Mr. Wendorf to death. Then he finds Mrs. Wendorf in the kitchen. There was a short verbal exchange. . . . She threw coffee at him, scratched his face, and he beat her with the crowbar. Then he beat her and he beat her until literally he beat her brains out, on that night in that house."

King then made a preemptive strike against the defense's triumvirate of expert witnesses, Drs. McMahon, Meyers, and Krop.

He said, "The defense will present mental and psychological evidence. I advise you to treat them as you would any other witness, listen to what they know about the facts. They are like anyone else. They come with the presumption of expertise, but listen to what they had to work with, the facts they had and I think the same is true—you put garbage in, you can't help but get garbage out. So listen to what they tell you, because that will help you in assessing their credibility. You determine what the verdict will be. You will speak truth and justice in this case."

Making the opening statement for the defense, David Norris said, "This kid pled guilty, he was sixteen years of age at the time of the offense; in Florida anyone under sixteen is not an adult. Age will be a factor here. He grew up in west Florida. We'll also talk about how Rod Ferrell got involved in some of these vampire games . . . they almost consumed his life. His fantasy subsumed his real life because that life was so painful. You'll hear about that.

"You'll hear from his mother, from doctors, school records so you will see how the doctors came to their decisions. You'll hear a lot of evidence about how he was abused as a child, exposed to fantasy games, abandoned by his father at a very young age.

"You'll be asked to give Rod life, because that's what he wants. You'll hear he was born with a cord around his neck, sufferered encephalitis as a child, head traumas; abused alcohol, Prozac and marijuana as a teenager. He doesn't deny that.

"Doctors will tell you he suffers from schizotypal disorder. You'll hear that this was a contributing factor to the events committed on November 25, 1996.

"You'll hear all this mitigation. One way you'll know about events is Rod admitted last week in court that he did it. He also cooperated with Baton Rouge and local law officers. . . .

"We believe he should be sentenced to life twice, with no possibility of parole. Thank you."

Both the prosecution and defense had laid out their strategies, telling the jury what they intended to prove in court. Now the contest was joined.

The prosecution called as its first witness Deputy Jeff Taylor, the Lake County lawman who'd been the first to respond to the crime scene. He told of finding the victims in the house and putting out the BOLO on the Ford Explorer.

The defense's cross-examination was perfunctory. There was no real disputing the physical facts of the crimes to which their client had already pled guilty, though there might be some advantage in shading certain fine points about the slayings in hope that it would win Rod some small gains on the benefit-of-the-doubt side of the ledger.

After the witness stepped down, Rod doodled on a yellow legal pad during the break.

Next called was Farley Caudil, a crime-scene technician in the county office. Brad King handled the direct, which started out quietly enough, but soon developed into a lively skirmish with the defense.

Caudil qualified as an expert witness. He said that he responded to a possible homicide with another technician, Jean Cushing, arriving at the scene about 11:45 A.M. They were occupied with evidence gathering outside the house until about 4:10 P.M. Before entering, the two donned white biohazard suits with attached shoes and hoods, also using gloves and face masks.

Caudil entered through the left side of the house, through a small utility room door which led to the family room. The lamp and TV set were still on. Richard Wendorf lay on the sofa on his back. Naoma Wendorf's body was on far side of the kitchen on the floor.

The prosecution moved to have photos of the crime scene entered into the record, prompting an objection from Defense Attorney David Norris, who argued that the photos would be prejudicial. The judge overruled the objection and the photos were entered into evidence.

It was time for a lunch break. Rod Ferrell held up his hands to be cuffed and was led out of the courtroom.

After lunch, Caudil returned to the stand.

The judge warned the jury that the photos would be graphic. The witness described the photos of the bodies. He pointed out a pair of glasses found on the kitchen floor. Photos showed Naoma Wendorf's body lying facedown and bloody shoe prints beside it.

Caudil identified a photo of Richard Wendorf on the sofa, saying that it accurately depicted the scene as he found it. He identified a photo of Naoma Wendorf, saying that it accurately reflected the body as it was found.

The defense moved to strike this and asked for a mistrial. Pictures of the crime were just too inflammatory. Judge Lockett denied the motion.

The prosecution asked Caudil to examine an exhibit of some things in a sealed plastic bag. Caudil was familiar with the items, which he had identified in his official report as bone fragments. He now clarified that point by saying that they were actually skull fragments, prompting another defense objection and motion for a mistrial.

It was denied.

The witness told where he found the skull fragments. "Two were under the dining room table, the third was on top of the vacuum cleaner near the victim's body in the dining room."

Caudil described how he tested for shoe prints using magnetic fingerprint powder. He applied that powder to the floor, hoping to pick up shoe or footprints. He did see shoe prints, which he then lifted. He identified an exhibit which was a shoe print found in front of the refrigerator.

He'd used Amino Black, a chemical specific to proteins, to enhance the bloody shoe prints. State's Exhibit 1 was two footprints on a square of floor tile gathered by the use of Amino Black.

A defense objection was denied, and the exhibits were entered into the record.

Caudil's testimony continued. On November 28, midnight of Thanksgiving Day, he had been told to go to Baton Rouge. He loaded a crime-scene-unit kit on the back of a department tow truck and drove to Baton Rouge, leaving on November 29 at two P.M. and arriving in Baton Rouge at three P.M. There he met other members of the Lake County Sheriff's Office and met and photographed Rod Ferrell.

He now identified photos of Rod Ferrell—full frontal, profile, and soles of boots. The head shots depicted the scratches on Rod's face. Caudil had taken the photos himself, except for the boots. All five suspects had been photographed front and back, with special attention paid to such identifying marks as tattoos.

Caudil stated that he had received items of Rod Ferrell's clothing from Detective Al Gussler, in plastic bags. He took the clothes back to Florida, and put them in separate bags.

He now identified a package of those clothes, including a pair of Arizona-brand blue jeans and some other items, which was entered into the evidentiary record.

The State's third witness was teenager Audrey Presson, a former classmate of Rod's, who now resided in New York.

She'd known Rod from ninth grade at

Eustis, and described him then as "a regular kid with long red hair . . . kinda dorky, but just a regular kid." She believed that he had left Eustis in tenth grade.

She went on to say that she'd seen Rod the night before the deaths. On Sunday night at around 9:00, he'd come to her house with some other people. He led her to their car and introduced her to Scott Anderson and two girls. He said that one girl was his wife and had his child inside her and the other girl was his "prodigy" and Scott was his "son." They had talked outside for about thirty minutes.

During that encounter, Anderson said, "We're going to have some fun tomorrow night." Rod said he was in Eustis on "unfinished business."

The prosecutor asked, "What did he mean by that?"

She said, "My impression of unfinished business is that someone has done you wrong and you've come to do something to him. It's not pleasant."

On cross-examination, Candace Hawthorne got the witness to state that Rod was "mellow . . . easygoing" before leaving Eustis. "He was just very docile. Wouldn't give you trouble if you didn't give him trouble," Presson said.

After he had moved, they talked over the phone about vampirism, witchcraft. She knew Jeanine LeClaire, "his girlfriend." Post-summer 1996, he had the Marilyn Manson look down pat—black clothes, eye makeup, cuts all over his arms.

Candace Hawthorne asked, "Did you still consider him your friend?"

"He was still my friend," Audrey said.

"Did his behavior change?"

"He was even more laid-back."

"Did he say anything about killing anyone's parents?"

"No."

The defense elicited the fact that when Audrey Presson had last seen Ferrell, he was wearing black jeans, boots, a long black coat, black shirt, and dark glasses. "His entire arm was covered with cuts, some were fresh, some were old, some scabby," she said. "They said they were going to sleep in the car, Rod and his friends. When they said they were going to have some fun, I thought they were going to party."

Presson said that she didn't practice witchcraft anymore, "because it's scary, it's a side of life I don't want to be involved in. I decided not to be involved in it right after Rod had killed, uh, I mean allegedly killed the Wendorfs."

That ended the cross-examination. Brad King requested that Audrey Presson be available to be brought back to the stand if the situation should so require. The judge okayed that request, and the witness was excused.

Next on the stand was prosecution witness

Dr. Laura Hair, the county medical examiner, with Brad King on direct examination.

She had performed detailed autopsies on the victims at the medical examiner's office, examining Naoma Wendorf at eleven P.M. and Richard Wendorf at two A.M. She explained to the jury that an autopsy is done to determine the cause and manner of death. It included measuring and taking pictures of wounds, and identifying such features as scars. Then the body is opened and the organs in the thorax, abdomen, and head are examined.

She reported that Richard Wendorf was 173 pounds and 67-inches tall, and that she had counted 22 wounds on his head. She then identified the autopsy photos.

The defense objected to introducing the photos into evidence and was overruled. A grim sequence followed as Dr. Hair described the head wounds, going through them by number and describing the incredible destruction they had wrought.

Members of the victims' families wept, their heads bowed, while Rod Ferrell sat blank-faced. The medical examiner continued. "Some wounds penetrated the frontal lobe of the brain; there's a hole so you can see into the skull. . . ."

She called attention to a cluster of nine separate wounds on the right side of Richard Wendorf's chest. At first, she hadn't known exactly what to make of them, and thought they were burns. Closer examination showed they were abrasions, probably caused by blunt impact.

Early on, there had been some wild speculation in the media that the "burns" were cult marks. But the so-called burns turned out to be gouges caused by Ferrell's stabbing the victim with one end of the crowbar.

The witness stated definitively that the "cause of death of Richard Wendorf was chop wounds with lacerations to the head and skull fractures."

The questioning now moved on to Naoma Wendorf, with Brad King introducing autopsy photos showing wounds and the defense objecting. The objection was again denied, and the photos were entered as evidence.

The hour was late and the judge put the court in recess until nine the following morning.

Day Two

The next day, Brad King resumed his direct of the medical examiner, focusing on her autopsy findings on Naoma Wendorf. Dr. Hair began by explaining that defensive wounds are caused when a person is trying to protect himself or herself from an attack by a weapon. They can be on the arms, or on the legs when people draw up their bodies to protect themselves from an attack. The wounds on Naoma Wendorf's arms were consistent with defensive wounds. Those types of wounds imply someone is conscious. Dr. Hair did not find such defensive wounds on Richard Wendorf, which was consistent with someone not realizing he is being attacked.

She said, "The actual cause of Mrs. Wendorf's death was due to head wounds and lacerations. But wounds numbers 13, 14, and 15 severed the brain stem from the body. The brain stem connects to the spinal cord at the base of the [skull], controlling most of the basic life functions. Severing the brain stem would cause instantaneous death.

"It's like someone cutting your head off, basically. There might be some jerky movements, but basically no voluntary movements at all."

The witness stepped down, and Brad King called to the stand Jim Binkley, a crime-scene investigator for the LCSO for approximately five years.

The witness recalled that on November 25, he was called to the victims' residence, where he took photos of the interior, made measurements that were later used to reproduce the floor plan of the residence, and collected evidence. He now identified certain items of the State's exhibits. Exhibit XXX contained a human tooth, found near Richard Wendorf's body. Exhibit YYY was a pair of the victim's glasses.

The defense's objection was overruled and the items entered into evidence.

Brad King asked, "Did you assist Dr. Hair in removing bodies?"

"Yes," the criminalist said. He then described the process of getting fingernail residue: an investigator uses a special clipper for the actual nail, lets it drop directly onto paper, folds the paper and seals it in an envelope.

An exhibit of right- and left-hand fingernail scrapings and clippings from Naoma Wendorf was entered into the record. So were swabs of bloodstains that Binkley had taken from the kitchen floor.

Also entered was an arrest photo of Rod Ferrell's face in profile, showing scratches on his face, and a full-length photo of him.

After Binkley, Baton Rouge Police Officer James Welbourne testified about the arrest of Rod Ferrell and associates. He was followed by Lake County Detective Al Gussler, who detailed his experiences in the pursuit and capture of the five suspects.

Brad King asked, "Notice any markings on the defendant's face?" Gussler answered in the affirmative, stating that Rod had pointed them out himself. Gussler identified Rod as the defendant sitting in court.

Since admitting guilt, Rod Ferrell's defense came down to mitigating factors, such as his age at the time he committed the crime—16—his emotional age, drug use, and his mental and emotional disturbance at the time of the killings. A trio of expert psychiatric witnesses would testify in his defense.

The first of these to take the stand was Dr. Wade Meyers, now called out of the preset sequence of prosecution witnesses by the defense in hopes of countering some of the damaging testimony about the brutality of the crimes.

Boyish and earnest, Dr. Meyers took the stand to testify to Ferrell's alleged inability to appreciate the criminality of his conduct, saying that a battery of psychiatric diagnostic tests indicated that Rod Ferrell was suffering from a "schizotypal" personality disorder, aggravated by an unhappy childhood and allegations that he had been sexually abused by his grandfather.

He also cited Ferrell's obsession with vampirism and the occult, alleging that his participation in "violent destructive fantasy games" impaired his ability to deal with reality.

Brad King opened what would be a vigorous cross-examination by asking, "You were hired to evaluate, not to treat?"

"Correct," Dr. Meyers said.

The prosecutor noted that although the doctor had diagnosed Rod Ferrell as schizotypal, based in part on the results of his personality disorder test, Ferrell had actually scored higher in the paranoid category. King said, "It looks like he scored lower for schizotypal than he did for antisocial personality, didn't he?"

Dr. Meyers said, "Yes."

"His highest score was for delinquent behavior, which is the same as antisocial behavior?"

"Yes."

"Those are the same kind of behaviors that are antisocial, correct?"

"Yes," Dr. Meyers said,

The prosecutor switched to another tack. "You accepted the allegation that Rod's grandfather sexually abused him?"

"What do you mean?"

"Did you believe it?"

"I believe some sort of abuse occurred."

"Did you ask his grandfather?"

"Yes."

"What did he say?"

"He said no. Which is what I would expect," Meyers said.

King honed in on the issue of Ferrell's veracity. "He told you he leaned over Mrs. Wendorf because she was still breathing?"

"Yes."

"You're an MD. . . . Now if you heard the cause of death was a severed brainstem, wouldn't this strike you as medically impossible [that she was still breathing]?"

"Yes."

"Now, when something's not true, wouldn't you want to try to get the truth from him?"

"Yes," Dr. Meyers said. "But had I done that, I would have sacrificed the integrity of the interview."

"Wouldn't it have helped your interview to challenge his lies? But you didn't do that. Why?"

"Because if I challenged him in the beginning, he would have clammed up."

King drilled in. "Now when Dr. Krop examined Rod and challenged him about his claim to have multiple personalities, he admitted that he didn't have them, didn't he?"

"I can tell you he doesn't have multiple personalities," Meyers said.

"He did say he would lie to get out of trouble?"

"Yes, he even admitted it on the Aschenbach test."

Brad King read aloud from the test: " 'Question: does he lie to get out of trouble a lot?' What was his answer?"

"Yes."

"We talked about the DSM-IV test; it lists every kind of disorder. Now for schizotypal, it's just that he doesn't interact the way people think we should?"

Dr. Meyers said, "Correct."

"Now let's go through what you didn't diagnose him with, conduct disorder." Brad King had the DSM-IV test entered into evidence, and began reading from its definition of conduct disorder, which stated that if the subject met any of three of the listed criteria within the required time period, then he could be diagnosed as having conduct disorder.

"Now, criterion one—often threatens or bullies others. You read the record of his threat to cut a teacher? You read about Mr. Ferrell throwing a knife at his mom and it stuck in the wall?"

Dr. Meyers said, "Yes."

"Now as to criterion number three, uses instrument to cause serious physical harm to people. He's already pled guilty to this?"

"Yes."

"Now number four, he's physically cruel to people?"

"Well, I didn't see a pattern of this for over a year."

"Now, physically cruel to animals. You know he beat cats against a tree?"

"Yes."

"That he broke into an animal shelter and hurt dogs?"

The objection which that brought from the defense was overruled.

King said, "Do you remember reading a statement in which he said that he'd done worse to dogs than he did in the incident with cats?"

Dr. Meyers said, "No."

King went back to the conduct disorder list. "Number ten, broken into house or car—done that, right? Number eleven, often lies? Number fourteen, has run away from home?" The answer to all three categories was yes. "Number fifteen, often truant from school from age thirteen?"

Dr. Meyers said, "Yes, he'd been truant for some time."

"Now that contributed significantly to his academic performance, culminating with his threatening a teacher and being expelled?"

"Yes."

Now the prosecutor zinged it home. "When

I spoke to you last Tuesday, you said you didn't diagnose him with conduct disorder because you didn't think it was fair to him, correct?"

"I don't believe I said it in those words," Dr. Meyers said.

"You said, this is a lot of stress for him to deal with and I didn't want to diagnose him with having conduct disorder, correct?"

"Yes, he'd been through a lot in a year."

"But you said he could be diagnosed with it?"

"Yes, he came close."

Brad King returned to the time of the murders. "Mr. Ferrell knew right from wrong that day, correct?"

Meyers said, "Yes, but I think his ability was impaired."

"He was thinking when he broke into the Wendorfs' house and beat them each twenty times in the head, didn't he?"

"Yes."

"Now he lied to you when he blamed it on someone else?"

"Yes. He said he often lies to get out of trouble," Meyers said.

By the time that Brad King's cross-examination was over, he had proved that no matter what else he might be, Rod Ferrell was a liar and, more damagingly, that that fact had been minimized in the evaluations of the expert witness who had diagnosed him.

And what good was a diagnostic evaluation predicated on lying responses?

Seeking to regain some lost ground on re-direct, Candace Hawthorne tried to establish that Rod Ferrell had told the truth on the test. "His high score was for delinquent behavior, which he could have avoided by lying?"

Dr. Meyers said, "Yes."

"Now, why did you diagnose what you did and exclude others?"

"I picked the ones that I thought best de-scribed him as a person."

Meyers went on to say, "I thought he had a lot of odd beliefs, in magic. . . . Other odd beliefs that he could be killed and go to a higher plane, that he could go through walls, etc. He felt he could get special powers from a book. He's talked about hearing voices, strange smells and so on."

Candace Hawthorne asked, "Did you ever see his drawings?"

"Yes. His drawings were of demons, weap-ons, knives, clubs, of warriors in very elaborate battle gear, great deal of aggression, fear—those things come out of his drawings." He added, "The drawings showed a very disturbed personality, suspiciousness, fear."

On recross-examination, Brad King queried Dr. Meyers about Exhibit KKK-3, a 1994 article the witness had written regarding kids involved in satanism and the occult. "Did you use this study in your evaluation of Rod?"

"It gave me some pointers," Dr. Meyers said.

"What were they?"

"Kids involved in satanism and the occult

are more likely to have identity problems and use of hallucinogens. Identity problems mean that they were confused about who they were inside, confused about religious and moral beliefs. Mr. Ferrell's problems led him to gravitate toward these beliefs."

King asked, "But involvement in the occult was not what caused him to go into the house and commit murder?"

"I think, I think, yeah, that's right."

"This article also says that belief in the occult does not have a link to violent behavior?"

Dr. Meyers said, "Yes."

"You said Mr. Ferrell was incapable of an intimate relationship. Did you see the tape of him and Charity Keesee in Baton Rouge Police Department, kissing and hugging for an hour?"

"Yes, but in general, people say he's odd, keeps to himself."

Brad King pressed a previous point. "You said it wasn't fair to label him with conduct disorder because of outside stress on his life?"

"When I said fair, I meant a fair diagnosis," Dr. Meyers said.

That concluded the day's testimony. Court was adjourned and recessed for the weekend.

Day Three

Court resumed on Monday.

The judge told the jury that starting the next day, court would begin at an earlier time, convening at 8:30 A.M. with a one-hour lunch break, in order to try to wrap up the trial by Friday afternoon. The trial might go into Monday, but would almost certainly finish by that day.

The prosecution called Timothy Bryant Petree, a forensic serologist employed by a Florida crime lab, whose specialty was the examination of blood and semen stains. Petree was an expert in stain identification.

After being sworn in, Petree took the stand for Assistant State Attorney Jim McCune's direct examination. A State's exhibit of fingernail scrapings and clippings from Naoma Wendorf was entered into evidence.

Petree explained that his task had been to look for the presence of blood on the pieces of evidence he was examining, then determine if it was human blood and if so, whose. After getting the screening test results, Petree had identified human blood on four of the State's exhibits, most notably Rod Ferrell's Arizona-brand blue jeans.

Petree was now handed gloves and scissors to open a sealed evidence bag. After visually examining Rod's jeans for reddish-brown stains, inside and outside, he put the jeans on display hangers to better show them to the jury. Stepping down from the stand, he pointed out the stained areas.

Using sanitary gloves to avoid contaminating the evidence, he now put stickers on the stained areas, which had been circled earlier for identification purposes. While he did so, the court was hushed, silent.

Petree testified that all five stains had tested positive for human blood—the blood of the victims.

The next exhibit entered into evidence was one of Rod's boots. The witness stated that stains on the boot had tested positive for human blood identified as the victims'.

Petree unsealed an exhibit, a kitchen tile with a shoe print on it, holding it up for the jury to see. He also showed them Richard Wendorf's ripped, bloody T-shirt.

The exhibits were all entered into evidence. Later, the prosecution would bring in its DNA experts to tie all the exhibits together into the scenario of the double homicides. For now, the important thing was to establish the scrupulousness and integrity of the evidence-collecting process.

Of course, the prosecution was not exactly unmindful of the psychological effect that seeing the bloodstained garments and other exhibits would have on the jury.

The defense was also aware of the possible effect on the jury. They decided to call out of order one of the defense witnesses.

The judge instructed the jury that the next witness would be a defense witness, and Dr. Harry Krop took the stand for Candace Hawthorne's direct examination. Goatishly bearded and broad-shouldered, Krop was one of the three expert psychiatric witnesses at the core of the defense's efforts to save Rod Ferrell from the electric chair.

Candace Hawthorne began by bringing out Dr. Krop's background and qualifications. A clinical psychologist, licensed since 1971, he maintained a private practice employing 13 to 14 mental health professionals. His specialty was forensic psychiatry, with a workload comprising about 60 percent criminal cases, and 35 percent custody cases.

An expert in assessing mental competency, he did custody case work where he evaluated what would be in the best interest of the child: civil work, clinical work, also therapy, but in the legal arena—he started the first child sex-abuse program in Florida. Working with victims and perps since 1977, it was probably the largest such program in the state. He was also a nonteaching assistant professor at the University of Florida.

Krop's practice entailed a lot of sex-abuse work. He would get referrals from the state attorney's office, for people on probation with the condition that they get counseling; he also got referrals from the State Division of Youth Services.

The witness had done evaluations of about 700 people in first-degree murder cases, and had testified evenly for both the state and defense.

The judge accepted him as a qualified expert in forensic psychiatric and sexual abuse.

Candace Hawthorne asked him to explain

his methodology, how he made his evaulations. Dr. Krop said, "In forensic evaluation, most information comes from sources other than the client. In criminal cases like this, clients may try to appear 'crazier' to avoid punishment (a condition which psychiatrists call 'malingering'). To get the mental state, it's important to talk to the family, get records, talk to people who have talked to the client. That's the main difference between forensic and traditional psychiatric evaluation."

This gave the defense a segue to the material it really wanted to get into evidence, Rod Ferrell's dysfunctional family background. Candace Hawthorne asked Dr. Krop about the circumstances of his first meeting with Ferrell, which had taken place at the Marion County juvenile detention center on December 10, 1996. At that time, Krop had interviewed the subject for 90 minutes, and also given him a series of psychiatric tests for an equal amount of time.

What was Dr. Krop's first impression of the client? "I saw a relatively scared, anxious individual who was fairly intelligent," he said. "He did not appear to be out of touch with reality when I spoke to him."

Candace Hawthorne asked, "What did he tell you?"

Dr. Krop said, "That he had been accused of murder, knew the victims . . . that he had made a confession, but that it was not a true confession, because he felt pressured or coerced to provide a statement to Louisiana and Florida police. . . . That he had been awake for a week, felt very tired and vulnerable when talking to the officers.

"Rod thought he was being forced to say he was the killer. He talked about his family background. Born in Murray, Kentucky. His father left when he was only a few days old. He didn't like his mother's boyfriends. He had no contact with his father until age seven or eight, visited him for a two-year span. His dad taught him to play D&D [*Dungeons and Dragons*, a fantasy role-playing game]. No contact with the father after age nine. His mom remarried briefly; Rod didn't like him. Mom had other live-in boyfriends, none of whom he liked. He was an only child.

"For most of his life, he lived with his mother and maternal grandparents. Asked to describe his mother, he said she loses her grip on reality and has mood swings. . . . Described his grandparents as 'die-hard Christians.' Was religious himself until age thirteen.

"Rod was expelled in tenth grade in Murray, Kentucky. He's moved back and forth between Eustis and Murray. He was not going to school at the time the incident [the Wendorf homicides] happened. He said they thought he was turning the school into a 'cult.' Said he was trying to make a fashion statement and people took it as a cult. Said he always felt different, but didn't feel he should be punished for it. Said people in Murray discriminated against him. Said he defied authorities, didn't do schoolwork and that's why he was suspended.

"Rod felt he was well-liked in Eustis, but discriminated against in Murray. He said his family was lower middle class, but said he would have money available whenever he needed it. Said he loved his girlfriend Che. His first voluntary sex contact was at age nine or ten with a sixteen-year-old girl. Described himself as a nymphomaniac, but since his involvement with Che, he was in love with her and stopped being promiscuous. He said he was born with an umbilical cord around his neck, and showed scars where he had cut himself.

"He talked about alter-egos [multiple personalities], but I did not take them seriously," Krop added.

At that meeting, Dr. Krop had given Rod the MMPI and other diagnostic tests. Candace Hawthorne asked, "Any conclusions?"

"I felt he was a competent, fairly intelligent individual who was able to communicate clearly and knew what was going on legally, in a naïve way. He knew he was facing life in prison or death. He was coherent enough to assist his attorney. I also felt that he was malingering, trying to communicate that he was a seriously mentally ill individual, that is, that he was delusional or had multiple personalities. It was hard for him to accept that he had killed people, and had a need to explain it as mental illness," Dr. Krop said.

Through Dr. Krop's opening testimony, the

defense had sketched in the outlines of the big picture of Rod's dysfunctional family background that they hoped would provide the mitigating factors needed to convince the jury to not vote for death.

Now, Candace Hawthorne moved to color in those outlines, as she questioned the witness on information he had received from Rod during their third meeting, in March, 1997. She said, "Did he talk about sexual abuse that day?"

"Yes," Dr. Krop said. "Rod told me that he was involved in a cult called Black Mask, which he said was a huge group of adults and children. He said he was introduced to the cult by his grandfather [Harold Gibson] at the age of six, its focus was dark magic. The goal of the cult was to release evil into the world and to extinguish light. He said he was viewed as a gifted child and was sodomized by several of his grandfather's friends. He told his mother about it, but felt very helpless. He said he couldn't remember whether his grandfather was actually present at the incident."

The witness stated that he had interviewed Sondra Gibson, Rod's mother, after she had been arrested and charged with soliciting sex from a minor.

He said, "I did have an opportunity to form my own professional opinion of Sondra Gibson during the interview. She said she had been arrested for having sex with a fourteen-year-old boy. I had seen letters to the boy, with clear deviant references. The boy and his older brother were associated with the defendant. The older brother was one of the leaders of the vampire cult Rod was involved with and had introduced him to the group. The guy's name was Steven Murphy, Rod referred to him as his 'sire.' The fourteen-year-old was named Josh.

"Sondra Gibson said the charges were vindictive because she had once called the police on Steven Murphy after an incident involving him and Rod. She said that the letters were taken out of context and weren't sexual in nature. . . . After reading the letters, I realized they were not necessarily taken out of context."

Dr. Krop felt Sondra Gibson was immature emotionally and enmeshed with the teenagers. This was the result of pathological relationship with another individual who was also part of same delusional process. In other words, she and Rod mutually reinforced their world of dark occultism and vampirism.

He said that both mother and son shared a somewhat similar diagnosis of personality disorders. In Rod Ferrell's case, this meant that he showed schizotypal, narcissistic, and depressive personality traits. "All of this means that the individual has unusual thought processes . . . that can extend to unusual beliefs, including delusional beliefs like magical beliefs—such as having certain occult powers."

Candace Hawthorne asked, "Could he have

appreciated and conformed his conduct to requirements of law?"

"He certainly could have appreciated his conduct, but he is a seriously disturbed individual and was seriously disturbed on the day of the offense. His ability to conform conduct was impaired that day due to disorders and to substance abuse." (Krop refers to the "Dragonfly" LSD Rod claimed to have taken on the night of the killings.)

Dr. Krop went on to say, "This is one of the more dysfunctional families that I have experienced out of seven hundred cases. No positive parental male role models. . . . And it's clear Rod has not had a positive female role model. Sondra Gibson is very disturbed, dependent, has been involved in pathological relationships herself. She has prostituted herself and drank heavily. She is an extremely dysfunctional and inadequate parent and tried to compensate by being a friend.

"He needed a parent, not a friend. This very chaotic family background has caused him to react by rebelling. The rebellion takes the form of this vampire cult, the ultimate rebellion."

The defense asked what the prognosis would be for Rod if he escaped the death penalty.

"If he's sentenced to life, he can function well in a prison situation," Dr. Krop opined. "He has his art, is relatively intelligent. He can function better in the structure of prison than in the lack of structure he has had in life."

The defense's strategy was to highlight Rod Ferrell the victim. On cross, Brad King put the focus on Rod as victimizer. "He indicated that he and Scott went through the house like in the army, searching methodically?"

Dr. Krop said, "Yes. They pretended they were in some kind of military maneuver."

"When he met Mrs. Wendorf in the kitchen, they both froze. She said, what do you want? Then she threw coffee and scratched him in face?"

"Yes."

"Now, Rod said to you that Scott hit her from behind? He said Scott was the one in charge, Scott told him what to do?"

"Yes."

"In fact he said Scott threatened to hurt someone, 'like that bitch'?"

"Yes."

"Later he said he saw Mr. Wendorf's body on the couch, didn't know how he'd been killed?"

"Yes."

"And that his reason for telling police he did it was that Scott had been his friend for eleven years?"

"Yes, and because he was essentially the leader of the group," Dr. Krop said.

Brad King now showed that he had done his homework on the Murray vampire clan's folkways. "You had discussions with him about the code of the vampires? And part of code was that vampires did not kill and did not take things forcefully from others?"

"Correct."

"Doctor, you don't feel the vampire issue had anything to do with this incident?"

"No, but it's more complex—vampirism is an expression of his personality disorder. . . . I truly do not think Rod believed he was a vampire."

"And the killings did not occur because Rod thought he was a vampire?"

Dr. Krop said, "No."

The prosecution now turned its attention to State's Exhibit-EEE, a letter that Rod had written on January 10, 1998, to his mother, Sondra Gibson. "In this version of events, he says they went in and found both Wendorfs dead and he essentially blames Heather?"

Dr. Krop said, "Yes. I think all along Rod has tried to figure out how to minimize not the murders per se, but minimize his responsibility in that. . . . I'm not a human lie detector, but the manner he said what he said, seemed truthful."

Brad King switched tracks, focusing on the ramifications of a potential life sentence for Rod Ferrell. "You said you believe he will be good candidate to be in the general population of prison?"

King then cited a disciplinary report regarding a fight Ferrell had had on December 3, and another report from June 1997 about how he had been seen assaulting another inmate.

Dr. Krop conceded, "He had four or five reports of a disciplinary nature."

"Including setting off a fire?"

"Yes, in April 1997."

King now referred to State's Exhibit-FFF, a statement by Lake County Corrections Officer Desiree Nutt regarding a disturbing conversation she had had with Rod on December 3, 1997, where he boasted to her of his escape plans and schemes.

He said, "This statement, in this exhibit, about taking innocent persons hostage, guards, etc., does that change your opinion about releasing him into the prison population?"

"I don't think it makes a lot of sense to tell a guard about escape plans—it goes along with his bravado, his act," Dr. Krop said.

"So you're not giving credence to this?"

"I don't doubt he said it, I'm just saying it goes along with his extreme immaturity."

"You read the statements from Shannon Yohe? . . . Assume for me that Mr. Ferrell did in fact on Monday afternoon tell Shannon Yohe that he was going to kill the Wendorfs, and that on Monday evening those things happened—would you not have to give credence to what he said—even though it doesn't make sense that he would tell someone he'd do such a thing and then do it?"

"Well, I think he believed some of these things."

"Doctor, in such a case, would you want to

be the one to find out whether he's fantasizing or telling the truth?"

"No, of course not."

On redirect, Candace Hawthorne tried to make the point that Rod often said things that he didn't mean, as a way of showing off and expressing his adolescent bravura. She recalled the incident which had led to Rod's expulsion from high school in Murray.

She said, "Regarding Rod's alleged threat to a teacher, there was a report where Rod was being escorted by a PE [physical education] teacher where he made the comment that he was mad enough to slit her throat."

"No, he did not threaten her," Dr. Krop said. "He made the comment to another teacher, because he was trying to comfort his girlfriend [Charity Keesee] and the PE teacher would not allow him to stay and do so, and he got angry.

"After Rod had made the comment to the other teacher, the teacher told Rod, you don't really mean that, you don't want to cut her throat, and he admitted that he didn't really. His comments are part fantasy, part frustration, part immaturity."

On recross, Brad King kept his parting salvo short and to the point. "For the victims, it wasn't bravado, he said what he was going to do and he did it?"

Dr. Krop said, "Yes."

The prosecution resumed its case, with Judge Lockett telling the jury that the next witness would be testifying for the State. Anne Montgomery was the director of operations of Reliagene Technologies, where she ran the forensics department. The company performed DNA testing.

On direct examination, Jim McCune had the witness establish that foreign DNA was found under Naoma Wendorf's nails. Ms. Montgomery stated that tests proved that that foreign DNA belonged to Mr. Ferrell.

Brad King then examined Deborah L. Fisher, a senior crime lab analyst for the state of Florida, who qualified as an expert on identifying shoe prints. She said that shoe prints were found on the kitchen floor of the murder house, including two shoe prints made in blood that were found beside Naoma Wendorf's body. The latter were made by her killer as he straddled her to deliver the death blows.

They were not only shoe prints but boot prints, boot prints which she positively identified as having been made by the boots Rod Ferrell had been wearing when he was apprehended.

Desiree Nutt was the author of the statement now labeled as Exhibit-FFF, which Brad King had cited during his quizzing of Dr. Krop. She now took the stand as a witness for the prosecution, with Brad King on direct.

On December 3, 1997, while employed as an officer by the Lake County Department of Corrections, she'd had a conversation with Rod Ferrell, whom she now identified as the individual sitting at the defense table. He had approached her while she was posted at her administrative station and commented on the security of the jail. First, though, he'd asked her a question about DNA, which she hadn't been able to answer.

He'd then asked about the surveillance cameras in the facility's air vents, causing her to write a report about the exchange to the jail's supervisors. She'd taken brief notes at her desk while talking to Ferrell.

Now, she read from the report she had made. Ferrell had said, "Are there cameras? I know there are manned gun posts on the roof . . . but if someone wanted to get out, they could go through the vent. . . . What I thought was, I could take out an officer in the shower room, and go through the vent. I would take hostages, innocent ones. I could take out so many of the dumb deputies. I'm an amateur assassin, but I probably won't take you all because I know you."

On cross-examination, the defense asked, "Does it seem logical that an inmate would confide their escape plans to you?"

Ms. Nutt said, "Yes, some of them do. Some of them are bragging."

"Running at the mouth?"

"Yes, I would say he was bragging."

"Inmates want to be respected by other inmates?"

"Yes."

The witness was excused and the court recessed.

Day Four

The next day, court convened at 8:30 A.M. For the prosecution, Jim McCune called Shannon Yohe. She and Rod Ferrell had been best friends in ninth grade, until he moved to Kentucky. She didn't have much contact with him after he moved.

She recalled that on Sunday, November 24, 1996, Rod had called her from the K-Mart in Eustis, the first time she'd heard from him in a long time. He came over to her house in a red car with Scott Anderson, Charity Keesee, and Dana Cooper. Ferrell made phone calls to Jeanine LeClaire and Heather Wendorf. He had Shannon make the call to Jeanine, because her parents didn't like him. He then spoke to Jeanine.

The next day, Monday, the group showed up at about five or six P.M., complaining about their car's bad tires. Rod called Heather, who gave directions to her house, while Rod drew a map.

After the call, they all sat talking in the kitchen. Ferrell said he wanted to kill Heather's parents. When Shannon Yohe asked why, he said he wanted their car. He told her he wished he was in their house so he could break their necks. He said that was his favorite way of killing.

"Then Dana Cooper drank some blood out of his arm and said she liked blood from his neck better," Yohe said.

Scott Anderson asked her if she wanted to know his favorite way to kill, but was interrupted before completion. The others were talking outside but stopped when Yohe neared. Then they left and she didn't see them again that day.

Under questioning, Shannon Yohe stated that on both days that she had seen him, Rod Ferrell did not slur his speech or have glassy eyes, and did not appear to be under the influence of any kind of intoxicating substance.

On cross-examination, the defense's Bill Lackay had the witness recall the Rod Ferrell she had known before he'd moved away to Kentucky. That Rod had gotten her to write poetry and was not into vampire games, as far as she knew. He dressed like a normal teenager before the move, nothing out of the ordinary. He was not a cigarette smoker then.

She said the Rod Ferrell who came in November 1996, was a different Rod Ferrell. He had different hair, was dressed all in black, and had cuts on his arm.

The defense asked, "You did not take Rod seriously that night [of the murders], because he runs his mouth a lot?"

"Yes," Shannon said.

Next taking the stand for the prosecution was Suzanne LeClaire of Eustis, a high school teacher and mother of two teenage daughters, one of whom was Jeanine LeClaire.

She recalled that on Sunday evening, November 24, 1996, her daughter Jeanine had received a phone call from Shannon Yohe, a friend from high school that she hadn't spoken to in awhile.

The next day, November 25, was Jeanine's birthday. During the family dinner at about 6:30 P.M., Heather phoned Jeanine, who seemed irritated with her. To Suzanne LeClaire, this did not seem normal. Jeanine said she'd call back.

Later, the witness noticed that Jeanine was not in her bedroom and went to look for her outside. It was a school night. Mrs. LeClaire saw her daughter standing near a tree at the end of the driveway.

Jeanine wanted to wait there in case Heather came by. She said Heather was talking about running away, and she wanted to talk to her. Suzanne asked Jeanine if she was planning to go with her. Jeanine said she didn't know, she was confused.

Suzanne went inside and tried to call the Wendorfs to warn them. The operator said their phone was out of service.

The defense chose not to cross-examine the witness.

Next came a series of law-enforcement officers and personnel appearing for the prosecution. Seminole County, Florida, Deputy Sheriff Charles Frazier testified as to how he had discovered the abandoned red Buick Skyhawk on November 26, followed by Lake County Sheriff's Office crime-scene technician Ron Shirley describing how he had processed that vehicle for evidence and discovered through the Vehicle Identification Number that it belonged to Scott Anderson's father.

Detective Al Gussler identified a blowup of the record of transactions on Richard Wendorf's Discover card and a Tallahassee Wal-Mart receipt from November 26 signed "Richard Wendorf," one day after he was dead. BRPD Detective Dennis Moran described the circumstances as Rod Ferrell and his associates were brought into the station under arrest from Thanksgiving's Day eve to the afternoon of the following day.

The defense cross-examination of BRPD Detective Thomas Dewey yielded a memorably ripe exchange, as the defense sought to establish Rod's state of exhaustion and debilitated physical condition at the time of his arrest. Bill Lackay asked, "Rod Ferrell rode in your car? He had pretty bad body odor?"

"Yes, sir, he did have a stench," Dewey said.

Sgt. Ben Odom detailed the circumstances of the arrests and the events before, during, and after Rod's first videotaped confession. Brad King said, "Did you ask if he was under the influence of alcohol or any controlled dangerous substance?"

Odom said, "Yes. He said no."

"Did you threaten or promise Rod anything to get the statement?"

"No."

"Did you withhold food or drink or anything?"

"No." Odom then identified an exhibit which was the videotaped confession.

Brad King asked, "As a result of that interview, did you find that certain items including a crowbar had been thrown in the Mississippi River?"

"Yes."

"Search for it?"

"Yes."

"Ever find it?"

"No," Odom said. "The Mississippi River in Baton Rouge is approximately a mile wide. Twenty to thirty feet from the bank, it goes down forty feet pretty drastically. The current is swift; in November it's pretty high, pretty dangerous. The dive team did not know how far it was thrown. It was a small pry-bar crowbar."

This meant that the murder weapon was gone and not to be recovered.

On cross-examination, Bill Lackay got it into the record that Heather Wendorf had been driving the Explorer on the night of the arrests. He then queried Odom about Rod's first confession, asking, "Under Louisiana law regarding juveniles, you have to have a parent or guardian present during an interview?"

"Yes," Odom said.

"But no contact was made to Rod's parents or guardians?"

"No."

"And you didn't tell him that he had the right to have a parent there?"

"No, we weren't operating under Louisiana law," Odom said. The crimes had been committed in Florida, where the law allowed for juveniles to be interviewed without the presence of parents or guardians. That made Rod's confession legal and admissable evidence. The time that Odom had spent on the phone with Florida authorities prior to Rod's midnight confession had not been wasted.

Brad King recalled Detective Al Gussler to the stand to identify an exhibit which was the complete unedited videotape of Rod's second confession.

Court was then recessed for the lunch break.

When court reconvened at one P.M., Judge Lockett spoke with attorneys for both sides over the timing of the afternoon's presentations. Brad King said he planned to play two tapes, each of them about fifty minutes long, followed by victim impact statements. The defense wanted to play a taped plea and also had some witnesses on standby.

When the jury returned, Judge Lockett said, "Folks, we're going to play these tapes for you. It's important that you can see and hear them.

I'm going to cut the lights. We'll take a break after the first tape."

The two videotaped statements from Rod recounted slightly different versions of the crimes. The first was made to Sgt. Odom, with Dewey and Moran present. Rod signed the consent form at a minute or two after midnight on Friday the twenty-ninth and the interview began.

For the jurors sitting in the darkened courtroom or for anyone not living on the dark side of the moon, it would be some show.

The flickering video monitor opened on the minimalist setting of the interview room, with a table, some chairs, a blank wall and ceiling. The scene was projected in a washed-out lunar-gray light, shedding an eerie phosphorescent glow over the jury box where twelve citizens sat and watched.

Rod Ferrell was in his full Mr. Spooky glory, with dyed black hair, black clothes, black fingernails. His face was scratched where Naoma Wendorf had clawed it with her nails during her death struggle. In the video, Rod seemed wasted, played out, withdrawn—all passion spent. There was a stillness about him. As he described his crimes, his hushed voice was by turns portentous and gloating.

It began with Odom reading Ferrell his Miranda rights. Rod, leaning on his hand, said he understood. He was barely audible.

Odom first got Rod's name, date of birth, and home address. "Okay, Rod, you know that you are under arrest and are now a fugitive from Lake County Sheriff's Office in Lake County Florida?"

"Yes."

"How far did you go in school, Rod?"

"Tenth."

"Can you read and write?"

"I've lived more knowledge than school ever thought of."

"I understand."

"The reason why I did this bullshit," Rod said vaguely.

Odom asked him if he's had any controlled dangerous substances. "Okay, and you have a mental disease, are you seeing a psychiatrist for anything?"

Ferrell answered, "I was seeing a psychiatrist. Don't know what for. Never paid attention."

"Who sent you, your parents?"

"The school, the sheriff's office, my mom. Basically, the whole city." Rod said he'd agreed to give a statement: "As long as I get to see Che."

"Okay, not a problem . . ."

"It's not because of the trouble. It's because I don't have any concern for life anymore. My own, especially."

"Perhaps you say that . . . but I know you're still a young guy and, ah, you've got a lot of living in front of ya," Odom said.

Rod Ferrell began his confession.

". . . Che and I've been seeing each other

for eleven months now and are engaged and she's pregnant [she wasn't] and all and I told Che beforehand that I was going to take her with me and just take like a half-ass road trip because I was sick of Murray, because all the cops were bugging me there for something I didn't do and I'm sorry [for knocking cops to other cops] . . ."

Odom said, "That's okay."

Ferrell said he got together with Charity Keesee, Dana Cooper, and Scott Anderson, put all their stuff in the red Skyhawk: ". . . and we drove out to where Scott's brothers were because he was supposed to drive them home that night and we had Che go and tell them that we had been kidnapped by Steven Murphy, better known as Jaden.

"And after that we took off and hit the road."

It took about a day to reach Eustis. Then: "I looked up some of my old friends to drop by and say hi and shit and I went by Jeanine LeClaire's house, that's Zoey's best friend, you know her as Heather."

"Jeanine LeClaire?" Odom asked.

"She's my ex-girlfriend. She wanted me to come back and pick her up."

On Monday, he contacted Heather/Zoey because she wanted to leave with them, too.

On Tuesday, the group was pulled over by a state cop on Lake Joanna Drive, who ran IDs on them which came up clean, so he let them go. But the stop spooked them. Rod went to the pay phones at K-Mart, called

Heather and said they were leaving that night and to tell Jeanine LeClaire the same thing and that they would be by to pick them up when it got dark.

They went to the Wendorfs' house first, Heather came down the road about an hour after dark. She, Che, and Dana Cooper got in Scott Anderson's car—"the car he took from his mom"—and drove to see Heather's boyfriend while Rod and Scott stayed behind.

> Ferrell: "After we made sure that they were gone, we walked down the road to Heather's house.
>
> "We walked up the driveway, looked around the house just to check the perimeters; we saw they left all the doors unlocked, went to the garage, looked for special items, found special items."
>
> Odom: "What kind of special items? Weapons?"
>
> Ferrell: "Yeah, that's all I was concerned about; weapons, food, and cash.
>
> Ferrell: "Went into her house, her mother was taking a shower, her father was asleep on the couch, so I took the liberty of rummaging through the house and getting something to drink, because I was thirsty.
>
> "Scott was following right behind me like a little lost puppy and then before her mother got out of the shower, I went

to her dad and smacked the fuck out of him until he finally quit breathing, so, yes, I'm admitting to murder."

Odom: "Okay."

Ferrell: "Actually it took him about twenty fucking minutes to stop, I swear, I thought he was immortal or something."

Odom: "What did you hit him with?"

Ferrell: "A crowbar. I was going to use a machete or chainsaw, but that was too messy, just nasty."

Odom: "Crowbar's pretty messy, too, you know."

Ferrell: "No, it only got a little blood spot on me—surprisingly—but anyway, so after that I basically picked his body up, screwed him around and looked for his wallet and stuff and that's where we found his Discover card.

"And about two minutes after that I flipped him back over, the mother came out of the shower with a nice hot cup of coffee that she spilled all over me, 'cause she was asking me what did I want, 'cause she thought I was just robbing them."

Odom: "She hadn't seen her husband yet?"

Ferrell: "No, I made sure that he was hidden. I didn't want her to freak. . . . She just basically looked straight at me and said, 'What do you want?' By that time, you know, it was pretty obvious, I had blood on me and a crowbar in my hand. I was fixing to say, 'Yeah, I want to have coffee with you, son of a bitching smart-ass.' But anyway, then that's when she lunged at me, 'cause I was actually going to let her live, but after she lunged at me, I just took the bottom of the crowbar and kept stabbing it through her skull and whenever she fell down I just continually beat her until I saw her brains falling on the floor, 'cause that pissed me off. That's how I got these [scratches on his face]."

Odom: "She scratched ya."

Ferrell: "She clawed me, clawed me, spilled fucking scalding hot coffee on me, pissed me off."

Odom: "Okay."

Ferrell: "So I made sure she was dead. Rummaged through the house looking for car keys, money, whatever. Thought about waiting for Zoey's sister, but decided nah, why bother. Let her come home, have a mental breakdown, call the police, which I was correct, she did. Anyway, went through the parents' bedroom, found the keys to the Explorer which you've now impounded, casually walked outside afterwards, unlocked the door, peeled out of the driveway."

Odom: "Where was Scott during all this time?"

Ferrell: "Oh God, he totally froze. He's

never seen people get killed before because he was hyped about telling me how he was going to kill them, so basically he is just an accessory.

"After that we drove over to Jeanine's house looking for the girls because they thought we were only getting the girls to run away with us, which was very far from our minds at that point in time 'cause I didn't want to be followed, so we drove back over to Jeanine's house. At that point in time we drove the Explorer so she [Heather Wendorf] kind of realized what happened to her parents, she flipped for about a hundred miles or so."

Odom: "Heather did?"

Ferrell: "Yeah, she goes by Zoey. She looks to me as her father or something."

Odom: "What all did you all take out of the house?"

Ferrell: "We took her mother's pearls, which were around her teddy bear's neck. We took her father's knife. . . ."

Odom: "What about the knife, was it still in the car?"

Ferrell: "Ah, Zoey had it on her 'cause it was her father's knife and she wanted to keep it as a souvenir I guess."

Odom: "Where were you guys going?"

Ferrell: "You mean after Florida? . . . The place we actually went to was New Orleans. We got pulled over by the cops there, too. We got pulled over five times on this whole trip and never got caught 'til now, 'til we checked into a hotel."

Odom: "Why did you let one of them call? Who called their grandmother? Did somebody call South Dakota?"

Ferrell: "Yeah, that was Che. . . . She was freaking out and she's basically the only thing I care about in this world, so. . . ."

Moran: "Bingo, that's who got you [busted] when she made the phone call."

Ferrell: "Oh, I know. That's when I told them, get out of town now, but they didn't listen to me. See, they never listen to the leader."

Odom: "Where were you going to go?"

Ferrell: "Don't know, don't care."

Odom: "Just ride 'til you lit somewhere?"

Ferrell: " 'Til I found a nice forest area. I was just going to fucking ditch the fucking Explorer in some lake and start going through the fucking woods, killing deers or whatever I could find for meat. [Pause] It was her grandparents that turned them in?"

Odom: "Ah, I don't know for a fact. Did you all ever discuss these homicides, prior to the day you went over there, with anybody that you can remember?"

Ferrell: "We never thought about it until about ten minutes before we did it."

Odom: "So . . . it wasn't a planned thing 'til you went over there?"

Ferrell: "It wasn't premeditated—it would be like spontaneous because if you premeditate something, it's too easily planned out and easily known."

Odom: "Did you know Zoey's parents prior to this?"

Ferrell: "I'd never even seen them before until I found them that night, so I wasn't even, hell, I went to the wrong house first. Didn't kill anybody though 'cause I looked in and saw there was little kids and that's my rule, I don't kill anything that's little. Now adults, that's perfectly fine, sixteen and up."

Odom: "Have you considered staying there [the Wendorfs' house] and waiting for Jeanine LeClaire?"

Ferrell: "No, 'cause Scott wanted to stay at the house just to dump the corpses in the pool . . . and I was like for one thing that's just sick and for another—no . . ."

Odom: "Dana and Zoey and Che weren't involved in this right?"

Ferrell: "Those three were basically just the ones we kind of kidnapped. . . ."

Odom: "But they went along agreeably, right?"

Ferrell: "Che had no choice. I told her either she agreed or I'd hogtie her, take her with me. Dana came with Che because she was worried about Che. Zoey came along 'cause she's been planning to come with me for about a year because we had planned on whenever I moved back into Eustis, her and Jeanine were going to come up here and we were just like going to go somewhere 'cause I still have a lot of friends in New Orleans and that was where I was going to live.

"And if Che didn't freak out, that's where I would have been right now. What can I say, it's a bitch about living in the big cities, you learn to be good friends with the cops and crime lords."

Dewey: "Rod, you said that Scott never saw a murder before. Did you see a murder before then?"

Ferrell: "I've fucking seen murders like all my life, ever since I was five 'cause my grandfather for one, he's never been caught either."

Dewey: "You saw these people murder other people?"

Ferrell: "He's part of an organization called the Black Mask. When I was five, they chose me as the Guardian of the Black Mask and the Guardian has to become one with everybody. In other words, they raped me. And they have to sacrifice a human to the Guardian, so they sacrificed someone right in front of me."

Dewey: "What city was that in?"

Ferrell: "It was in Murray."

Dewey: "Would you call that a cult?"

Ferrell: "Yeah . . . I never became part of them."

Odom: "Kind of tough when you're hard core, isn't it, man?"

Ferrell: "Two things bother me: what happened whenever I was five and the fact that I never will get to see Che after this. . . . I've been hanging around gangs and cults and all that shit all my life, so I've seen like sacrifices and drug buys. . . ."

Odom: "I'm just asking, Rod."

Ferrell: "Killing is a way of life, animals do it, and that's the way humans are, just the worst predators of all actually."

Odom: "How old is Che?"

Ferrell: "Sixteen . . . she is carrying around my kid. She's almost two months pregnant. Like they say, shit happens."

Odom: "Well, Rod, I'm not going to sugarcoat this thing, buddy, 'cause you know what you've done."

Ferrell: "It's pretty simple, I'm fucked."

Odom: "The guys from Lake County, the detectives, are on their way here. . . ."

Ferrell: "Is it actually possible for somebody my age to get like a death penalty?"

Odom: "It depends, I don't know what the laws are in Florida. When you are sixteen years old in this state you can be tried as an adult and you're subject to adult penalties."

Ferrell: " 'Cause what I was thinking, what I would have done if I was an adult would equal the death penalty. So I was kind of hoping, you know, I was like, please go ahead, ha!" [Laughs]

Odom: "To be straight up with ya, yeah, it's probably going to entail the death penalty."

Ferrell: "Yeah, there you go. [Laughs] I'm sorry, this is just like a big fucking joke. My life seems like a dream. My childhood was taken away at five. I don't know whether I'm asleep or dreaming anymore so whatever, for all I know I could wake up in five minutes."

Odom: "Rod, I can assure you it's not a dream."

After that, the interview trailed off into a dying fall, as Rod tried to take the opportunity to pay back a real or imagined grievance by accusing his stepfather Darren Breven, now residing in Pontiac, Michigan, of allegedly dealing drugs out of a pizza parlor that he owned. For whatever reason, the would-be vampire fell right into the snitch game, as the first videotaped confession ended.

The jurors had only drunk half the bitter cup of Rod Ferrell's revelations, for they had yet to see the second videotaped confession, the one Ferrell had made to Detectives Al Gussler and Wayne Longo, with the latter handling the majority of the questioning. The tape was loaded into the monitor and the real killer video began.

Gussler: "You still hanging in there, Rod? Okay. Today's date is November 29, 1996, approximate time is 17:38 hours. Present for the interview: Sergeant Wayne Longo LCSD, Florida; Detective Al Gussler, Lake County Sheriff's Office, Florida, and would you give us your full name, sir?"

Ferrell: "Roderick Justin Ferrell."

Gussler: "You're aware, I'm sure, why we're here to speak with you this afternoon?"

Ferrell: "Yeah."

Gussler: "Okay, and that being what?"

Ferrell: "Let's see, the murders of Heather Wendorf's parents."

Gussler: "Did you know their first names by any chance?"

Ferrell: "Uh, no."

Gussler: "Okay, Mr. and Mrs. Wendorf."

Ferrell: "That's the most I know."

Longo: "Rod, do you have any parents?"

Ferrell: "Well, my mom, Sondra Gibson and my real father, Rick Allen Ferrell, my stepfather, Darren Breven, and my second stepfather, Kyle Newman."

Longo: "You don't have a problem talking with us without them present or anything, do you?"

Ferrell: "I don't give a shit."

Longo: "I just want to ask and make sure you're comfortable with us and everything else."
Ferrell: "Well, my life's fucked, so—"
Longo: "Okay."

At this point Ferrell was once again read his Miranda rights.

Gussler: "All right, having these rights in mind, do you wish to talk to us now?"
Ferrell: "Most definitely."
Gussler: "Yeah. Good. You just roll and we'll listen."
Longo: "What did you talk about while you and Heather were at the cemetery? . . . Did you discuss with her about her parents at that time? You didn't mention anything to her and ask her about if she wanted her parents killed?"
Ferrell: "Ah, within the year I jokingly said it once, but I never thought I would do it."
Longo: "She's mentioned that you said it several times . . . over the course of several months, that you have said that to her? . . . Is that true or—"
Ferrell: "Well, I'm saying she didn't point out ask me. She didn't say, oh please kill my parents."
Longo: "I'm telling you she's telling us—that you asked her, 'Do you want your parents killed?' "

Ferrell: "Like I said, I said it once because she kept throwing the hint to me and then I just go what, do you want me to kill your parents."

Longo: "How was she throwing you a hint?"

Ferrell: "Like she was saying . . . shit like, both my parents have a misfortune or an accident or something it would make it a lot easier to run away. Things like that."

Longo: "Did you say anything to her at the graveyard about that again?"

Ferrell: "I was just asking her if she was sure she wanted to leave because I knew it had been a year and she'd gotten a steady boyfriend, the only thing she was flunking in school was French. . . . It seemed like a halfway good life at least, so I was asking her for sure if she wanted to leave with us."

Longo: "Nothing about hurting the parents though?"

Ferrell: "Nothing about death or anything besides just running away. . . . But then that night after the state cop pulled us over, and all that shit, we called her back. We told her that we were leaving tonight, to get ahold of Jeanine, get her shit packed, get ready. She told us that she wanted to go see her boyfriend, Jeremy, so I told Che and Dana to take her and go see Jeremy and they asked me why I was staying behind.

"I told them that we would meet them at Jeanine's house. They asked us how we would get there. I said walk. So I told them to go really slow. Scott knew what we were doing because he was coming with me."

Longo: "And that was? Fill in the blanks for us, Scott knew you were doing what?"

Ferrell: "Oh, we decided at that point before, because I pulled Scott to the side because I got to thinking about how Heather's parents would probably react and I didn't want to be found, for one, and I said how do you feel about taking someone out and he's like, no problem, so we decided that we would go into the house, at least hogtie her or something, her parents."

Longo: "Uh-huh."

Ferrell: "Didn't exactly plan on beating them to death . . ."

Longo: "Did the girls, the three girls that were at the car, did they know what you were up to when you were going up to the house?"

Ferrell: "No, they didn't. . . . I didn't tell them anything—because I wanted to keep them out of it."

Ferrell continued, stating that he and Scott Anderson entered via the unlocked garage, after first prowling the house "perimeters" for "access." He had a bow staff, broken in two, so both he and Scott were armed.

Ferrell: "We went into the garage. I used my lighter to look for some kind of better weaponry because I only have a stick—I knew a stick couldn't do shit."

Longo: "What were you planning on doing with it? I thought you were just going up there just to hogtie?"

Ferrell: "I was saying just in case they attacked me. . . . Because I didn't know how her father—like how big he was or what. . . . So I was taking precaution. I was looking for something stronger."

Longo: "And you found?"

Ferrell: "A crowbar. . . . I figured it surpassed wood by far. I was going to take the money that they had on them and their vehicle, that was it."

Longo: "How did you know they had any money?"

Ferrell: "Taking a guess. . . . I know Heather's parents. I know Heather's sister. I mean Heather's sister owns a cell phone, they own a big Explorer and they own the house."

Longo: "You already had Heather in the car, is that correct? Why not just take her and go?"

Ferrell: "Because there was no way we had enough room in the Buick for that amount of package . . . people and items.

"[Richard Wendorf] was watching TV. . . . I checked out the layout of the

house. I looked through the windows to
see what was going on. . . . I was afraid
that he was going to come after me so I
had the thing [crowbar] propped up
ready just if he came at me I was going
to slug the fuck out of him. So what happened is he did turn around and started
to get back up, so then I did waylay his
ass and I didn't stop because he was still
like breathing and stuff. I just kept beating him and beating him and beating
him and beating him. . . ."

Longo: "And he was sitting up or laying
down when this was happening?"

Ferrell: "Well, after I waylaid him, he got
unconscious."

Longo: "Laying right there on the couch,
okay."

Ferrell: "Because it was as he was starting
turning around, I saw he was coming out,
I just boom, right across the temple of
the head. It knocked him out cold and
while he was cool, I figured now or never,
because if he gets up, I'm a fucking dead
motherfucker. So I just beat him until he
died."

Longo: "Did you strike him anywhere
else with the crowbar or just in the
head?"

Ferrell: "I striked him once in the chest,
because he wouldn't stop breathing, so I
stabbed him in the heart. . . . I took the
bottom of the crowbar and *splack*.

"Her mom came out through the kitchen area holding a very hot cup of coffee and she asked me what I wanted and I flat out told her I wanted the keys and she was like freaking, she thought that Zoey was still in the house so she started to come after—"

Longo: "Did she know who you were?"

Ferrell: "No, they have never seen me before. But as you can see, she clawed the fuck out of me."

Longo: "Let me see. All those scars right there on your face are from her?"

Ferrell: "Who knows? Okay, this isn't good, she was supposed to stay in the shower 'cause she asked what I wanted. She was like, first thing she said, she kind of like did that melancholy thing where she goes, 'Zoey,' like that, really quiet and she like started to lunge at me. She spilled her coffee on me, like all over me, then she clawed my face and grabbed my wrist and that's when I took the straight end of the crowbar and just started bashing the back of her head."

Longo: "So she was running away from you when this happened?"

Ferrell: "No, she was holding on to me. . . . She had her fingernails embedded in my skin and until she let go, I was going to beat the fuck out of her and finally—

"But anyway, then the hot coffee

started steaming, so it pissed me off so I just plain out gave a crescent kick [karate-type move]. Kicked her on the ground and then continued to beat her there until she stopped breathing."

Longo: "Okay, why not wait three more hours until she goes to bed, take the keys and you all leave?"

Ferrell: "Because I'd heard Zoey mention . . . that the keys were in the parents' room and I didn't want to take a chance of them getting up and happening what happened.

"After we left New Orleans . . . Che was totally freaking out and I didn't want her to freak so bad to cause any stress to the baby.

"We were right next to the U.S.S. *Kidd*— at a pay phone. Only a few blocks from here actually. She called her mom. Her mother was asking way too many fucking questions. I knew she was going to turn us in. I told Che to hang up right then and get the fuck out, don't tell her where the fuck we were because I knew she was going to turn us in. . . .

"Within the next half hour, the police pulled up at the hotel and that's whenever I just walked straight to the cop car and put my hands behind my back and said, okay, let's go and then I came and slept in this room and on goes the story and that's it."

Longo: "Did you get those cuts on your arms from the murders?"

Ferrell: "No, it's self-infliction. . . . Physical pain to override the mental."

Longo: "You ever heard the term 'over the edge' or 'over the other side' or 'over'?"

Gussler: "Crossover?"

Longo: "Crossover?"

Gussler: "Crossed over."

Ferrell: "Yeah, I heard that from Jaden."

Longo: "From who?"

Ferrell: "Jaden Steven Murphy."

Longo: "What does that mean?"

Ferrell: "It is supposed to be where you go from human to vampire. . . . You cut yourself, let them drink it, it runs through their veins for a few moments and then your blood becomes tainted and you drink from them and become the untainted. You go around feeding on humans."

Longo: "Do you do that?"

Ferrell: "All the time.

"Suicide has never worked for me so that's why I was kind of hoping at this rate now I could maybe be tried as an adult and get electrocuted or something. Not that I'm throwing a hint."

Longo: "You want to die?"

Ferrell: "Oh, yes, definitely."

Gussler: "Rod, just one thing if you would. You said when you start swinging the crowbar on the male subject [Richard Wendorf] that you really felt, I was trying to think of the word, you felt good, you felt . . ."

Ferrell: "There was a rush to actually—"

Gussler: "A rush, okay. That's—"

Ferrell: "To feel that fact that I was taking a life because that's just like the old philosophy about if you can take a life, you become a god for a split second and it actually kind of felt that way for a minute, but if I was a god, I wouldn't exactly be here, would I?"

Longo: "How many times did you hit him?"

Ferrell: "Around fifty."

Longo: "Together, total or each?"

Ferrell: "Total for him—for her about thirty, really fucking hard hits 'cause his face was just, it looked like a rubber mask. It didn't even look real and her head, her brains were just like oozing out of her skull."

Longo: "Uh-huh."

Ferrell: "So that's when I basically knew, yeah, they're dead so I got nothing to worry about."

Longo: "Did Scott do anything, stop you from doing it, watched you—"

Ferrell: "He just watched and smiled."

Longo: "He got a rush, obviously, too then? Is that what kind of smile you are referring to?"

Ferrell: "He was like a happy, almost like a kid at an amusement park for the first time. I mean the minute she rushed in, he was like—when she grabbed me, he was like, yeah, and I was like, after she is down, I turned around and looked at him and then I just went boom, boom, made sure she wasn't going to get back up because she was a stubborn—"

Longo: "Uh-huh."

Ferrell: "—persistent little bitch and also the fact that she spilled hot coffee and clawed me didn't exactly make me too happy, so that's why her brains were coming out and his weren't."

Longo: "Uh-huh."

Ferrell: "I'm very nice unless you're not nice to me."

Longo: "Anything else you want to tell us? I think we've covered about everything."

Ferrell: "Like I said, I give detail. I've got a question for you all."

Gussler: "Go ahead."

Ferrell: "You seriously think I'm fucked?"

Gussler: "Hard to tell; we can't guess the system, man."

Ferrell: "I'm fucked."

That ended video confession number two. The monitor screen went dark, the courtroom lights came up, and the judge announced a fifteen-minute recess.

* * *

The recess done, the prosecution called Paula Queen, Naoma Queen Wendorf's oldest daughter from a previous marriage. She told the jury how her mom was unique. "She raised four daughters. She was honest. She liked to talk about old times. She liked to do a lot of craft things. She had real good friends and she taught us girls each to how to do things. . . . I didn't realize how tough it was until I had kids of my own."

Robert Wendorf then took the stand. He was Richard Wendorf's younger brother. He told the jury how Richard Wendorf and his other brother Billy were twins, and how the twins were always together. "Ricky was a great brother, he was always what a brother should be. He was honest, hardworking . . . a good provider. A sensational father.

"He always decorated the house with lights at holiday time. Jennifer was talking about how the lights were so balanced, he told her she should balance her life, too—not all work, no play.

"He was a loving son and grandson. He was always visiting our mother's house and fixing things. His grandfather, ninety-nine, lives with Mother and he was always going over to help.

"I've said all this to express what a loss it will be to all of us. Loss to the family and to the world," Robert Wendorf concluded.

That ended the prosecution's case. Now it

was the defense's turn. The expert psychiatric witnesses that it had called out of order earlier had been put on the stand to counter some of the negative effects of the State's case.

The defense's first witness was Rick Ferrell, Rod's father. Bill Lackay asked him on direct, "Do you feel like you abandoned Rod?"

"No, I do not," Rick Ferrell said. "Sondra would be friendly one minute and the next minute she would be very difficult to deal with. I believe that it would have made a difference if I and my mother [Betty Jane Ferrell] had been able to raise Rod."

Next called was Diane K. Smith, the manager of the Southside Manor Apartments in Murray. During Candace Hawthorne's direct, Ms. Smith said how she had seen Rod Ferrell and Sondra Gibson going up and down the road, not socially. She thought they were girlfriend and boyfriend, not mother and son, because they were holding hands. They were both dressed in black, black everything including nail polish.

They moved out in November 1996. She inspected the apartment after they moved out. They paid zero rent, because they had zero income. It was a subsidized apartment.

Candace Hawthorne asked, "Anything unusual in the apartment?"

Ms. Smith said, "The main room had a few holes, nothing unusual. But the master bedroom had a pentagram on the floor. It was Sondra's room."

Day Five

On day five, the defense brought out the big guns to demonstrate just how dysfunctional Rod Ferrell's family really was. They began by showing a videotaped deposition made by Betty Jane Ferrell, Rod's paternal grandmother. On the tape, she told how she was raised most of her life in West Virginia, moved to Kentucky in 1969, and resided there 19 years.

She and her husband had adopted Rick Ferrell, Rod's father. She said that she knew nothing of Satan and denied her husband was the one who allegedly raped five-year-old Rod. [It was Harold Gibson, Sondra Gibson's father, whom Rod had named as his alleged rapist in the revels of the Black Mask cult.]

On the video deposition, Betty Jane Ferrell recalled wistfully of Rod, "He was a sweet little boy, the sweetest little thing."

Ashley Elkins took the stand. She lived in Murray, where she was a senior in high school. She'd known Rod for two and a half years and had met his mother. She was also the onetime girlfriend of Jaden Steven Murphy, Ferrell's vampiric "sire."

She testified, "A bunch of kids would visit Rod's house. Rod's mother would rub the boys, touch them, flirt with them. They're about Rod's age, mid-teens, a little older."

She said that Heather Wendorf called her house sometimes, and sometimes she wrote letters. Heather used to contact Rod through Ashley when his phone had been disconnected. The calls from Heather were before November 26, 1996. She'd read four letters Heather wrote to Ashley's brother, who never wrote back. In one of the letters, Heather said she wanted to get rid of her parents because she wanted to be with "him"—Ashley assumed it was Rod—and that was the only way they could be together. There was a drawing of a teddy bear with a noose around its neck in the letter. Her brother threw the letters away because he didn't want anything to do with her or Rod.

On cross-examination, Jim McCune asked, "Is it true Rod Ferrell always tried to intimidate people?"

"Yeah, he wanted me to be scared of him. He wanted everyone to be scared of him," Ashley said.

"Is it true that Mr. Ferrell only cared about Mr. Ferrell?"

"That's how it seemed to me."

"Now, did he make any threats toward you?"

"One time, he called me names and said he was going to spread my guts all over the walls so that everyone could see them and smell them," Ashley Elkins said. She didn't take him seriously, but she stopped seeing him at that time. She was angry at him, thought a friend wouldn't say such things. Then he started following her.

Ferrell told her he was powerful, could hurt people.

Candace Hawthorne called Jaden Steven Murphy to the stand. He was husky, looked like he could take care of himself, and was well-spoken, articulate. He wore an ankh pendant, the ancient Egyptian symbol of life. Jaden Steven Murphy was his real name, though not his birth name.

He said he used to wear all black and was into vampirism. That was not why he and Rod Ferrell became friends. It was more that they dressed alike and were both outcasts. "We didn't fit in with the redneck or prep genre in the school."

Ferrell's hair was strawberry blond when they had first met. Later, he dyed it black. Murphy turned Ferrell on to playing *Vampire: The Masquerade*, a dark fantasy role-playing game. The game was a mélange of occultism, Bram Stoker, Anne Rice's vampire novels, horror movies, English Hammer fangs-and-gore films, and similar elements. Game players would create fantasy characters and enact them in scenarios taken from the game manual. It was a live-action game, a kind of fantasy theater in the round, played in various locales that fit the Gothic mood of the mythos.

The largest number of people that had ever

played in Jaden Murphy's game was twenty. The games would run from dawn to dusk, played out in graveyards, under railroad trestles, in empty fields and lonely woods.

Murphy was the game master, directing the action. His game-master book contained different scenarios, rules, and codes of conduct, serving as a template for his "vampire clan."

He told how he crossed Rod Ferrell over. "I had been telling Rod about my lifestyle—I couldn't fly, I just had a craving for blood, human and animal. The first time I tasted blood other than my own I was five. We don't have certain gods we worship. I took a knife and cut my arm, and he took from me, and he did the same, and I took from him."

Candace Hawthorne said, "Were you then known as Rod's sire?"

"Yes, more or less, I was the one who embraced him and crossed him over into our way of life." But Murphy stressed that he was not responsible for him if he messed up or anything.

Jaden Murphy was not into drugs at the time, not for the last four years. He was into self-mutilation and cutting himself even before the game, to relieve emotional pain and stress. He was dating Ashley Elkins at the time.

He knew Sondra Gibson. She was sending his younger brother Josh very sexually oriented letters and sent him a key to her apartment asking him to embrace her so she could be his eternal bride. "My mother was furious, could have pressed charges."

Later that summer, he did have a falling out with Ferrell. He went over to hang out at Rod's. Rod and his mother were fighting with each other, their "normal pattern." Then Sondra and Jaden got into a beef. She said he was controlling Rod. "Rod wasn't listening to her, blah, blah." Rod was being cocky, said he felt Jaden was standing on him. Jaden grabbed him by the throat and slammed him against the wall.

The relationship was deteriorating anyway, because Ferrell was getting too intense, drawing outside attention to the vampire clan.

Candace Hawthorne said, "You're known as the 'Prince of the City' in Murray."

He said, "Yeah, that's an ongoing joke."

"Didn't the prosecutor from Murray visit you to take a blood sample?"

"Yes, they found fingerprints on the [Wendorf crime] scene that they couldn't identify," Murphy said, looking at Ferrell and smirking. He knew that at one point Ferrell had tried to hang the murders on him.

The witness then read a love letter written to him by Sondra Gibson, quoting her: "'If I could have one wish it would be to spend my life with you.'" On the letter was the ankh symbol. Basically she was proposing marriage, he said. The letter was signed "eternally, Star, Mistress of the Dark."

McCune took the cross-examination, asking

straight out, "Why were you smiling at the defense table?"

Murphy said, "It's been some time since we've seen each other and we're close."

"Do you love Rod?"

"I love Rod."

"Are you a vampire?"

"Yes, I was into this lifestyle even before this game. I mean I'm not eternal, I'm only eighteen years old."

"So it's a lifestyle thing?"

"Yes."

"You don't have fangs do you?"

"No."

"Isn't one of the laws of being a vampire that you don't kill?"

"Yes, we have to live the laws man has set as well. We're not supernatural beings that can twist things."

"Your fight with Mr. Ferrell was provoked, wasn't it?"

"Yes . . . I heard around town that he planned to take my life and that of my fiancée at the time, Ashley Elkins. I went to confront him."

On redirect, Candace Hawthorne got him to say that he didn't take that threat seriously because Rod Ferrell had never shown aggression toward him or Ashley. He also didn't believe the source of the rumor.

When Jaden Steven Murphy wrapped up his testimony, Ferrell blew him a kiss. That would put him in solid with the jury. Rod Ferrell, aka Vesago, the sorcerer's apprentice who had rocketed beyond fantasy into blood and death.

April Doeden, from Murray, knew Jaden Murphy. She'd met Rod Ferrell at a game of *Vampire: The Masquerade,* and had gone out with him in 1996. As the year progressed, he dyed his hair black and started wearing black nail polish. He talked in Gothic rhymes and poetry. "But everyone did that." They did hang out in cemeteries.

She testified that she had seen a pentagram in Sondra Gibson's bedroom.

She was around once when Heather Wendorf called Ferrell from Florida and heard her asking him to come get her. "She said the only way I can see getting out of here is killing them," April testified. She believed that Heather was talking about her parents. The witness was bringing a cordless phone from the other room, while Ferrell was on the other line, which is how she'd happened to overhear that part of the conversation.

On cross-examination, Brad King brought out some interesting facts. April Doeden had been engaged to Rod for a period of months. "He thought of you as his light and Charity Keesee as his darkness, correct?"

"Yes."

"He pretended to believe that the child you had was his child?"

"I have heard that."

"But you know for a fact that it wasn't his."

"Yes."

April said she was not involved in vampirism. She believed herself to be a good witch, if anything. Yes, she'd heard of Heather Wendorf and Jeanine LeClaire.

Brad King said, "Rod had said they were his little women and they followed him?"

"Yes."

Lazetta Crews was Rod Ferrell's aunt, Sondra Gibson's sister. Their father was Harold Gibson, Rod's alleged pedo-rapist and satanic cult initiator. Under oath, Ms. Crews described three incidents that had taken place before the age of twelve where her father had initiated inappropriate sexual behavior with her.

Once, he had pulled the car over to the roadside and started kissing her. Another time, he placed her on a bed and rubbed against her body. The third time he tried to mess with her, she told him to get away. He told her, it was no use to tell her mother, it would only hurt her, so she didn't.

Sandy Crisp was Rod's cousin. His mother was Lazetta Crews. She testified about what she knew of Sondra Gibson's relations with men. When she was twelve, Sondra had shown her photos of some of her men friends. They were usually pictures of men dressed as women, with makeup on. The witness said that it had been shocking to her.

Sondra Gibson was into vampirism. She made it sound like Rod's vampirism was all right. She thought it was wonderful, she was really into it. Ms. Crisp stated that she had seen Sondra going out nights dressed in black, walking down a street at night in an area known for illegal activity, drugs and prostitution.

Candace Hawthorne called Sondra Gibson to the stand to tell her story. She began, "I am Sondra Joanne Gibson, also known as Star. I am thirty-five. I was pregnant at sixteen, Rod was born at seventeen."

She had worked in Missouri at Faces, a nightclub. She was a dancer. "Yes, I did work as a prostitute. At that time I was on [the drug] ecstasy, speed, alcohol, anything I could get pretty much."

Her parents were very strict, religious, members of the United Pentecostal church. Rod was taken to church. She thought Darren Breven could have introduced Rod to dark occultism, because he was that kind of person—"mean."

She'd go to social functions with her son and his girlfriends. She was dressing all in black and wearing black nail polish.

Candace Hawthorne said, "Did you write letters soliciting sex from a fourteen-year-old named Josh?"

Sondra Gibson said, "Yes."

"Why would you do something like that?"

"I was having problems with his older brother Jaden Steven Murphy. He was going around town saying I was his woman, his vampire bride and he was the prince of the city."

She said that she did talk about "people floating by her window." She denied ever having told anyone that her son had sex with her—"That's ridiculous," she said.

"Did you ever tell anyone that Steven [Murphy] raped you repeatedly in occult sessions?"

"I don't believe I said that."

Candace Hawthorne showed her a report that said she had. Gibson said, "The doctor misunderstood who I was talking about."

She said that she'd had her phone shut off because she had a thousand dollar phone bill one month, due to Rod's calls to Heather and Jeanine. She'd started dating apartment handyman Kyle Newman, who was on probation and who inscribed tattoos on Rod's arm.

"You knew about it?"

"I was sitting right across the table from him when he did it," Gibson said.

On cross-examination, Brad King had Sondra Gibson identify a Valentine's Day card she sent to Jaden Murphy. She said she was/is in love with him. The prosecutor turned his attention to an exhibit which was the medical record of Rod's birth, documenting that there were several people in the room at the time of the birth. The record said that the newborn was crying lustily, there was nothing wrong with him. Rod hadn't been born with a cord around his neck, as mother and son liked to claim.

Gibson disagreed.

Brad King said, "So these records are wrong?"

"Yes, they are wrong."

"Rod was supposed to go back to court on November 26, 1996. That's the same night the murder occurred, isn't it?"

"I wouldn't know," Sondra Gibson said.

So ended day five of the trial. Day six, devoted to the testimony of Ferrell's high school principal, social workers who had dealt with mother and son, and the like, was largely uneventful.

Before putting the court in recess for the weekend, Judge Lockett instructed the jury, "Do not discuss this case with anyone. Do not read or watch television about this case. We will start with closing arguments on Monday."

JUDGEMENT DAY

Court reconvened on Monday, at nine A.M., day seven of the trial. Rod Ferrell looked worried as the jurors entered their box.

Brad King delivered the prosecution's closing argument. "This is one of the more serious decisions any human being can be asked to be made about another. Decision to decide an appropriate sentence for Rod Ferrell. It seems we've tried many people in this trial—Heather Wendorf, Harold Gibson, the Kentucky school system, Kentucky juvenile system, etc. But we're here to try Rod Ferrell."

He drew a contrast between the State's expert witnessses and those for the defense. "Our State expert, shoe print expert, her opinion is based on hard scientific evidence, with methodology to it. Ms. Montgomery did likewise—she had hard DNA evidence based on scientific principles."

But mental-health professionals, he argued, trained to help people who want and need help, go astray when outside their area of competency. "Rod Ferrell was not asking for help, he was asking for something else: a life sentence.

"Ferrell just flat out lies to Dr. Krop, says I've got these multiple personalities, and even the doctor says these tests are not reliable. Dr. Meyers gives his tests in early July, and has to say some of them are just not right.

"On and on the lies continue and the tests continue. There are things you can draw from what experts have said—that he lies to get what he wants, that he manipulates, that he has an average intelligence, that he knows right from wrong, and that he can understand responsibility and consequences.

"The law gives you a clear understanding of how to apply that idea [of self-determination] to this case. It's aggravating and mitigating circumstances.

"The first aggravator is, Mr. Ferrell was previously convicted of murder, armed robbery and armed burglary. The second is, were these murders committed during the course of certain violent felonies? Yes, armed robbery and burglary. Third, they were committed to avoid arrest. Fourth, they were done for financial gain. Fifth, the result of these murders on those involved—heinous, atrocious, and cruel—did the victims have an understanding of what was going to happen to them before it happened ?

"Last circumstance, is the crime cold, calculated, and premeditated?"

The prosecutor answered his own questions. "What you have is, he left Kentucky to go on a road trip. He left because he had law enforcement after him, he was due in court on Monday, he wanted to get out of town. He was the leader, the undisputed leader of four. He came in part to get his little women in Florida and he came to conclude some unfinished business. Now Monday, flat tire. He goes to Shannon Yohe's to make calls to Heather and Jeanine, and tells Shannon about his plans to kill the Wendorfs for their car. And it is interesting that before this trial, you never heard anything about rescuing Heather Wendorf from her abusive parents. He talks about wanting a car.

"When they get to the Wendorf house, they talk about going into the home, into the garage, and searching for better weapons. They go into the house and pull phones from the bedroom, so they won't get caught. . . . Then he goes to Mr. Wendorf, and you heard him talk about deciding, might as well do it, and beating him and beating him because he doesn't want him to be alive. And then Mrs. Wendorf walks in, and throws coffee at him. The fight starts here, and that entire time across the kitchen, she's fighting.

"She's no match for a young man with a crowbar. They take the keys, abandon their car, then they go to New Orleans. Ladies and gentlemen, those facts prove each of the aggravating factors. Commits murders, commits them during armed robbery and burglary, committed them to avoid arrest, committed them for pecuniary gain, and Naoma Wendorf fought him, knew what was going to happen.

"She gave him a fight for her life, but she lost, she paid the penalty for that. And finally, you know that it's cold, calculated and premeditated. . . ."

Brad King continued, "You say Mr. Ferrell is a person who can think, rationalize, make decisions. And it's true I wouldn't presume he's the same as you and I. He's not, because he has the capacity to look at the situation and decide, I want what I want and I'm gonna take it. And there are not many who live by that code.

"Even as he walked in the house, he could have said, this isn't the right thing to do. But he didn't choose to do that. He chose instead to do what he did. Even after beating Mr. Wendorf to death, he could have said no, I'm gonna leave one parent alive. But no. Ladies and gentlemen, the time for mercy has passed.

"There is only one penalty when someone has chosen to act so despicably, and that is, Mr. Ferrell, you have forfeited your right to live here on earth. That was his choice. Now is the time that Mr. Ferrell has to be held to account."

Candace Hawthorne closed for the defense. "Two weeks ago, Rod Ferrell stood up in this courtroom and pleaded guilty to these charges. His decision has not been to avoid blame. He took responsibility on November 28 and 29 when he talked to the Baton Rouge police . . . and in this court.

"It is our position that justice will be served by a life sentence, punishment will be served by a life sentence. Mr. King wants you to ignore certain issues in this case. He wants you to forget that a very significant part of this case is Heather Wendorf, the daughter of the victims. We cannot ignore that, you cannot ignore that in your decisions.

"That Rod would choose such a bizarre fantasy world shows just how bad his life is. Choices? He didn't have the tools to make the right decision."

She argued that the "abuse" of Heather Wendorf may not have existed, but Rod Ferrell thought it did. "As the doctors told you, this was an act of absolute rage. Rage doesn't come just because you want to rob someone's car; it comes from years of pent-up anger. Feeding into that was the fantasy and vampirism.

"There is the defendant's age. I submit that you may consider that he's approximately the age of three emotionally. . . . And you heard from his mother, she just had no clue. She failed to give him any values, she allowed him to smoke, use drugs, put an upside-down cross in the home. . . .

"Rod grew up in an emotionally disturbed family. Rod felt persecuted by society. Rod was under the influence of drugs at the time of the crime.

"We have seen no evidence from the State that Rod wasn't abused. In fact, we have evidence that he probably was. These occultists, the sacrifices, they may very well have occurred. In a child's mind, the child may believe that a person has been killed in sacrifice when they haven't been. This child probably believed everything he was shown. Rod has taken responsibility for what he did—he said 'I did it'—in Louisiana and in court.

"Rod is able to function in a prison environment. . . . Finally, he will never be part of our society again. He will be segregated from the rest of society until he dies.

"When Rod went into that house, he couldn't stop the rage. His decision-making process was flawed. . . . You won't decide this case in rage; you'll decide it with common sense and collective judgment. We all wish Rod had that common sense, but he didn't. Please make the right decision and sentence Rod Ferrell to life in prison."

After deliberating for four and a half hours, the jury reached a verdict. On both counts of first-degree murder, in a unanimous decision, they voted to recommend the death penalty for Roderick Justin Ferrell.

The defense attorneys later received a letter from the jury foreman which said that the jury had found no mitigating factors.

On February 27, 1998, Judge Jerry Lockett accepted the jury's recommendation and sentenced Rod Ferrell to death in the electric chair, making him the youngest person to sit on Florida's death row.

After sentencing Rod Ferrell to be executed, Judge Lockett took the unusual step of urging the prosecution of Heather Wendorf, saying, "There is genuine evil in this world" and that there were still unanswered questions about Wendorf's role in her parents' slaying.

Sondra Star Gibson said her son did not deserve the death penalty and endorsed the judge's suggestion of pursuing charges against Heather Wendorf. "There's one person walking around who's just as guilty as he is," she said outside the courtroom following her son's sentencing.

Heather Wendorf was investigated by a second grand jury, which also declined to indict her.

Georgia v. *Crowder:*
THE TOMATO PATCH MURDER

MISSING PERSON

At midday on Monday, May 19, 1997, in small-town Ludowici in Long County, Georgia, 19-year-old Billy Crowder was tending to a bit of household gardening. Slim, wiry, with short dark hair, he fit the image of the quiet type who keeps to himself. Now, he eyed the newly planted rows of slender green tomato plants set in a bed of freshly turned earth. The tomato patch lay about five feet away from the east wall of the one-story concrete blockhouse where he lived with his sister, Katie, 17, and their grandfather, Thurman Martin, 64.

Earlier that day, Crowder and his friend Jason Jordan, 18, had driven into the nearby town of Jesup, where they'd gotten the plants at an agricultural supply store. Jordan had actually done the planting for the tomato patch.

It hadn't required much work because the digging had been done the night before.

Now Jordan had left the scene, leaving Crowder alone with the pale green shoots embedded in the dark reddish-brown earth.

Looking around, Crowder could see the familiar small-town landscape where he'd lived all his life.

Almost directly across the street from the Martin house was the residence of the chief of police and his neighbor, a member of the Georgia Public Service Commission. About 150 yards away lived the mayor pro tem, while three quarters of a mile away stood the sheriff's department.

Ludowici, population, 1,600, was a farm-based society, land bound, conservative, setting a high store on kinfolk and continuity, a town where everybody knew everybody else . . . or at least thought they did.

Tending to the tomato patch was just one more routine chore, judging by Billy Crowder's demeanor. He knew all about chores. To him, it seemed like he had been doing them all his life, every spare minute of the day when he wasn't going to school. Both he and Katie. There was no end of household chores for either of them.

He carried out his task with the same methodical determination and quiet competency with which he performed all his work. He was mechanically minded, handy, good with cars and guns.

He was a good shot, a member of the high school shooting team, and a good hunter, too. He and his granddaddy Thurman Martin had once run a pack of hunting dogs for the town hunt club. As Crowder recalled it, he had done all the work and his granddaddy had taken all the money. Then Thurman had had some trouble with the club and the arrangement was no more.

Widely regarded in the area as a local "character," Thurman Martin was a rough-and-ready relic of the town's rowdy past. Located in rural southeast Georgia not far from the Florida border, Ludowici (*Luh-do-wiss-see*) was notorious from the 1950s to the early 1970s as one of the most piratical flyspecks on the regional map. Situated on Highway 301, the town was one of the speed-trap capitals of the world, preying on vacationers and tourists driving through to the playgrounds of Florida. It was a stereotypically sleepy, dirty, little country town straight out of the *Dukes of Hazzard* and *Smoky and the Bandit*, only for real.

Those were the days when carnival booth operators were given the okay from higher-ups to run games of Razzle-Dazzle, an incredibly complex gambling game whose one certainty was that no honest player could win. Sore losers were liable to get hit on the head and wake up on the other side of the county line, picked clean of their valuables. Sometimes they never woke up. The honky-tonk joints were flush with moonshine whiskey and whores, and "cuttings" were common. Big-time political bosses like Colonel Ralph Dawson ran the county as their own private property.

It had gotten so bad at one point that the town was blacklisted by the AAA Auto club. Governor (and future president) Jimmy Carter had begun an investigation into the area, but it was called off after the death of Colonel Dawson. The opening of an alternate route, Interstate 95, had put an end to the bad old days, but there were still many people around who had lived through those times.

Thurman Martin was a survivor of that era. He liked to boast of his "insider" connections to the ruling clique. The extent of his involvement with the town's dirty side is uncertain, but it seems likely that he was familiar with its movers and shakers and that he carried out errands for them. He bragged about his ability to whip a folding knife from his pocket, "cut" an opponent, and repocket it in quick-time. Photos of him depict a hard-bitten, unsmiling individual.

Originally from Glennville, Georgia, Martin had been many things in his life. At one time, he'd owned and run a drinking club, no job for the fainthearted. Mostly he'd been a trucker while Billy and Katie Crowder were growing up, but in recent years a back injury had forced him to retire from the road. These days he ran a little automobile repair shop out of a corrugated-metal shed on the property.

Billy did most of the repair work, while Thurman collected the money.

The white concrete blockhouse was a onetime Church of God church, which Martin had rebuilt. He resided there now with Billy and Katie. His wife, Lula Kate Martin, had lived there until she'd died in February 1997. Billy Crowder loved and revered her; she'd been like a mother to him. More than a mother.

His and Katie's real mother was Thurman Martin and Lula Kate's daughter, Diana, known to family and friends as Diane. Only her husband, John, called her Diana. Within days of Billy's birth, she had given him to her parents to raise. Or maybe Thurman had just taken him; the truth of the matter was hazy.

Diane was a troubled soul who'd been married five times and had been treated for mental problems. Billy's daddy was a Crowder, so that was the name he bore—Billy Crowder.

Thurman and Lula Kate's other offspring, Edward Dean Martin, "Dean," had been in prison since 1978, serving a life term for beating and raping a woman.

When Lula Kate had first taken sick, Thurman Martin had sent for Billy's sister, Katie, who was then 12 years old, moving her into the house to tend to her ailing grandmother. After Lula Kate's death, Diane, 35, had separated from her current husband, John Stanton. Spouse number five was 54-years-old, four years younger than her father. Leaving their house in Brunswick, Georgia (about 50 miles away) they moved into a trailer in back of the Martin house, so Diane could continue to look after Katie.

Sunday night, May 18, Diane and John Stanton had stayed in the trailer, but early the next morning they had left for Augusta to see a doctor as John Stanton was deathly ill with bone cancer. They returned about noon, in time to see Billy tilling the tomato plants.

Katie was somewhere in the house. Outside, it was nice and quiet, peaceful.

Thurman Martin was nowhere to be seen.

Later that day, Billy Crowder contacted the Long County Sheriff's Department, his phone call taken by Sheriff Cecil Nobles. Crowder said that his grandfather was missing, and hadn't been seen since the previous night.

The sheriff was not overly concerned. There was nothing sinister or even unusual in a man absenting himself without so much as a by-your-leave from home for a day or two, or a night or two. Especially not a man like Thurman Martin.

Two hours later, Crowder followed up with a second call. Such concern over a missing person in so short a time frame struck Sheriff Nobles as suspicious. Nobles, some 60-odd years old, was round faced and wide built, with an easy, agreeable manner. In Long County, the sheriff was an elective office, and the voters had kept him in that office for over thirty years.

Thurman Martin had spent most of his life in Ludowici. Sheriff Nobles had known him for some 45 years.

Nobles later recalled, "Things just weren't adding up, to report someone missing way before dark. This man has lived in this county all his life. I'm sure he's been out down there in the swamp hunting and fishing a lot and out of town. It's very unusual reporting someone missing three, four hours before dark."

The next day, Billy Crowder came into the sheriff's office to file a missing person report. Chief deputy and veteran investigator Ty Smith took the complaint. Crowder said that Thurman Martin was last seen on the night of May 18, and that three pairs of his pants, shirts, and underwear were missing.

Crowder also spoke of Diana and John Stanton's Augusta trip, saying that they had left early on the morning of the 19th, returning around noon. He also said that two men, acquaintances of Martin, claimed to have seen him on this very day, the 20th.

Already suspicious, Sheriff Nobles found his misgivings growing as he reviewed the case: "After talking to Billy Crowder and Katie Crowder, they mentioned that three pair of trousers was missing. And so they wanted to lead us that maybe he had gone off with another truck driver down the road.

"How would he know that three pairs of

pants would be missing?" wondered Nobles, skeptical of the specificity of the information. "But we kept questioning around town, and we suspected something wasn't adding up."

Nobles was suspicious enough to get in touch with the nearest branch office of the Georgia Bureau of Investigation. The GBI is a statewide agency empowered to assist local law-enforcement investigations, a particularly useful asset for sheriff's departments in rural counties with far-flung territory, sparse population, and underfunded operating budgets.

About two days after the initial complaint, Nobles contacted the GBI office in Moultrie, requesting their assistance in the matter of Thurman Martin, which was now listed as an official missing persons case. And so it was as a missing persons case that it entered the GBI files.

On May 22, 1997, members of the Long County Sheriff's Department met with GBI agents to discuss the case. GBI Special Agent Ron Brooks, clean cut, athletic, intent, would handle the case from the bureau's end, teaming with Long County Sheriff's Department Deputy Sonny Chambless, the department's chief investigator. Together, they worked the initial investigation.

Ron Brooks later told *Court TV,* "We didn't really have a prime suspect at that point in time because it was a missing persons case. And so the standard procedure for us is everybody's a suspect till they're cleared.

"We didn't know whether or not we had a crime at that point in time. 'Cause he's a missing person doesn't mean you have a crime; it simply means that he may have walked off on his own. He could've gone back to driving a truck, he could have done a number of different things. So we were just trying to find him and following the leads wherever they went."

When a citizen in a small town goes missing, it makes a big hole.

Bennie Griffin, the town barber, knew Thurman Martin from the old days. He had given haircuts to three generations of Martins: Thurman, his son, Dean, and grandson, Billy. A few days after the disappearance had become common knowledge, Billy dropped by the barbershop.

Bennie Griffin recalled, "I didn't know what had happened to Thurman Martin. I suspected Diana Crowder, his daughter, of having something to do with the disappearance, but I never suspected Billy. Billy and Thurman was too close to suspect anything like that.

"Diane is a little off in the head and her and her daddy didn't get along too good. And she had threatened to kill him before. He told me that."

As it happened, Bennie Griffin was not alone in thinking that if Thurman Martin had met with foul play, the culprit might not fall too far from the family tree. Cecil Nobles was thinking along similar lines. "At first when it happened, we really suspected the daughter,

Diana Crowder, and the son-in-law, John Stanton. We suspected those two would be involved in it."

It was no secret that there was bad blood between Thurman Martin and his daughter, so much so that when he turned up missing, she topped the list of likely suspects. But there was no reason to suspect Billy Crowder. The sheriff asked around and was told by people who knew them that Billy and his grandfather were close, that there was no indication of a problem there.

Bennie Griffin spoke for most of the townsfolk when he said, "I knew him, Thurman Martin, for at least thirty-five years and he was real strict on his grandchildren, because he'd had problems with his own children. But I never dreamed that Billy ever had any bad feelings about his granddaddy. I thought he loved him, 'cause he was with him all the time. And Billy was as nice-mannered a boy as they are in this county—yes, sir, no, sir. Never been in any trouble."

But there was more than just family matters to investigate. Brooks and Chambless probed into the doings of a female associate of Thurman Martin's, an alleged crack-taking, black prostitute who traded sex for drugs. An interesting line of inquiry, especially for what it said about Thurman Martin, but one that had yet to produce any tangible results.

Then came a bombshell development.

Earlier, on Thursday, May 29, GBI SA Ron

Brooks had interviewed John Stanton at his Brunswick residence, with Diana Crowder present. The debilitating bone cancer was eating John away from the inside, forcing him into a quasi-invalid retirement and afflicting him with intense pain that was being treated with a morphine patch.

On May 31, Brooks received a phone call from John Stanton, charging that Diane had been raped by her father, Thurman Martin. The alleged rapes had occurred not in the past when she was a minor, but recently—specifically in the time since the death of her mother, Kate, and the time when Thurman Martin had gone missing. Diane claimed that he had raped her four times on four separate occasions. John said that this was the first he had learned of the alleged rapes.

On June 10, 1997, Diane Crowder swore out warrants against Thurman Martin for the four rapes. With foul play seeming likely in Thurman Martin's disappearance, the sudden surfacing of the rape charges could well be interpreted as a kind of preemptive strike, laying the groundwork for an abuse defense. Incest-rape was a motive for murder, perhaps even for a plea of justifiable homicide.

Meanwhile, a promising lead was developing in a different sector of the investigation.

Chambless and Brooks continued doing the legwork, canvassing the area, interviewing neighbors, friends, and associates. One person they would have liked to talk to was currently unavailable.

Jason Jordan, Billy Crowder's buddy who had gone with him on the day of the disappearance to buy the tomato plants, had left his hometown of Jesup and gone to live in North Carolina.

About a week or so into the investigation, Sheriff Nobles was contacted by a potential female informant. He assured her that he would protect her anonymity. She offered information on a principal in the case.

Around that time, while following up different leads, Ron Brooks interviewed Toni Shacklefort, Jason Jordan's girlfriend. The girl he had left behind. During that interview, she indicated that Jordan may have been involved in the disappearance of Thurman Martin, and gave several reasons why she had come to that conclusion, mainly involving potentially incriminating statements he had made to her and others.

Following up that lead sent the investigators to North Carolina, where they interviewed a number of Jason Jordan's known associates. Returning to Long County, they did some more interviews.

Then they asked Jason Jordan to come into the GBI office in Moultrie for an interview. During that interview, they confronted him with their knowledge that he had made statements to several of his associates about his being present when a father or grandfather was killed and buried. Jordan admitted to making such statements. However, he denied making a statement where he first asked an acquaintance if the other had ever killed anyone. When the other said no, Jordan had allegedly said, "Well, I did, and you'll hear about it in a few days." He had then left for North Carolina.

Following that interview, Jason Jordan was asked to take a polygraph test, to which he agreed. The results of the polygraph showed deception. He was called on it and cracked, admitting that he was present when Thurman Martin was killed.

Jordan kept on talking. Based on the information provided by him, Ron Brooks drafted several search warrants: one for the residence of Thurman Martin, one for Diana Crowder's trailer, and one for the house of John Stanton.

After the warrants were drawn up, Brooks and several of the other agents decided to ask Billy Crowder if he would take a polygraph examination, which he agreed to do.

Crowder now says that GBI agents "told me they told Jason he didn't pass it [polygraph test], but [earlier] he told me they said he passed it with flying colors. And if he could pass it scared and jumpy as he was, I figured I could, too. So I agreed to go take one."

What Crowder didn't know was that the police were now sure Jason Jordan was involved in the murder.

Crowder was not under arrest. The GBI had merely "requested" that he take a polygraph, an "invitation" that he was legally free to decline. Crowder made some half-hearted attempts to get out of it at the last moment, he says, telling agent Ron Brooks that he wanted a postponement to work on somebody's transmission. According to him, Brooks said that it would be impossible to cancel—"it would screw up a bunch of work and throw a bunch of things off."

Subterfuge and subtle psychological pressure tactics have always been part of an investigator's tools, and are perfectly legal. The law has no quarrel with the use of cunning to trap a suspect.

The GBI's Moultrie office, where the polygraph would be given, was about a hundred miles from Ludowici. On July 3, 1997, the day before Independence Day, Billy Crowder got into a GBI car for the two and a half hour drive to Moultrie. The agents who drove Crowder there occupied the time by making small talk, much of it about hunting.

Again, Crowder was not under arrest. The examination was strictly voluntary. At any time, he could have requested that the agents drive him back home, and they would have had to comply. But he didn't. At Moultrie, GBI polygraphist Rodney Rance administered the exam to Billy Crowder.

At the same time, in Ludowici, the GBI's Walt Lanier and another agent were meeting with Katie Crowder. They interviewed her, asking her what she knew about the disappearance of Thurman Martin. At a key point in the interview, they revealed that they knew that Martin was no longer among the living.

While Billy Crowder was being polygraphed, Ron Brooks was contacted by Lanier, who told him that Katie had broken down and confessed that she had cleaned up blood and a shell casing at the instructions of her brother.

That, added to the fact that Jason Jordan had flunked the polygraph test and implicated Billy, led Brooks to think that "we had a pretty good chance of getting a confession out of Billy."

During the post-polygraph interview, Crowder maintained his ignorance of the whereabouts of his grandfather. Brooks told him that the polygraph showed "deception." Crowder stuck to his story, hanging tough, denying that he had any part in the disappearance of Martin.

Brooks confronted him with the fact of Katie's confession. Billy leaned forward, saying that "it didn't matter what Katie said, it didn't matter what the black box [polygraph] said, I never shot my granddaddy with that rifle."

Brooks said, "Rifle? What rifle? Who said

anything about a rifle? Only somebody who was there could have known that."

That tore it. As Billy Crowder later recalled, "After that I was just tired of it, tired of looking over my shoulder. That's the reason I confessed."

Slumping back in his chair, he said, "I swore since I was six years old that I would kill my granddaddy."

Sometimes teary-eyed, but never crying profusely, he told what had happened on Sunday, May 18, 1997.

Crowder said that on that day, he was at the Martin house working on cars with Gene Ryals, a neighbor of about his own age. He and Ryals washed and waxed Thurman Martin's car, but mistakenly used the wrong kind of wax, giving it a kind of two-tone appearance. Thurman was upset, and Crowder told Ryals to go home. When Crowder was alone with his grandfather, Martin started beating him, cursing and hitting him.

According to Crowder, this was no one-time occasion, no fit of pique or temper. This was standard operating procedure for Thurman Martin, the way he treated all his family behind closed doors where outsiders couldn't see. The way he'd been treating Billy since he was six years old. Billy and his sister, Katie, were virtual slaves, forced to spend all their non-school hours working away at chores, subjected to Martin's endless bullying, harassment, and verbal and physical abuse.

Crowder said, "Thurman started slapping me and hitting me. And that kept on for fifteen minutes. And he knocked me down and I would stand back up. I never would draw a hand against him. He just kept on, I don't know how long it was."

Thurman Martin was no feeble senior citizen. He was a tough old bird who hit hard. He gave Billy a "beatdown," cursing, spitting, slapping, punching, and kicking him. Crowder begged him to stop, but never raised a hand against him, like always. Billy's nose was bloodied and the blood ran down his face.

"I remember blood coming out my nose and tasting it in my mouth," he said.

At the same time, Martin taunted him, twisting the verbal knife by making ugly remarks about his dead grandmother—Martin's late wife, Lula Kate—who had raised Billy like a mother and whom he revered.

Crowder told GBI agents, "The last thing I really actually remember knowing what I was doing, he said, 'You ain't going to never amount to nothing like that bitch of a grandma you had.' And next thing I knew I had a rifle in my hand . . . 'cause I loved my grandma more than anything in the world."

But it didn't all happen quite that fast. A number of twists and turns still lay ahead before Thurman Martin met his fate. There was still some distance to go before Billy used that rifle. But with the taste of his own blood in his mouth as he picked himself up off the ground, the wheels were set in motion.

John Stanton had come up from Brunswick the day before, spending Saturday night in the trailer with Diane. Sometime on Sunday, Billy Crowder told Stanton he was going to kill Thurman Martin. Some gauge of the situation and the kind of regard Thurman Martin was held in by his own kin and in-laws may be seen in the fact that not only was Stanton not surprised, but that he made no attempt to dissuade Crowder.

Later, Billy Crowder contacted Jason Jordan in Jesup. "Early that evening I guess you'd say, I called Jason and said I need some help. And he said all right. He knew how he [Martin] treated me and all. I went over there and he was ready."

In the strange story that unfolded, the role of Jason Jordan is perhaps the most cryptic part of all. The family may have had their reasons for doing what they did, but where did he fit in? And why? Just to help out a buddy? Apparently Jason Jordan knew something of the abuse.

That evening, Billy Crowder drove over to Jesup, where he and Jordan went to a local supermarket. Using common everyday household items bought in the store—the cardboard roller from a roll of aluminum foil and a number of washers—Crowder made a silencer while they were in the parking lot. He'd learned how to make it from *The Poor Man's James Bond,* a kind of underground militia-type manual that described how to make such devices.

Crowder and Jordan then drove back from Jesup, going to the trailer on the Martin property, where John Stanton and Diana Crowder were. Thurman Martin and Katie Crowder were in the house, presumably asleep. Billy brought in the silencer and a rifle, a Ruger 10-.22, .22-caliber weapon. There already were some weapons in the trailer, three or four firearms belonging to John Stanton, brought from his home in Brunswick. There was a Mac-10 and a .9-mm pistol.

The trailer was the staging area. Crowder and Jordan changed clothes, donning camouflage outfits, as though they were going hunting. Together with Stanton, they armed themselves, with Crowder taking the rifle and silencer. Diana Crowder was present. Sometime between 11:30 at night and 12:30 in the morning, the three men went from the trailer to the house.

They stood silently outside, in the dark. Crowder stealthily removed a pane of window glass, opened up the window, and climbed through it into the quiet house.

Once inside, he padded to the door and let in Stanton and Jordan, weapons and all. They went to Thurman Martin's bedroom. Martin lay in bed, on his side, sleeping. Crowder put the rifle with its homemade silencer to the back of

Martin's head and pulled the trigger. He fired several more times until the gun jammed.

The silencer must have been effective, because none of the neighbors, not the chief of police nor the mayor pro tem, nor anyone else reported hearing gunshots that night, or anything that sounded like gunshots. One might wonder what Katie Crowder heard, if anything, and if she did hear it, what she did.

Crowder used a pocket knife to clear the jammed rifle. Then John Stanton took hold and fired two times into the back of Thurman Martin's neck.

Jason Jordan was supposed to take his turn next. The plan was that each one would shoot Thurman Martin, sealing them in conspiracy, mutual reliance, and silence, like a blood oath. That way, they'd all be equally culpable, and they'd each have something on the others to bind them to silence. One couldn't talk without self-incrimination.

It had been Jordan's plan, but he was no longer playing. He refused to shoot, saying that Thurman Martin was already dead.

Thurman Martin didn't need any more killing. He'd never be deader. Still, it was a chink in the wall of solidarity of the conspirators.

A .22 round is small caliber but high velocity. It would have drilled pencil-thick lines through Thurman Martin's skull and brain. Head wounds bleed heavily. There would have been plenty of blood around, on the bed and headboard. Maybe some bits of scalp with hair and flesh on them flying around, too. Gunsmoke would have been thick in the air, even with the windows open.

The trio took down a plastic shower curtain. Thurman Martin's corpse was gathered up with the bloody bedspread and mattress cover and folded in half, then rolled up inside the shower curtain and the package tied with yellow nylon rope.

They went outside and dug a hole in the ground near the house. Billy Crowder and Jason Jordan did the digging, while John Stanton stood by and watched, due to his health. After about three hours of digging in that hard Georgia red clay, they had a hole that was between three and four feet deep.

The trio went back inside the house, carried the body outside, placed it in the hole, and covered it with dirt.

The tools were cleaned up, and Stanton went back to the trailer. Diane had been in the trailer the whole time. Sometime between three and four in the morning, Diane went to the house where Katie was and allegedly woke her up, telling her that Thurman Martin wouldn't be bothering her anymore. Katie went back to sleep.

Billy Crowder steadfastly maintained that Katie had no involvement with the actual crime.

In the house, in Martin's bedroom, lay the dead man's wallet containing somewhere between 600 to 800 dollars. Billy took 20 dollars from it and gave it to Jason. Whatever Jordan's motivation for joining in the murder conspiracy, it wasn't for cash.

On the day after the murder, Billy Crowder gave the rifle and silencer to John Stanton to get rid of. Stanton subsequently threw the murder weapon off a bridge into the ocean. A few days later, Crowder gave Stanton 200 dollars of the money, for a trailer payment. Crowder used the rest of the money to pay bills and put food on the table.

As to the missing persons complaint he filed on Thurman Martin, Crowder said, "We only said things that he had said, that he was tired of having to feed everybody, and he was going back on the road."

Some of the details were fleshed out later by investigators, but that in essence was the crime as told by Billy Crowder. After his verbal confession, he wrote out a statement reiterating his account of the crime.

During the interview, when asked where Thurman Martin was, Billy Crowder replied, "Ever see that movie *The Last Supper*?" The modest independent film was a black comedy about graduate students who invite obnoxious social types to their house for dinner, poison them, and bury them in the vegetable garden for fertilizer.

The mention of the film led to some speculation that perhaps it had helped inspire the crime in a kind of copycat scenario, but Crowder later maintained that only in the last few days before his arrest had he seen the film, when it was playing on TV, and that it had nothing to do with plotting the crime.

Ron Brooks had crime-scene technicians on standby, ready to move when Billy Crowder revealed where Thurman Martin was buried. He called them on the phone and gave them the go-ahead.

Brooks prepared to transport Crowder back to Ludowici. Crowder was now officially under arrest, and pursuant to bureau regulations, he had to be handcuffed during the trip. He was a prisoner. He'd been caught.

At one point they stopped at a roadside stand and bought Crowder a jumbo-size drink of ice tea, then continued onward. By the time they got back to Long County, the searchers had already located Thurman Martin's body and were in the process of digging it up.

Sheriff Nobles had gotten a call from Ron Brooks, telling him exactly where the body was buried. Nobles was pleasantly surprised. That early morning trip to Augusta by John Stanton and Diana Crowder on Monday morning after the murder had led him to theorize that the body had been gotten rid of somewhere between Augusta and Brunswick, a lot of ground to cover. He hadn't expected the grave to be so close to home.

He went to the Martin residence. In the yard was a rusted Oldsmobile and an abandoned pickup truck. The body of Thurman Martin was buried there, if the confession was true. Nobles later recalled, "They told exactly where he was buried. They had the tomato plant over the grave. We knew right where to find the body and we saw some fresh dirt that had been dug. So it was very easy to find."

The crime-scene techs didn't have to look any farther than the tomato patch. In the 45 days since they had first been planted, they had grown ping-pong-ball-size green tomatoes. The criminalists used flexible fiberglass probing rods, like blind people's canes or fishing rods, spearing the soft bedded tomato patch. Between 3 and 4 feet down, they found something.

The sheriff had a backhoe on-site and its bulky metal claw tore up the earth and opened up its burden for all to see.

In the shallow grave, wrapped in a plastic shower curtain, lay the partly decomposed cadaver of Thurman Martin.

As the sheriff later said, "Digging a body up, that's a bad thing to happen, especially when this man had been buried forty-five days." It was a hot day.

The dead man had been buried with his watch, a Timex. It was still keeping time when Thurman Martin was unearthed, after all those weeks of being buried underground.

Other crime-scene techs worked inside the house, uncovering evidence. In the bedroom where the murder had taken place, they found bloodstains or bloodlike stains on the wall that hadn't been cleaned up yet.

Elsewhere, at the Glenn County Police Department, John Stanton was picked up and taken into custody at approximately 5:54 P.M. and given his Miranda rights at 6:05 P.M.. After arresting him, GBI agent Walt Lanier interviewed him. Stanton stated that Thurman Martin had "raped" Diana Crowder. For the next four or five hours, he labored over a handwritten 26-page confession, exasperating the arresting officers with the sheer length of it.

The statement cleared up the mystery of what had happened to the murder weapon. Stanton said he took the scoped .22 rifle, and threw it off Turtle River bridge on Interstate 95 into the river. The silencer had been made of paper, so he burned it.

Five people were now under arrest in connection with the death of Thurman Martin: Billy Crowder, John Stanton, Diana Crowder, Katie Crowder, and Jason Jordan.

When the news became public, barber Bennie Griffin spoke for many in town when he said of Billy Crowder, "He completely fooled me and the rest of the people around here, too."

PRETRIAL

The case would be tried in Atlantic Circuit Superior Court, a six-county rural circuit in southeast Georgia. Hal Peel was one of a rela-

144 BLOOD AND LUST

tive handful of area lawyers who handled the
cases of indigent defendants.

On the Monday following the arrests, Hal
Peel was in court in Bryan County. The judge
called Peel and two other lawyers to the bench,
advising them that they were going to be rep-
resenting some people in Long County who
were accused of murder. There was a bond
hearing at five P.M. that afternoon in Ludowici.
Peel went down there, meeting for the first
time his client, Billy Crowder.

Peel was bespectacled and bearded, earnest,
empathetic. He told *Court TV,* "Right up front
we knew that here was something wrong because as a rule people don't band together
and kill the patriarch of their family, so we
knew that there was something going on
there. . . . We didn't realize the extent of it
until we got into a little bit more."

It was an open-and-shut case on the facts of
the crime. The law had the defendants nailed
dead to rights on the murder. They had confessions, too. Jason Jordan, John Stanton, and
Billy Crowder had shot Thurman Martin dead
in his sleep. There was no getting around that.

Not long before, the Georgia Supreme
Court had set a precedent with the Smith case,
a ruling that provided a basis for the Battered
Person Syndrome defense. Furthermore, the
law said that if BPS was the defense, it must
be the sole defense. The law stated that if such
a charge were presented to the jury, the defense must call the defendant and expert wit-

nesses who would show that the defendant was indeed suffering from BPS, which encompassed a cluster of behavioral traits, including suffering from such things as Post Traumatic Stress Disorder (PTSD).

Proceeding according to Superior Court rules, the defense notified the prosecution of their intent to introduce documented evidence of some 35 prior acts of violence by Thurman Martin against the accused and other family members.

District Attorney Dupont Cheney assigned Assistant District Attorneys Tom Durden and John Dow to prosecute the case. In the preliminary stages, Dow and Long County Sheriff's Department Deputy Sonny Chambless interviewed the same witnesses that the defense would later call, such as Thurman Martin's neighbors, the Ryals.

The defendants were held in various area jails—Billy Crowder in Statesboro, where Peel went three or four times to get bail reduced. Crowder was let out on bail, living with his cousin Pam Beasley and her family for the nine months before the trial.

First came the trial of Jason Jordan, who was tried separately for the murder of Thurman Martin in April 1998, at Long County Superior Court, Judge Robert A. Russell III presiding.

Jordan had a tough row to hoe. There could be no BPS abuse defense for him. Although he had not fired a shot into Thurman Martin, in the eyes of the law he was still as guilty of murder as if he had.

Of all those involved in the case, Jason Jordan is the hardest to read. The other defendants were tied to Thurman Martin by blood and cohabitation, but not him. What was his motive?

Just an ordinary guy helping out his buddy, Billy? Sure, helping him out by conspiring with him and other family members to kill a hated grandfather. By all accounts, Jason Jordan was gung ho to do the deed, coming up with the all-for-one, we-all-killed-Thurman-Martin plan, then getting cold feet when it was his turn to pull the trigger. He might as well have, for all the good his abstention did him in court.

It wasn't a greedy crime, though he took a 20-dollar bill from Thurman Martin's cash. He wasn't charged with robbery.

His motives were obscure, but this much was known: Jason Jordan couldn't wait to talk up his role in the kill. He hungered for the respect and status that came with having taken a life. He couldn't wait to start making his big brag about it. He talked it up to his girlfriend and associates in Ludowici, and did the same in North Carolina.

He was the weakest link in the chain. Billy Crowder and the others were able to maintain the front that Thurman Martin had just gone missing. Jordan shot off his mouth, got caught up in the investigation, and pretty much cracked once the law started speaking sternly to him. Once caught, he fingered everyone else.

After a speedy trial, on April 22, 1998, after deliberating a scant 18 minutes, the jury returned the verdict, finding Jason Jordan guilty on the counts of murder and hindering the apprehension of a criminal.

Judge Russell gave Jason Jordan a life sentence on the murder charge, tacking on an additional five years on the charge of hindering.

Now, for no discernible reason except perhaps a burning desire to play the big shot, he would spend life in prison. Plus five years.

Pam Beasley was present at the trial. Afterward, she called Hal Peel, whose heart sank when he heard the news about the verdict, and the speed with which it had been delivered. The next day, his concerns were eased somewhat when Pam Beasley told him that she had spoken to a juror after the trial, who indicated that the jury had no compassion for Jason Jordan because they felt he had no justification for what he did.

That news cheered Peel somewhat, since he felt that his client did indeed have such "justification" for his act. Peel hoped that would give them a better shot at beating the murder charge.

The next legal milestone was the disposition of the Diana Crowder and Katie Crowder cases. They had helped clean up after Thurman Martin was killed and each ultimately pled guilty to hindering the apprehension of a criminal. Diana was sentenced to a year in prison, and Katie got five years probation, with six to eight months to be spent in a detention center.

Hal Peel noted, "Katie got a great deal . . . they simply did not have enough evidence to charge her with murder. She ended up eventually pleading to lesser offenses for probation and then some detention center time, which was great. That was an excellent deal."

But Peel had no such incentive to cut a deal for Billy Crowder. The DA's office wasn't dealing. Peel offered to plead Billy Crowder guilty of manslaughter, but the prosecution said no. They called it murder and were going for a conviction.

THE TRIAL

Billy Crowder and John Stanton wanted to be tried together because they had similar defenses. Trial was set for the week of June 15, 1998, but a bizarre series of events caused a postponement.

Jury selection was set for Tuesday, June 16. On Sunday, John Stanton checked into a hospital, complaining of intense pain from his bone cancer. He was given morphine intravenously, in addition to his morphine patch, which he'd had for some years. His physician,

Dr. Moran, said he thought John was faking some of his pain, but couldn't be certain.

On Monday, Judge Russell was notified of the hospitalization, and called Stanton's doctor, who repeated his belief that Stanton was probably faking some of his ailments. The judge ruled the trial could go on, directing that an ambulance transport Stanton to court on the following day, Tuesday, June 16.

John Stanton entered, escorted by two emergency medical technicians, who slowly walked him into court in full view of the jury pool. After sitting down, Stanton appeared to pass out. His lawyer shook him, trying to bring him around, but Stanton was unresponsive, seeming semicomatose and unaware of his surroundings.

The judge wanted to begin individual voir dire, the questioning of the individual jurors, as had been done in Jason Jordan's trial. He had both defendants, their lawyers, and the prosecution taken into the grand jury room so the jurors could be questioned in private. In the room, outside of the view of the jury pool, Stanton's condition appeared to worsen. His breathing was labored, he lapsed into unconsciousness. He had to be tied to his wheelchair to keep him from falling to the floor. The EMTs discovered his blood sugar level was dangerously low.

Throughout all this, court personnel stayed in touch with Stanton's doctor over the phone, who doubted that the patient's condition had been caused by morphine. A sheriff's deputy was sent to Brunswick to transport the doctor to the courthouse.

On the way back to court, the deputy and Dr. Moran were involved in a serious car accident. The deputy's cruiser was totalled, after being struck by a car driven by an elderly woman. The doctor ended up back in the hospital, so the judge and lawyers went there to question him.

The doctor said he believed Stanton's failing condition was caused by low blood sugar, not morphine, and that the plunge might have been caused by anxiety. He stated that Stanton was in no condition to help in his own defense.

Judge Russell then reluctantly delayed the trial.

The defendants were each being charged with four counts: murder, armed robbery (for taking the victim's money), hindering the apprehension of a criminal (for burying the body and filing a false missing person's report), and possession of a firearm during the commission of a crime. Under the murder count, jurors would have the option of convicting each defendant on a lesser included charge of voluntary manslaughter.

The potential sentences were these:

For murder, life with the possibility of parole (which generally means a defendant must serve 7 to 14 years before becoming eligible for parole).

For armed robbery: 10 to 20 years OR life with the possibility of parole.

For hindering the apprehension of a criminal: 1 to 5 years.

For possession of a firearm during the commission of a crime: 5 years tacked on to any other sentence.

The judge's sentencing discretion allowed him to run the sentences for murder (manslaughter), armed robbery, and/or hindering the apprehension of a criminal, either concurrently or consecutively. But the mandatory five-year sentence on the firearms charge would have to be served after every other sentence was completed.

John Stanton's lawyer, John Cloy, planned to argue a form of self-defense, claiming that Billy Crowder and Stanton acted to protect themselves and other family members when they killed Thurman Martin. He would also mount a "good character defense." The judge would allow a certain number of witnesses to testify to his client's good reputation in the community, though specific testimony regarding Stanton's good deeds would not be allowed.

In Georgia, a jury can actually acquit a defendant based upon good character, as long as the evidence against the defendant is also considered.

Crowder's lawyer Hal Peel would use the justification defense. Peel would argue that Crowder was the victim of physical and emotional abuse at the hands of Thurman Martin from the time he was a baby and the only way to break free was to shoot Martin in self-defense. Peel would call to the stand neighbors who would say that they had witnessed Martin's abusive behavior over the years, and family members who would testify that Billy, Lula Kate Martin, Katie Crowder, and Diana Crowder all tried to escape from Thurman Martin many times, but always returned home after Martin allegedly threatened them.

He would also claim that Billy Crowder and other family members got PTSD from Martin's abuse, and that that condition made them unable to exercise the option to simply walk away.

The defense boiled down to "Guilty, with an excuse." They weren't going to argue the facts of the case, that Billy Crowder and John Stanton had conspired to kill Thurman Martin in his sleep. They were going to argue that Martin was the kind who needed killing, and that the particular brand of abuse he'd allegedly inflicted on the family over the years had so traumatized them that they believed that they had no way of escaping Martin except by killing him.

The prosecution would argue that even if Thurman Martin had been mean or abusive, that this still was no justification for his being shot dead in his sleep (and robbed). There were

other means of dealing with him. Despite what
the defense alleged, there were no reported incidents of such abuse against family members,
no police arrests or even complaints. There
were a couple of incidents regarding John Stanton, but the prosecution would seek to minimize those.

They would maintain that the complaints
were overblown, exaggerated. The level of
physical abuse claimed by the youngsters
would surely have resulted in hospital stays,
medical reports, reports being filed by school
authorities.

Buttressing their claim was the fact that
Thurman Martin had no police record to
speak of. The fact that they had questioned a
crack-smoking prostitute regarding his vanish-
ing showed that his reputation was less than
spotless, but Tom Durden dismissed as "folk-
lore" the deceased's claimed exploits, such as
cutting out a man's guts and making him take
a drink of whiskey, pulling knives.

Katie Crowder had made no previous claim
of sex abuse. Diana Crowder had made her
claim only after Thurman Martin was dead.
Both the prosecution and defense seem to
have regarded Diana as a loose cannon. The
judge and sheriff both wanted her banned
from the county for the duration of the trial.
She ended up not being banned, but was not
allowed to testify and stayed away from the
courthouse. The defense made no objection.

The defense would counter the prosecution's claims by saying that they helped to make the defense's case. History was destiny, and the history of old-time, low-down Ludowici had worked for Thurman Martin. He had been an important figure in the local power structure and as such enjoyed protection and immunity against arrests.

In other words, he had clout with the police and the legal-political system, and that this influence stopped family members from making a getaway or even filing a complaint.

A more subtle point was this: Thurman Martin didn't really have to have the influence he claimed he had. What was important was that his family members believed it was true, and acted accordingly.

In the trial of Jason Jordan, the people had rendered their verdict and condemned him quickly. But Jordan wasn't family. Billy Crowder and John Stanton were. The defense argued that that made a difference, all the difference in the world, the difference between life and death, murder and manslaughter.

Thurman Martin was about to be put on trial, posthumously, by the defense.

Hanging over the case was the long shadow of the Menendez brothers, who had claimed that sexual abuse had justified the shotgun slayings of their parents. Their plea had tended to discredit the abuse excuse among Americans.

* * *

On July 13, 1998, jury selection took place. The process was a lengthy individual voir dire, with the jury pool sequestered and examined one at a time. This procedure was favored by both prosecution and defense, who felt that potential jurors would speak more freely, openly, and honestly without their friends and neighbors watching.

A 30-person jury pool had been impaneled. When it came to disallowing jurors, according to Georgia law in a noncapital offense case, the defense was given 12 strikes and the State, 6. If each side took the maximum number of strikes allowed, 18 jurors would be removed, leaving 12 to make up the jury.

The individual questioning was long and tiring, lasting a marathon eleven hours with breaks, stretching from 9:00 A.M. to 10:30 P.M. A twelve-member jury was selected, with seven women and five men, and two male alternates.

Once impaneled, the jurors would be sequestered until they had reached a verdict, with one exception. One juror, whose very pregnant wife was due to deliver the couple's sixth child at any moment, was allowed to return home each night (under strict instructions not to discuss the case).

The trial began on Tuesday, July 14, 1998 at Long County Superior Court in Ludowici, with the Honorable Robert A. Russell III presiding. Prosecuting the case was Tom Durden, Chief

Assistant DA for the Atlantic Circuit, State of Georgia, and Assistant DA John Dow, while attorneys Hal Peel and Joey Sapp appeared for the defense of Billy Crowder and attorney John Cloy for the defense of John Stanton.

The jury was sworn and then Prosecutor Durden made his opening statement. He began with the basics, explaining the charges to the jury. He said, "Georgia law says a person commits murder when he causes the death of another human being."

He went on to explain the charges of armed robbery, hindering apprehension of a criminal, and possession of a firearm during the commission of a felony. Unknown to all, one of these lesser charges would prove vital to the outcome of the case.

"How is the State's evidence going to show the guilt of John Stanton and Billy Crowder for this crime?" he asked, then answering his own question by stating that the evidence would show that John Stanton and Billy Crowder did commit these crimes—"That's what the evidence will show you."

He said, "Murder cases generally fall into three categories: who done it, how did it happen, and why did it happen?"

He went on to say that the defendants would offer the abuse excuse, that Thurman Martin was mean to them. "But you'll hear from witnesses who never heard any such abuse." And Thurman Martin wasn't present to defend himself from such charges. Even the alleged abuse was no justification for shooting the man in his sleep.

"It was an unjustified killing," Durden argued, "which under Georgia law is murder."

He added, "Before he was buried, it gets even more macabre. They take and rob their relative, take money out of his pocket. This killing was unmitigated, unjustified, unexcusable, and at the appropriate time I'm going to ask you for a verdict of guilty as charged on each count. And you'll agree that each of these defendants is guilty of each crime. Thank you."

Now it was time for the defense to make its opening statement. Hal Peel declined to give an opening for Billy Crowder. John Stanton's attorney, John Cloy, exercised his option, beginning by introducing his client to the jury.

"A lot of what the State has told you is true, but it is a why-done-it," he said, putting the emphasis on "is" in rebuttal to the prosecution's opening remarks. "The evidence will contradict the State's theory. Thurman Martin was a wildcat."

The dead man's public and private faces were opposite, the attorney said. "To the family, he was a terror, he picked on the weak. He raped his own daughter, he attacked his grandson, he abused his granddaughter."

He spoke of John Stanton's bone cancer: "He's been picked on and abused by Thurman Martin repeatedly." Addressing the issue of the lethal assault, he wondered, "Was it really armed robbery, or was it really self-defense? Maybe Thurman Martin was asleep, but if you're infirmed and weak, how do you deal with a wildcat?

"The jury's duty is to 'seek the truth'—in this state, contrary to what you were told [i.e., by the prosecution], there are occasions where justification is allowed. You've got to decide whether or not it was justified, keep an open mind."

That closed the openings. Now, the State would present its case, calling as its first witness Long County Sheriff's Department Deputy Ty Smith, who had handled the initial missing person's report on Thurman Martin. John Dow conducted the direct examination.

Dow established the timetable of the complaint, with that witness stating that he took a missing person report from Billy Crowder on May 20, 1997, though Thurman Martin had allegedly last been seen on May 18. On May 19, Crowder had offered the information that three pairs of pants, shirts, and underwear were missing, with the implication that Martin had taken them with him and gone out on the road.

The prosecution also elicited the fact that Crowder had stated that one of the missing man's known associates had seen him on May 20. Also, that Crowder said that he had last seen Thurman Martin "around eleven P.M. on May 18."

The witness had also spoken with Billy Crow-

der on May 22 at ten A.M., when the defendant
had offered additional minor information that
buttressed his story that Thurman Martin was
alive.

There was no cross-examination by the defense.

Dow next called GBI Special Agent Gerald
Hill, a crime-scene specialist who was called
into the case on July 3, 1997, to assist in the
investigation at the Martin residence.

Hill was shown photos of the scene and
identified them for the record. The first group
showed interior views of the house, including
Thurman Martin's bedroom. One such photo
depicted adhesive markers pointing to some
bloodstains behind the headboard, on the
wood paneling. Another showed a close-up of
the stains on the paneling. Others imaged the
area behind the headboard, showing signs of
"some wiping"—that is, of an attempt at con-
cealment and deception.

A second set of photos entered into evidence featured exterior shots, including the
garden area in general and the tomato patch
in particular.

Hill then established his background as a
qualified crime-scene technician and was so ac-
knowledged by the court.

More photos were introduced into evidence,
with the witness identifying them: "This is a
yellow probing device, a fiberglass rod about
five feet long. We use that to probe the soil. . . .
We hit some soft soil.

"This area with wooden markers, on the east side of the house, is where the digging was done.

"During the digging process, this is a green shower liner we came across." He noted a white spot at the "fleshy portion of the foot."

"Now here's a closer view of the digging . . . we found things around the shower liner, including a mattress pad and a yellow nylon rope. The liner was removed and put in the body bag with the body."

The last photo was a close-up taken after the shower liner had been removed, showing a white mattress padding which was wrapped around the body, with yellow nylon cord around the mattress cover.

Dow asked, "Those pictures fairly and accurately depict what you observed?"

"Yes, they do."

On cross-examination, John Cloy asked the witness if he had been personally acquainted with Thurman Martin, to which Hill said no.

Tom Durden took the direct for the State's next witness, Dr. Mark Koponen, an investigator and medical examiner with the GBI. Describing his official duties, Dr. Koponen said, "I'm responsible for death investigation." He went on to explain that he was a forensic pathologist by profession. The court accepted him as a qualified expert in the field.

Prosecution and defense both stipulated that the chain of custody from the time of the removal of the body was complete. On background, Dr. Koponen explained that the GBI crime lab conducts autopsies for law-enforcement agencies throughout the state. "Cases are called in to our investigators, and the body is brought to our office, where an autopsy examination is conducted."

He stated that on July 4, 1997, he performed an autopsy to determine the cause of death of Thurman Martin. Autopsy photos were entered into evidence, handed to the court reporter and marked. He then stepped down from the stand to better display and explicate those photos to the court.

Indicating the first photo in the series, which showed some irregularly shaped lumps of metal, he said, "This depicts projectiles that I recovered from the head of this gentleman. Four small projectiles were recovered from the skull, from the remnants of the brain."

The next photo showed four gunshot wounds to the back of the victim's head. Dr. Koponen pointed out four entrance wounds where the bullets had gone in. "The wounds are oval to almost circular in shape, varying from a quarter-inch to a half-inch in diameter." He then showed a third view of the wounds.

Durden asked, "Did you arrive at an opinion about this manner of death?" Dr. Koponen said, "This gentleman died as a result of four gunshot wounds to the head, and he was a homicide victim."

"Was he awake or asleep?"

Before the witness could reply, Judge Russell called a sidebar conference, after which Durden rephrased the question.

"What you observed, is what you found consistent with a man having been shot in his sleep, while he was laying down?"

"That is certainly possible, yes."

That ended the direct. On cross-examination, co-counsel Joey Sapp asked the questions on behalf of his client, Billy Crowder. He said, "Were there degenerative changes in the deceased's liver, of a kind consistent with extreme alcohol consumption?"

Koponen said, "The body was badly decomposed, but the liver showed no gross evidence of cirrhosis."

"Was he a heavy smoker?"

The doctor didn't know. Sapp's line of questioning seemed designed to slip evidence regarding Thurman Martin's lifestyle into the record by the back door.

On cross-examination for John Stanton, John Cloy asked, "Could any tests determine if Thurman Martin had neurological diseases?"

No, Koponen said, the body was too decomposed. "There was so little left of the brain that nothing meaningful could be done." Under Cloy's questioning, the doctor conceded that "a person could have a normal-appearing brain and yet have a severe pathology."

Cross-examination ended, the witness

stepped down, and the jury was excused for a morning break.

When court resumed, the prosecution called GBI Special Agent Ron Brooks, with Tom Durden on direct examination. In a special sidebar hearing held outside the presence of the jury, Brooks stated that Billy Crowder had been properly Mirandaized, and that his statement was made freely and voluntarily.

This was important, because if the defendant's Constitutional rights were found to have been violated, the State's case would have been in serious jeopardy. The exchange that followed between the prosecution and defense was not mere quibbling, but a kind of jousting where the defense probed for a weak link in the law-enforcement arrest procedure, some lapse in the process that could possibly be exploited for big gains.

Hal Peel cross-examined the agent, probing the circumstances of Billy Crowder's polygraphing and confession. "Was Billy aware of his rights, as a citizen not under arrest who could have left any time up to confession?"

Ron Brooks said yes, going on to explain that the decision to administer the polygraph test was made after Jason Jordan had taken one, and the interview with Billy Crowder was done after he was polygraphed.

Hal Peel said, "At any time during the ride

between here and Moultrie, could he have gotten out of the car and left?"

Brooks said, "Yes, any time he wanted to."

"Was he a suspect at the time you took him to Moultrie?"

"At the time of an investigation, unless they're one hundred percent cleared, everybody's a suspect."

"You treated him real nice to get him over there?"

Ron Brooks wasn't going to fall into that trap. "We treated him the same way we treat everybody, with respect and dignity."

Peel said, "At the time you had him, were two other agents over here with his sister?"

"Correct."

Brooks continued, saying there was no talk regarding the case during the two and a half hour drive to Moultrie, but after confessing, on the return trip Billy Crowder had continued to give details about the case.

Peel said, "What was his demeanor?"

Brooks said, "At different points he was okay; at some points he was upset, crying a little bit, disturbed."

"Did he make any reference to any abuse he'd received?"

"He indicated that he swore since he was six that he'd kill that man; he told us his grandfather had mistreated his grandmother on numerous occasions, that he was all the time hollering at her."

"Did he get into any details with you about any other type of abuse?"

"I specifically asked him earlier, because we'd heard rumors that he might have been abused," Brooks said, "and he denied that his grandfather had ever beaten him."

Peel focused on the witness's statement that he'd heard "rumors" of abuse, asking where he'd heard such rumors.

Brooks said, "Around the police department . . . a neighbor told us she had seen Thurman Martin 'whup' Billy before. It was something that comes up; in the course of an investigation; you hear a lot of things."

"Did you hear that from several different members of the sheriff's department?"

"I don't remember."

That ended that line of questioning for now. Next came a detailed discussion about the Mirandaizing of Billy Crowder, the timing and atmosphere, what and how much he grasped of the situation. Ron Brooks conceded that he didn't tape record the interview, such taping not being a part of GBI procedure.

The witness stepped down. Billy Crowder was offered the chance to testify in this sidebar hearing, but declined. There were no other witnesses.

Reviewing a summary of his findings, Judge Russell determined that Billy Crowder had been properly advised of his Miranda rights, that "the defendant understood them, voluntarily waved them, and gave a statement freely.

Therefore I will find the confession was freely and voluntarily given."

A similar sidebar hearing was then held to determine if defendant John Stanton had received his Constitutional rights. GBI Special Agent Walt Lanier was called to the stand, with Tom Durden on direct examination. Lanier said that John Stanton had been properly Mirandaized at the Glenn County Police Department, where he had been taken into custody.

On cross-examination, John Cloy inquired about Stanton's medical condition at the time of the arrest. Lanier said that John had taken his medication during the interview, during which he had written out a lengthy 26-page statement about the crime. It had taken him from 6:00 P.M. to 11:00 P.M. to write out the statement.

Cloy said, "Did you have a discussion with him about the problems he had had with Thurman Martin?"

Lanier said that the defendant had said that Thurman Martin "was a bad man, had treated his wife bad, had raped her, stuff along those lines."

Cloy asked if the witness had sweet-talked Stanton into confessing by intimating leniency. Lanier denied it.

For Billy Crowder, Hal Peel declined any questions of the witness on cross-examination, and Lanier stepped down. John Stanton was given the opportunity to testify, but declined.

The judge found that the defendant had voluntarily waived his Miranda rights.

The Miranda sidebar hearings having been concluded, the judge sent for the jurors, apologizing to them for the lengthy span of time they had been out of the courtroom. "We took care of some important issues, and we're ready to proceed."

The State resumed its case, calling Ron Brooks to return to the stand on Tom Durden's direct. The prosecutor first established for the jury that Billy Crowder had been properly Mirandaized, then asked, "Did the defendant agree to waive his rights and talk about the death of Thurman Martin?"

Brooks said, "Yes."

"What did he say?"

"Essentially, he confessed that he shot his grandfather."

Brooks then told of the interview following the polygraph test, during which Crowder's gaffe about not using a rifle to kill his grandfather had led him into a confession. Brooks asked where Thurman Martin was, quoting Crowder as saying, "Did you ever see the movie *The Last Supper*? It was about farmers who grew world-class tomatoes . . . they'd kill people for fertilizer."

Brooks added, "At that point in time, we knew where Thurman Martin was at, and called crime-scene techs in to exhume the body."

On cross-examination, John Cloy inquired about the search by Ron Brooks and Deputy Sonny Chambless of John Stanton's Brunswick residence, establishing that the law-enforcement agents had a proper warrant. Referring to a self-help book which had been found on the premises, Cloy said, "Did you not come across an item called *Stopping the Abuse?*"

Ron Brooks said, "Yes."

Switching tracks, Cloy began, "Did you speak to Dean Martin, Thurman Martin's son?"

"Yes, in state prison."

"Did you not discover—"

The prosecution objected to this line, an objection which was sustained by the judge, leaving unanswered the intriguing question of just what it was that Brooks might have discovered while interviewing Thurman Martin's convict son.

That ended the Stanton cross-examination. For Billy Crowder, Hal Peel returned to the subject of the abuse rumors, asking if Ron Brooks had interviewed the Ryals, neighbors who lived across the street from Martin. Brooks said that after Crowder had confessed, he had interviewed the rest of the neighbors who, unlike the Ryals, had nothing to say about any alleged abuse.

Peel asked if Brooks had known Thurman

Martin. The GBI man said, "I supervised his son on parole, so I know Thurman Martin and the family."

"What was he on parole for?"

"Rape."

"And he's serving a sentence now for rape?"

"Correct." The supervisory period had been from 1984 to 1990, during which time Brooks said he saw no evidence of any alleged abuse.

Hal Peel reiterated the line of questioning he had first developed at the sidebar hearing, regarding Billy Crowder's demeanor before and after the trip to Moultrie. The jurors got to hear it as Brooks told of the circumstances of Crowder's confession and his "I swore to kill him since I was six" statement.

Peel probed Crowder's "affect," that is, his facial expression. Brooks said that the defendant had had some tears in his eyes during the confession. The defense's questioning continued along that line, with Peel seeking to establish a kind of "numbness" in the defendant's demeanor. He asked if Billy Crowder's outward lack of emotion during the confession had surprised the GBI agent.

Brooks said, "Well, in this business you think you've seen it all; you never know how they're going to react."

Court went into recess for lunch. After the break, Hal Peel's cross-examination of Ron Brooks continued with the defense asking,

"You had received information that Thurman Martin had been abusive to his family?"

Brooks said, "Yes."

"Did you also learn that Martin had carried on a long-term affair while married?"

The prosecution's objection was overruled.

Brooks's response was hazy. "I don't specifically remember that; I think I remember somebody saying he had an affair."

Peel tried to bring in the matter of Edward Dean Martin, and this time the prosecution's objection was again sustained, with Judge Russell ruling out the use of such testimony. Also excluded was material concerning Thurman Martin's longtime mistress and, as Peel noted, "a lead that Mr. Martin may have provided drugs to a young black female."

Wrapping it up, Peel asked, "Is this a continuing investigation, or is this investigation concluded?"

Brooks said, "Any investigation is always continuing, until the jury reaches a verdict."

On redirect, the prosecution entered into evidence the warrants sworn to by Diana Crowder on June 10, 1997, accusing Thurman Martin of raping her on four separate occasions. "So they were only sworn out after the man was dead and in the ground?"

"Yes," Brooks said.

Now came a quick volley between the prosecution and defense. On recross, the defense established that the alleged rapes had taken place in the time period between the death of

Lula Kate Martin and the disappearance of Thurman Martin.

On redirect, the prosecution asked, "Did you ever find any evidence of rapes, other than John Stanton's and Diana Crowder's claims?"

Ron Brooks said, "No, sir."

Walt Lanier took the stand, with Tom Durden on direct examination. The witness established for the jury that John Stanton had been properly Mirandaized, and told of the defendant's written confession. He said that Stanton had said, "If I had knowed that her father had raped her, that she'd had a nervous breakdown, I would have taken his life then. Diana is a mental wreck, due to the rapes and mental abuse."

Stanton had further written, "The Crowders have stated they would always live in a state of fear; Thurman said he would burn the house down and them in it if he could. . . . He would accuse Katie of being a whore. He would say to Diana, 'Did John FUCK YOU?' He would say that I could not give her the pleasure he could—"

The confession went on to say that therapy had established that Diane had been raped by her father and by her brother, Dean. After her mother, Lula Kate, had died on February 8, 1997, according to the statement, the first rape had occurred ten days later, with Thurman Martin raping Diane in her mother's bed.

Stanton said that he had no knowledge of the rapes until after Martin was dead.

John wrote that he had complained to the IRS regarding Martin's illegal cash withholdings, and to other federal agencies about Martin's practices of illicit toxic dumping and dealing freon without a license, to no avail. "I tried everything for help, but none came."

More followed, regarding what a stinker Thurman Martin was, including "always at the eating table, he would curse God, and no blessing could be spoken over the meal." Martin was always served first, too.

According to the document, Thurman Martin no more respected God's laws than man's. "Even when he raped Diana, he told her the Bible said it was okay to have sex with her."

Stanton wrote, "I know I've done a terrible thing. I should have been mature enough not to let it happen. Thurman Martin has destroyed all of his family, even after he is gone. . . . Never will Diana's mind or body get over the constant flashback of her father raping her, like a TV nitemare. Diana did not plan this in any way.

"The sad thing is that many people know what was going on and nothing was ever done."

Lanier then told of how John Stanton had drawn a diagram to help locate the murder weapon which he had thrown off a bridge, and of the failed attempts of a police diver to find it.

On cross-examination, John Cloy established that Lanier had found a document entitled *Expressing Anger Safely* while searching Stanton's house. Lanier said, "I had anticipated some excuse of abuse in Mr. Martin's death."

The document was admitted into evidence without objection.

On redirect, referring to the document, Tom Durden said, "Anywhere in there, does it encourage violence?"

"No," Lanier said, "it speaks mostly of controlling your anger and walking away before anger becomes violence."

The witness was then shown another book, *The Poor Man's James Bond.* He said its contents included "Fireworks and explosives, pyrotechnics, arson by electronics, etc."

Tom Durden said, "It was found in John Stanton's home?"

"Yes."

On recross, Hal Peel asked, "You know of plenty of incidents where Martin had repeatedly done acts of violence against John Stanton?"

Lanier said, "All I know is that John Stanton said it."

"And you know he moved away to get away from Mr. Martin?"

"I don't know if that statement is true or not."

The State's next witness was the Long County Sheriff's Department's Chief Deputy and Investigator Sonny Chambless, a mild-mannered, white-haired lawman who would not have looked out of place behind the counter of a general store. Tom Durden used Chambless's appearance on the stand to introduce Billy Crowder's confession, which was entered into the record in a roundabout way. The confession itself was not allowed into the record, but the deputy's remarks about it were, allowing jurors to hear lengthy excerpts.

On cross-examination, Hal Peel probed for evidence of Thurman Martin's alleged abuse of his family. Chambless said that he was unaware of any complaints being made on that score during his 22-year tenure as a Long County law-enforcement official.

Peel then tried to work in Billy Crowder's "demeanor" at the time of the arrest, saying, "You've arrested people accused of killing somebody numerous times?"

Chambless said, "Yes, sir."

"And do those people ever show a great deal of emotion when it comes to admitting it?"

"Some do and some don't."

"And Billy didn't?"

"He didn't show a lot of emotion, no, sir."

Chambless said that he had interviewed people who lived in the houses surrounding the Martin property and that nobody ever gave any indication of having seen abuse "except for one house [the Ryals']." He asserted that Katie Crowder had said nothing about Thurman

Martin's abuse during the case initially, but "she was pretty upset, and you couldn't hardly talk to her."

A key element of the defense strategy was the argument that Billy Crowder and other family members had been afraid to level abuse complaints against Thurman Martin due to fear that his "good old boy" connections with town officials would prevent any action from being taken. Hal Peel questioned Chambless on his background with Thurman Martin and the family, with the deputy testifying as to his lack of involvement with them.

On redirect, the prosecution asked, "When was the first time you heard about this abuse that was supposedly going on?"

Chambless said, "When we started getting statements admitting the murder; the first of it came from Billy." He denied having heard of the illegal dumping and freon-dealing allegations made by John Stanton against Thurman Martin.

On recross-examination, the witness made the point that now that Thurman Martin was dead there was nothing that could be done about the abuse allegations, but that when he was alive, "nobody ever reported anything to us."

Chambless was the prosecution's last witness. Tom Durden said, "Your Honor, the State rests."

* * *

The defense began its presentation on that same day, on the afternoon of July 14. Having passed on making an opening statement at the start of the trial, Hal Peel exercised his option to do so now, part of a strategy to maximize the effectiveness of his words now that the jury had gotten at least a glimpse of the private face of Thurman Martin.

He said, "A lot of times, the law is more understanding than those who are charged with enforcing it. The law says that in some times, homicide is forgivable, justifiable. That is our case to you. . . .

"Yes, Billy killed his grandfather. We merely seek through you the justification, the redemption that the law allows to a charge of homicide."

The first witness called for the defense of Billy Crowder was Pam Beasley, an attractive brunette who was Diana Crowder's first cousin and Billy's second cousin. Her father's sister was Lula Kate, mother of Diane and Edward Dean Martin. Now living in Jesup, she was born and had lived in Long County for 19 years, and had known Billy and Katie all their lives.

She said that Diane and her family had come to her house for help many times, fleeing Thurman Martin. "Many, many times," she said. "They were afraid, tattered, torn. Yes, they were bruised . . . clothes torn. It was just weird, bad."

The pattern was that the family would run

Crime Scene Video

Naoma Wendorf, 53, was found in a pool of blood in her kitchen.

Wendorf's glasses were knocked off during the struggle with her killer.

Self-styled vampire Rod Ferrell, 16, confessed to beating Richard and Naoma Wendorf to death.

Sondra Star Gibson, Ferrell's mother, on the witness stand.

Lake County, Florida Deputy Sheriff Jeffrey Taylor with diagram of crime scene.

Defense psychological witness
Dr. Elizabeth McMahon.

Judge Jerry T. Lockett.

Defense Attorney
Candace Hawthorne.

Rod Ferrell with defense attorney Robert Lackay as death sentence is read.

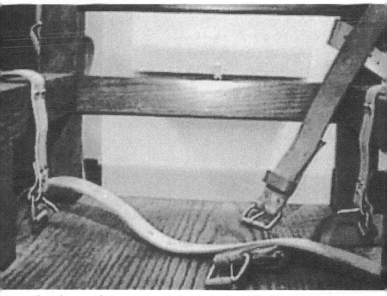

The electric chair awaits Rod Ferrell, the youngest person on Florida's death row.

Thurman Martin's grave site was hidden by making it a tomato patch.

Martin's home in Ludowici, Georgia.

Bed in which Thurman Martin, 64, was killed.

Billy Crowder, 19, killed Martin, his abusive grandfather.

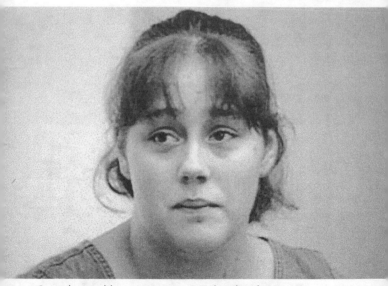

Crowder and his sister Katie, 17, lived with Martin.

Martin's son-in-law, John Stanton, 54.

Jason Jordan, 18, Crowder and Stanton each shot Martin
several times.

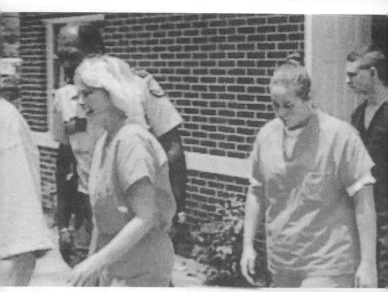

Defendants Katie Crowder (*right*) and her mother,
Diane Crowder, 35.

Assistant District Attorney Thomas Durden.

Georgia Bureau of
Investigation Special
Agent Ron Brooks.

Long County, Georgia
Superior Court Judge
Robert A. Russell III.

Long County, Georgia
Sheriff Cecil Nobles.

Billy Crowder at his trial.

Crowder was sentenced to life in prison plus ten years.

Prominent Delaware Lawyer Thomas Capano, 48, killed Anne Marie Fahey, one of his mistresses.

Missing person poster circulated for Anne Marie Fahey, 30.

ATTEMPT TO LOCATE
MISSING PERSON

ANNE MARIE FAHEY
WHITE FEMALE 30, DOB 1/27/66, 5'10", 128 LBS,
RESIDENCE: 1718 WASHINGTON ST.,WILMINGTON, DE.

SUBJECT ANNE MARIE FAHEY WAS LAST SEEN ON
THURSDAY, JUNE 27, 1996 AT 1718 WASHINGTON STREET, AT
APPROXIMATELY 2200 HOURS. SHE HAD DINNER EARLIER
BETWEEN 1900-2100 HOURS AT A RESTAURANT IN
PHILADELPHIA. HER VEHICLE, WALLET AND CLOTHING WERE
FOUND AT THE RESIDENCE. NO CONTACT HAS BEEN MADE
WITH ANY MEMBER OF HER FAMILY OR FRIENDS.

IF LOCATED PLEASE CONTACT:

DET.DONOVAN - WILMINGTON POLICE DEPT - (302)571-4512
LT.DANIELS - DELAWARE STATE POLICE - (302)323-4412

Fahey was murdered at Capano's home.

Capano used his brother Gerard's boat to bury Fahey's body at sea.

Debbie McIntyre, Capano's long-time mistress, gave him a gun five weeks before Fahey disappeared.

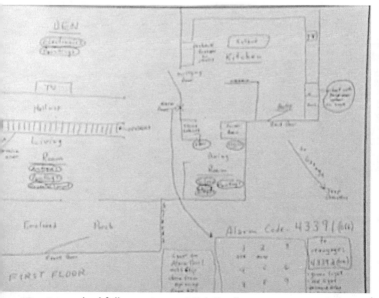

Capano asked fellow prisoner Nick Perillo to arrange for McIntyre's house to be burglarized and drew him a detailed diagram.

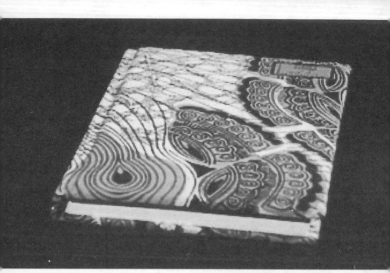

Anne Marie Fahey's diary.

Page from Fahey's diary discussing her love for Capano.

away. Then Thurman Martin would bring them back. She said that her father had had to brandish a gun more than once to make Martin back off.

She recalled that during the deathwatch when Lula Kate was in the hospital, she had seen Martin threaten John Stanton. "Thurman Martin said he'd blow his brains out." For Billy Crowder and the other family members, "It was just lifelong fear."

On cross-examination for John Stanton, John Cloy had the witness establish her background as a nurse and give John a good character reference.

On the State's cross-examination, Tom Durden said, "If you were presented with evidence that John Stanton shot Thurman Martin while he was asleep, that would change your opinion?"

"It would be so hard for me to say that, because I just know so many things," Pam Beasley said.

Durden asked why, if she had seen "hundreds" of incidents of abuse, she hadn't called the police. She said, "I never called them because my own life was threatened. This is an incredible story, is all I can tell you; this is not a fairy tale."

Next called to the stand was Sonya Harris, Pam Beasley's sister and Billy Crowder's second cousin. She expanded on some aspects of the previous witness's testimony regarding Thurman Martin's grip of fear on his family.

She was followed by her and Pam Beasley's brother, Mark Strickland, who stated that the family had run away from Thurman Martin "twenty, thirty times."

On redirect, the witness was asked why he didn't call the police. "Was that a matter that was looked at as being handled within the family?"

Strickland said, "Right."

"You didn't want to get a whole lot of others involved?"

"Right."

Lloyd Byrd was Diana Crowder's ex-husband, having been married to her in 1983. Speaking of that time, when Billy Crowder was six, he said, "Thurman beat Billy with a belt buckle, from head to toe. I've seen Thurman throw wrenches at Billy, and hit him in the back." He told of how Martin liked to boast of having gutted a man with his pocketknife and making him drink whiskey before letting him go to the doctor.

On cross-examination, John Dow asked, "Why did you allow the abuse to go on?"

The witness said, "I brought that up to Diane one time, and she said that it was none of my business, because he belonged to Thurman. She said that Billy belonged to Thurman, that he'd been over there since he was born."

"So his mother felt like he belonged to Thurman Martin?"

"That's what she told me."

On Hal Peel's redirect, Byrd was asked, "Do

you feel like Thurman Martin was a control freak?"

"Over the kids, yes."

On recross-examination, the prosecution asked, "Isn't it true that throughout her life Diana Crowder has had psychological problems?"

Byrd said, "Well, I couldn't tell; I know she didn't have no help for it."

"Who provided for Billy?"

"For the most part, it was Thurman Martin."

It was late in the afternoon and the judge decided to let the jurors leave, after once again admonishing them not to discuss the case during the evening's sequestration. He said, "Hopefully we'll have a chance of finishing tomorrow."

The next day, the trial resumed with Hal Peel calling the first of a string of witnesses who would testify to the reality of Thurman Martin's abuse of his family. Toby Prescott, currently employed by the Georgia State Prison Department, had grown up in Long County and knew Edward Dean Martin and Diana Crowder in high school. He told of witnessing an incident where Thurman Martin roughed up Diana and ran Prescott off their property.

Georgina Grippe, a native of Ludowici, said that as a young girl she witnessed Thurman Martin whipping Dean and Diana so hard that the blood flowed. Chris Carter, 19, had witnessed Billy's fear of Thurman Martin, but conceded that he saw no acts of violence.

Deona Walker, 18, red haired and round faced, a friend of Billy's, stated that when she was in tenth grade, she saw Thurman Martin beat Billy in the yard, where he was working on a car. "Billy was sitting under the hood, working, and Thurman hit him and knocked him on the ground. Billy was saying 'Please stop hitting me. Please don't hit me any more. Let me up, let me up.' "

Defense counsel Joey Sapp said, "Did Billy ever raise his hand?"

"No, sir."

"How would you characterize Billy and Katie's lives with Thurman? Would you consider them to be slaves?"

"Yes, sir," Deona said, weeping.

Counsel asked the witness, "What was your opinion of Thurman Martin?"

"He was mean."

The Ryals family lived across the street from the Martin house. Of all the neighbors who'd been interviewed by police investigators, they were the only ones who spoke of incidents of abuse committed by Thurman Martin against his family. Now, they would take the stand.

First up was Debra Ryals, who had lived in the house for roughly 17 to 18 years, about as long as Billy Crowder had been alive. Under Hal Peel's direct examination, she said, "Thurman was abusive to Billy and Katie, and they were terrified of him. I have seen Thurman beat that child in the face. People don't realize what kind of a man he was unless they lived by it and saw it. The abuse at the [auto repair] shop, the cussing all day long, that was every day, every day. . . . You never heard those kids scream or holler; they just took it."

She said, "My husband told him that if he didn't stop it, beating on Billy, that he was going to cut his guts out."

Debra Ryals had given the defense some strong testimony. On cross-examination, John Dow asked, "Have you ever spoken to the media about this?"

She said, "Yes, I talked to *Extra* and I talked to Channel 11 [WTOC-TV]."

After some back and forth with the prosecution, she said, "I don't believe in taking anybody's life, but that child was suffering for nineteen years."

Her husband, Leon Ryals Jr., known as "Junior," took the stand for Peel's direct examination. He put in some bad words for Thurman Martin, punctuated by some salty language. Recalling a confrontation they had had, he said, "I told him if he pulled the gun out of his pocket, I'd leave his damn guts laying on the ground."

It seemed like Thurman Martin wasn't the town's only colorful character.

Leon Ryals III, aka "Bubba," had once seen Thurman Martin give Billy Crowder a vicious beating in the auto repair shed in the summer of 1996.

Hal Peel began, "What is it that you remember the most about Billy and his interactions with his granddaddy?"

Bubba Ryals said, "They didn't get along; they was always fussing and fighting."

"Who did most of the fussing and fighting?"

"His grandfather."

"Did you ever hear Billy fight back?"

"No . . . he was probably scared of him."

"Did you ever yourself see Thurman hit Billy?"

"Yes, I saw it one time [in summer of 1996]. Thurman beat Billy down to the point that he was kicking him and spitting on him, and never once did I see Billy raise his hand to hit that man back."

"Would you describe what you saw?"

"He was standing up over him with a closed hand, and was hitting Billy in the face until he hit him all the way to the ground. And then he was kicking on him, and spitting on him."

Gene Ryals, 19, had known Billy Crowder for about 15 years and was working on cars with Crowder on the last day of Thurman Martin's life. He described some of the beatings he had witnessed. "It would be they'd be working on a car or something, and Thurman Martin would just start cussing, beating Billy and kicking him. He was just mean; he didn't have no reason for it, he just snapped."

Hal Peel said, "How did he look?"

"Terrifying."

"He foamed at the mouth?"

"Yes, sir."

"And he would just go off?"

"Yes, sir."

"That's when he would strike Billy?"

"Yes," Gene Ryals said. "I seen him hit him with welding rods, wrenches, hammers, anything he could get his hands on. . . . Billy just stood there and took it; that's the only thing he could do. Because he was scared for his life."

"How did you feel toward Thurman?"

"I was scared of him."

The witness described how he had occasionally eaten at the Martin house. "There was nothing ever good enough for Thurman, and he'd spit food back onto his plate and put it back in the bowl."

"So nobody else could eat it?"

"No."

Peel asked the big question. "What kind of person would you think Thurman Martin was?"

"Probably the cruelest man I ever met," Gene Ryals said.

On cross-examination, referring to the abuse, Tom Durden asked the witness, "Why didn't you tell the sheriff?"

"Because Billy told me not to."

The last of the Ryals to testify stepped down, and Katie Crowder took the stand. Thurman Martin's granddaughter, Billy's sister, she was sweet faced, slightly plump, soft, and vulnerable. She said that she'd lived with Thurman Martin "on and off my whole life," and that she had moved in on a "full-time basis" when she was twelve.

Hal Peel asked if Thurman Martin carried weapons. Katie Crowder said, "He's carried a knife, and on several occasions he's had a rifle." She stated that once, during one of the family's getaway trips while they were living apart from Martin, he called them on the phone and said that he'd had her and Billy in the scope of his rifle while they were playing in the park, and that "he could take us out any time he wanted to."

She said that she was "ordered" to come back to take care of her ailing grandmother, Lula Kate Martin; that Martin demanded it, telling Diana he would harm Katie if she didn't bring her in. Katie Crowder had taken care of the old woman, dressing and bathing her, in addition to cooking, cleaning, and keeping house. She said that she took care of the "inside" chores while Billy handled the "outside" chores.

Peel said, "Did your grandfather ever hurt you physically?"

Katie Crowder said, "He's left bruises on me, kicked me so hard in the behind I thought my stomach would come out my mouth. He busted my mouth, my nose . . . whatever he felt like hitting you with he'd use.

If he got mad at somebody else, he'd come home and take it out on you."

She went on. "I was scared. He threatened on several occasions to kill me, my brother, my mother. . . . You did not defy him. If he threatened to do something to you, he would do it to you."

Peel said, "Did you believe he'd kill you?"

"Yes, sir."

Asked if she'd ever seen Martin wield his pocketknife, she told how she'd once seen him try to stab a man in the yard, and on another occasion hold a butcher knife to her grandmother's throat and threaten to kill her. "He said if we called the police he'd kill us. Then he beat me, and said, 'You sorry little bitch, I'll kill you'. . . . Then he beat my brother, and then beat my grandmother again."

Peel said, "Do you remember a specific instance involving a feather duster?"

"Yes. After my grandma died, about a month later, he told me not to fix any dinner and to clean the house up. Then he started cussing at me, because I didn't have anything cooked. He slapped me with the back of his hand, and then he went inspecting the house.

"There was a feather on the floor I didn't pick up, and he made me get down on my hands and knees and pick it up with my mouth, and then he kicked me on my back end.

"He made me get a pan, and he hit me over the head. He hit me so hard over the head that he broke my headband, and it went so far into my head that after it was busted, it wouldn't even fall off."

Ever since his arrest, and throughout the trial, Billy Crowder had mostly kept a stone face. But now, seated at the defense table, listening to his sister's testimony, he wept.

Katie Crowder sobbed, too, as she recalled her grandmother's death and its aftermath. "I begged my mother to move back up with me, so she moved there. I was afraid of him, afraid of what he'd try to do . . . that he would try to rape me."

"Did he try that?"

"He tried several times."

"Did he ever?"

"No, because I fought him off."

"What was his condition when he was doing that?"

"Drunk . . . he'd touch you in places you weren't supposed to be touched," she said, adding that he threatened to kill her if she told Billy.

An eerie moment ensued a little later on, while Katie was describing how Martin had ordered her to take care of the outside gardening, including an earlier tomato patch of 6 tomato plants. He'd kicked and beaten her for overwatering the plants. It was an ironic forerunner of his own final involvement with a tomato patch.

On John Stanton's cross-examination, John Cloy elicited further information about threats made by Thurman Martin against his client, including the fact that Martin's threat of sniper fire against the youngsters came when they were at Stanton's gas station in Brunswick.

Dow took the cross-examination for the state, querying Katie Crowder about her claim of having been beaten every day for six years. "That would be a little over two thousand beatings?"

"Yes, sir."

More importantly, Dow established the fact that neither Billy Crowder nor John Stanton knew of Thurman Martin's rape attempts against Katie Crowder when they killed him.

Dow said, "Isn't it true that you've already entered a guilty plea?"

"I pleaded guilty, but I still maintain my innocence. But I felt the evidence the State had against me would convict me," Katie Crowder said.

The witness was excused, and Billy Crowder took the stand. He was now 20 and a half years old. Under Hal Peel's direct examination, he said that he'd lived with the Martins since he was 3 days old, that he thought of Grandmother Lula Kate as his mother, and that Thurman Martin would run off his biological mother Diana Crowder when she'd try to be around him.

He recalled the primal experience of his first real beating from Thurman Martin, when he was six years old, helping his granddaddy in the shop. "I was out in the shop, and I was getting tools for him. I couldn't find the right tool quick enough, and he slapped me, kicked me. He just done that two or three hours that evening.

"That time was more or less a beatdown, more or less kicking, bruises, and sore for about two weeks."

Of the beatings, he said, "I can remember certain ones more than others, but it was an everyday thing."

Peel said, "Do you remember what it would take in order to be on the receiving end?"

"It could be anything. If he ever started mumbling, you knew it was fixing to come on then."

"Gene said he'd seen Thurman throw some tools at you?"

"Yes, with eighteen-wheeler tire irons—it's an inch-thick steel rod. Sometimes, when he threw a screwdriver, the blade would stick into you. One time he directly stabbed me with a screwdriver, across my shoulder blade."

"When you were brought up, were you or Katie allowed to show emotion?"

"No, the night before my grandma got put on the respirator, he was complaining about the light bill. Her blood pressure went up, she couldn't stand violence. The next day, she went on a respirator. The nurses said she had from two to twelve hours to live. We was in there crying, and he said, 'Don't you cry again, you little son of a bitch, I'll beat the mother-fucking hell out of you.'

"Thurman Martin had like two sides. If you was around with anybody, none of this would go on, like a perfect little gentleman. Right when they'd leave, he'd pick up right where he left off."

He said that during his sister's testimony, she'd left out a few things, such as the time "he took a broom and hit her over the head two or three times with it."

Peel's line of questioning now sought to establish that Thurman Martin had made virtual slaves of his grandchildren. Billy Crowder told of the rigorous duties he'd had to carry out when Martin had run a pack of about 17 hunting dogs for the town hunt club.

"What would you have to do?"

Crowder said, "Give them their medicine, shots, vaccinations, keep the pens clean, sterilized them, change the water every day. I really didn't mind taking care of them, because I liked animals. A pleasure sport had become like school—basically, you'd dreaded doing it."

That ended when Thurman Martin "had a run-in with people at the hunting clubs."

The stress of life with Martin took its toll on Crowder. Increasing the tension were such episodes as the time Martin hit Lula Kate so hard he knocked her false teeth out. "I stayed up all the time; I didn't want to go to sleep, because I didn't want to wake up the next morning."

According to Billy Crowder, it wasn't pretty when Martin would go off. "First he'd start slinging stuff at the wall, and then he'd start slobbering. You couldn't even move, you knew better. Anything to trigger it would lead him to a total rage that would last ten minutes and then he'd become like a kitten."

"How did all of this make you feel?"

"Well, to see my grandma abused, my sister abused . . . it made you feel there was no hope. I knew they wouldn't do nothing to him. I've seen him get out of things, and I knew if you ever turned against him, raised a hand, spoke back to him, he'd kill you."

"Were you afraid of him?"

"Yes, I was."

Peel said, "Tell us about Thurman Martin and his knives."

"He could reach in his pocket with his knife closed and have it opened by the time it got out of his pocket. He told me he killed a soldier. He said you weren't a man unless you could open the knife out that fast, kill something, and then get it back in his pocket. I've heard a bunch of people talk about his character, and how bad he used be when he was younger. I was always scared of him. I didn't know what he was capable of," Crowder said.

Tom Durden took a skeptical tone on the cross-examination. "How many doctors did you see?"

Billy Crowder said, "He didn't believe in doctors; you just didn't go to them."

"So you've been stabbed, kicked, and scalded, and you never went to a doctor?"

"Yes."

Durden wanted to underline the deception that Crowder had used to try to escape detection for the murder. "How is it that now what you're telling the jury, you didn't tell Sonny [Chambless] and Ron [Brooks]?"

"Well, the first time they directly asked me about it they was asking me if I knew where my grandpa was. That night, when he was beating me, I tasted blood in my mouth. I snapped, done it, and snapped back. There was so much rage, to hate somebody so bad. I was scared and that's the reason I denied it."

"You denied it at first. You went so far as to call the sheriff and see Ty Smith about a missing person."

"Yes."

"He wasn't really missing at the time?"

"Well, he was to the town, but he wasn't missing; he was buried."

"How come you didn't tell Sonny Chambless and Ron Brooks about the blood in your mouth?"

" 'Cause that day I thought my life was over; I didn't know nothing and I didn't care."

Durden steadily turned the focus toward the crime. "The gun you shot your granddaddy with had a silencer on it. Tell the jury how you made it."

Crowder did so, describing how to make a silencer from common items bought at a store.

Durden displayed a copy of *The Poor Man's James Bond.* "Have you ever seen that book?"

"Yes, my granddad said he got it from the black market . . . that ain't the one [which tells how to make a silencer], there are other volumes."

"What kind of gun was it?"

"A Ruger 10-.22 [rifle]. It had the front sight sawed off."

"So this gun was rigged to be silent and to do maximum damage?"

"It was rigged to put the man who beat me and my sister—"

Durden asked the judge to direct the witness to answer the question and the judge did so. Durden said, "This gun was made to be silent and deadly?"

"Yes, sir."

Durden now tackled the ambiguous role of Jason Jordan in the crime. "When did Jason Jordan know for the first time what was going on?"

Billy Crowder said, "He made mention about 'why do you let that man beat the hell out of you?'—that evening was probably the first time."

"He knew when he put the silencer on the gun?"

"Yes, he was well aware of it then."

Crowder told how he and Jason Jordan

donned camouflage clothes and went with John Stanton to the Martin house to do murder.

"Jason carried the weapons. I don't remember what John did, and I went through the window and unlocked the door, then let them in. I went to the counter. . . . Then from there I got ready, turned the corner, and just fired."

"You don't remember how many times you fired?"

"No, sir . . . when I actually come to knowing what I was doing, it was after the shot rang out . . . and I just panicked."

"You shot first, then handed the gun to John?"

"It was handed at him, but he didn't want it."

"But the plan was for each of you to shoot, so nobody would spill the beans?"

"That was Jason's plan, that's what he said."

Then there was the theft of the dead man's money, an act which Durden felt knocked the legs out from under the abuse excuse. "After Jason refused to shoot, you took Thurman's wallet out of his pocket? About how much money was in it?"

Crowder said, "Best I can remember is about seven hundred dollars."

"He probably wouldn't have given it to you if you'd asked?"

"No, he never gave me much of anything." Crowder said that he gave Jason 20 dollars and gave John 200 dollars for a trailer payment.

Now for the disposition of the corpse. Durden said, "How did you wrap his body up?"

"It was a shower curtain, we just wrapped him up in it," Crowder said.

"You tied it around him?"

"Yes."

"Who actually dug the hole?"

"Jason dug it . . . I did dig a few shovels up."

Then there was the matter of the tomato patch, the symbol by which the case had become known. "How long after that did you all go to Jesup and buy tomato plants?"

Crowder said, "The next day."

"Who went and got them?"

"Me and Jason."

"Who planted them?"

"Jason."

"You were starting the cover-up then?"

"Yes."

"After the tomato plants were planted, Jason went to North Carolina?"

"Yes, he'd been planning that for a month or so earlier."

"Whose idea was it to throw the gun off a bridge?"

"I don't know; John was supposed to have got rid of it."

"You trusted him to get rid of the murder weapon?"

"Yes."

"After you all killed your granddaddy, what did you tell Katie?"

"I personally didn't tell her a thing. I did not want to involve her one bit," Crowder said.

On redirect, the defense sought to reinforce Billy Crowder's slave status and undercut the theft of the dead man's money by providing a rationale for it. "You weren't paid an hourly wage for work in [the] shop?"

"No."

"After your granddaddy was gone, did you take over paying the bills?"

"Yes."

"How did it feel not to be beat or cursed or kicked or spit at?"

"Like I was in another world," Crowder said feelingly.

"You felt good?"

"Yes, you didn't get kicked inside no more . . . there just wasn't no more of it."

"And it didn't happen to Katie Crowder anymore, did it?"

"No."

On recross-examination, John Cloy took up the theme on behalf of his client. "It didn't happen to John Stanton anymore, did it?"

"No."

Under questioning, Crowder told of a violent incident between Martin and Stanton, during which Martin had told Crowder to get a gun. "He didn't like John; he didn't like anyone my mom associated with. He went over there and said he would beat John up. He told me to get my target pistol . . . that he was going to kill him with it. I took a pin out of it and said I'd lost it. He got mad and slapped me and said he was going to kill John with his bare hands.

"I seen him take John and grab him by the throat and slam the side of his head into the truck. He struck him several times with his knife curled into his hand, to make it more solid."

On redirect, Hal Peel said, "Why didn't you leave the house?"

Crowder said, "Because my grandma had tried so many times and he always made us come back." He described the last such incident. "After my grandma come back, he said he was going to blow our brains out, that he was looking at us through a rifle scope."

"And you didn't leave after that?"

"No, sir, we didn't leave again."

The witness was excused, his place on the stand taken by Daniel Grant, a psychologist whose specialty was in clinical neural psychology and forensic psychology and who had been an expert witness some 20 or 30 times.

After voir dire by the State, the judge qualified Daniel Grant as an expert witness in neural, clinical, and school psychology, as well as in Post Traumatic Stress Disorder.

Hal Peel said, "Are you familiar with Battered Person Syndrome?"

Daniel Grant said, "Yes, it was originally called Battered Woman's Syndrome, but then they realized that men could have it, too. It consists of a cluster of things, which contains individuals who undergo or experience physical or mental trauma, usually both. They perceive that they have few alternatives; they feel trapped in a life of abuse . . . hopeless.

"No matter what you do, there's nothing you can really do to effect any positive change, to alter the abuse. You have low self-esteem, a sense of fear, a sense of terror, a sense of being controlled."

"Have you had the opportunity to interview Billy Crowder and others? What did Billy Crowder's test results reveal to you?"

"That he's experienced PTSD and depression over a long period of time."

"Would Billy Crowder fall within the BPS?"

"Yes, I think he does. He described himself as often feeling like a zombie; he's not allowed to have any feelings or emotions; they had to be buried. The children were taught to learn that if they showed any emotions, they would be abused more severely. So they essentially learned not to feel."

"Would the things that you've described be consistent with PTSD?"

"Sure—they all felt like there was no way to really escape or get away; even when they left, Mr. Martin would find them. There was really no escape, because he would stalk them. They were trapped."

Peel said, "People who are subjected to stress orders, such as a family unit or individuals subjected to repeated events of cursing, beating, or witness that happening to other members of the family, would those people be able to leave that type of environment?"

"That's often a problem you find with battered people, they don't leave," Daniel Grant said. "They were trapped, because if anyone left, or anyone told, and he got hold of them, they'd be injured, or he'd threatened to kill others who didn't get away."

Hal Peel offered a hypothetical version of Billy Crowder's case, and the doctor opined that a person in that situation might well think that killing was the only way out.

On cross-examination for the John Stanton defense, John Cloy questioned Daniel Grant about his examination and diagnosis of Diana Crowder. The psychologist said that he had spent a lot of time speaking to Diana and reviewing her medical and psychiatric records.

The defense asked, "How did she get those problems?"

Daniel Grant said that Diana's condition originated "from physical sexual abuse by her father," and that she'd been diagnosed by a number of facilities as having Multiple Personality Disorder. "Sixty-eight percent of the time, you don't develop multiple personalities without having sexual abuse prior to the age of nine."

The questions now turned to John Stanton's

physical and mental condition. Daniel Grant said that obviously Stanton was mentally affected adversely by his sickness. "Mr. Martin knew that John had cancer and was fairly weak. He was constantly belittling him, calling him names, referring to him as being weak. He hit him on the head so hard he knocked him on the ground, and threatened to kill him. He said he was going to get a gun and put him out of his misery.

"John also talked about how he had tried to get Diane away, and got her admitted to a hospital in Florida. No one knew where she was, but Mr. Martin was able to find her and called her up and threatened her. He speaks of the emotional impact of being a man and not being able to defend your wife . . . and he knew that this had been going on all her life."

When Daniel Grant ventured on characterizing Thurman Martin, the prosecution objected, prompting Judge Russell to ask, "Can you give an expert opinion without interviewing somebody?"

"Yes, a hypothetical one," the psychologist maintained. He went on to give a thumbnail analysis of Thurman Martin's type of abuser. "There's a constant anger, lashing out; they have a high rage level; are unaware or don't care about how what they're doing affects others. They have a sense of entitlement about their own needs, a sense of drive about having one's own way. He feels good by making other people feel bad. They're abusive over a period of time, not just isolated incidents."

On cross-examination, Tom Durden asked, "How do you know what was threatened?"

Daniel Grant said, "Just by what was reported to me."

"By whom?"

"Diana, Billy, Katie, John, and other people who said they heard him threaten their life."

Durden cut to the chase. "The bottom line: your analysis or opinion is really only as good, as accurate as the information given you?"

"Well, in part," Daniel Grant said, explaining that he used multitesting and responses to widen the field. "That's why I try to talk to as many individuals as I can, to get a better opinion of what really transpired."

Turning to the subject of John Stanton's bone cancer, Tom Durden asked, "Are you aware that, according to Dr. Moran, that it is in remission?"

"According to Memorial General Hospital in Savannah, it's not," Daniel Grant said.

"Dr. Moran testified that, in his opinion, John Stanton can turn it on or off as he wants."

"Yes, he said that, but he also said he wasn't competent to make decisions about his own medical care, so I was in a quandary about what he was really saying."

Daniel Grant stepped down, and Hal Peel said, "On behalf of Mr. Crowder, at this time we rest."

* * *

After a 15-minute recess, the trial resumed, with John Cloy presenting John Stanton's defense. His first witness was Neil Zellis, a police officer with the Glen County PD, who said that John Stanton did make a complaint about some kind of terrorist threat from Thurman Martin. But he admitted that the details were hazy and the paperwork minimal.

He was followed by GCPD Officer Leon Tucker, of Brunswick, Georgia, who said that on September 5, 1995, he went to investigate John Stanton's complaint of a terrorist threat by Thurman Martin. But on cross-examination, John Dow had the witness establish that no warrants were ever taken out by John Stanton against Thurman Martin. In other words, there had been a complaint, but there wasn't enough there to act on, and it had come to naught.

Cloy next moved to solidify the "good character defense," calling Billy Johnson, a friend of Stanton's who'd met him through their church and had known him for forty years. The witness said he'd believe John under oath. "Johnny's always been very, very straight with us."

On cross-examination, Tom Durden asked, "If John Stanton killed a man laying asleep in his bed, that would change your opinion of his character, wouldn't it?"

"Yes."

Clayton Johnson, another longtime acquaintance, gave John Stanton a character reference. "I've never heard anything bad about him at all."

When Durden sprang the same question on him—would it change his opinion of John's character if he killed a man laying asleep in his bed?—Clayton Johnson said his opinion might not change. "Not necessarily. It depends on what the circumstances was . . . as far as I know, he's all right."

Cloy now called John Stanton to the stand. Before Stanton could actually, physically take the stand, he was the subject of an exchange between the judge, prosecution, and defense. The witness's lack of health was stipulated to by all parties, who officially noted that Stanton had been diagnosed by his physician, Dr. Anthony Moran, as being afflicted with bone cancer, that he was under medication to kill the cancer, and was also on pain-therapy medication.

Now the witness could take the stand. As he rose from the defense table and shuffled across the courtroom, frail, stooped, and failing, it might have occurred to some of the spectators that they were seeing a dead man walking.

He was 59 years old, weak, and weepy. He spoke of Diana Crowder. "There's twenty years' difference in our ages, and I just fell in love with her, and I told her I wouldn't let nobody hurt her no more. We got married, and to my knowledge he [Martin] didn't hurt her anymore, but he would phone her, always harass her."

He said that when Diane was in the Woman's Institute of Therapy in Florida, she was diagnosed with 54 multiple personalities. He told of living with her in Brunswick, and how when Lula Kate died, Diane chose to go back to the Martin house, to Thurman Martin, because Katie Crowder had asked her to.

He recalled that Thurman Martin had never liked him, was always verbally and sometimes physically abusive to him, that he had called John's mother a "motherfucking whore." He said, "My mother died twenty days after Lula Kate . . . in between them twenty days, he raped my own wife in her own home, in my mother's bed, and then had the nerve to come to my own mother's funeral."

He said that he didn't feel he could go to law enforcement in Long County, but claimed that he did so in Glenn County, describing his making a complaint against Thurman Martin for terrorist threats. He told of his dire sickness.

His lawyer asked, "What did you weigh in 1990?"

"One hundred eighty-five pounds."

"What do you weigh now?"

"One hundred twenty-seven."

He said that Diane lived "in a trailer on the property next door to Thurman Martin's property. She stayed there, and part of the time she stayed with Katie to protect her."

He recalled the incident when he had gotten away from Thurman Martin before he could get his gun. "Yes, we [he and Diane] came to pick up a tire that belonged to me. Thurman Martin said, 'You're just a lying SOB . . . them's my blankety-blank tires' and told me how sorry I was, that he just thought he'd go ahead and kill me and put me out of my misery. He hit me and knocked me down. I told Diana to get in the truck and by the time he got back, we were gone.

"The Sunday before [Martin's death], the same thing happened; Thurman Martin took me and beat my head up against the side of a pickup truck. The man was a maniac, a total maniac . . . anything could just set him off."

John Stanton said that Diane had told him that on Mother's Day when she had gone to lay a wreath on Lula Kate's grave, Thurman Martin had said, "Kate, I've got your pussy, and I've got your daughter's, too."

On cross-examination, Tom Durden made the point that all John Stanton knew of the alleged rapes came from Diana Crowder, though Stanton countered that doctors and psychiatrists had known about it. Durden said, "They would have only known if she told them."

"Yes, sir."

Returning to the night of the murder, Durden said, "Did you know prior to that time that you were going to be involved in a killing?"

"No, there wasn't no plan, no pre-thing."

"Billy got in and went to Thurman Martin's room and shot him; how many times did you shoot him?"

"Twice."

"Billy handed you the gun?"

"No, the gun jammed. There was a period of time in between."

Durden pressed. "When you could have walked out, but you didn't?"

"I didn't," Stanton said.

The prosecutor continued. "Jason hands you the gun; you put it to the back of Thurman's head and fired twice more?"

"Yes."

"And Jason refused to shoot?"

"It was his choice not to."

"And then Billy took the wallet out."

"No, no, the man didn't have his clothes on."

"Where was the wallet?"

"I don't know, I wasn't there . . . I have no knowledge of it."

Durden said, "But you shared in the proceeds of what came out of Thurman Martin's wallet?"

Stanton protested, "It's not the way you think it was. . . . He did not give me the money that night. It was later in the week, when Ford Motor called me and told me that the payment on the trailer was not made. Then I went to Billy and he gave me the money."

"Bottom line, you got the money?"

"Yeah, it belonged to Diana."

And the body? "You wrapped him in a shower curtain, tied him up, and Jason and Billy dug a hole?"

Stanton said, "I was already inside the trailer when this went on."

"And the three of you put him in the hole and covered him up?"

"Right."

"Did you have anything to do with planting the tomato plants a day or so later?"

"No." Stanton said there was no plan, that "something just went wild—we'd just had enough. I was the protector of my family . . . I'm not a murderer."

He repeated, "It wasn't planned. It just happened."

On redirect, Cloy said, "Do you have any reason not to believe what your wife tells you?"

"No."

"Did you go there to take money?"

"No."

"What happened to Billy?"

"He just went crazy; the whole thing's crazy," John Stanton insisted. "This is just the craziest scenario that could ever be."

The witness was excused. John Cloy said, "That's all the witnesses I have."

* * *

The judge asked for rebuttal witnesses at this time. The prosecution called Cecil Nobles, the sheriff of Long County since 1969, who stated under oath that he had no prior knowledge of any abuse between Thurman Martin and his family, and that he personally was not intimidated by Thurman Martin.

On cross-examination, Hal Peel inquired about the relationship between Nobles and Thurman Martin, if any. Nobles said, "I knew Thurman Martin, but I was never close to him. I know he voted against me." Which counts for something to the holder of an elective office.

Peel teased the cronyism angle. "Thurman Martin used to come up here and push Judge Phillips around in the courthouse some?"

"Many times," Nobles said. Judge Phillips, the reputed successor to county political kingpin Colonel Ralph Dawson, had been paralyzed and put in a wheelchair after being shot by his wife.

Peel continued. "And Judge Phillips and you are friends?"

Nobles said, "Oh, yes, always been." He pointed out that Phillips had been Edward Dean Martin's defense lawyer on the rape charge, which would account for Thurman Martin's association with the judge.

Peel said, "Were you aware of any acts of violence Thurman Martin or Edward Dean Martin might have done outside the county?"

"No."

There were no other rebuttal witnesses, and

no sur-rebuttal. The jurors left the courtroom as the attorneys approached the bench to examine the judge's proposed verdict form. It laid out the options of murder, voluntary manslaughter, or not guilty for each defendant. All parties approved the form.

The jurors returned. Judge Russell told them that the evidence phase of the trial was now concluded, and asked the prosecution to begin its closing statement.

After first thanking the jury for its attentiveness throughout the case, Tom Durden said, "This is the part of the trial where we lawyers get to speak to you for the last time. It's our opportunity to point out what you've seen from the evidence. This is not the kind of case where the jury considers punishment. Your question on each of those charges is 'did they do it?'"

He urged the jurors to shun the abuse excuse. "Nobody in this courtroom is asking you to like Thurman Martin. If we allow this tomato-patch defense, then I submit the truth will not have been found, the truth will not be known. If we allow the excuses these men are offering to you for their actions, then we're kidding ourselves that we're meting out justice and truth.

"Thank you."

The Crowder closing was delivered by Hal Peel. "If you consider the rest of the story, you begin to see that there is evidence of justification. Killing is wrong, but what Thurman Martin did to all of his family was wrong. He was just a mean son of a bitch. I think he got what he deserved, and that is a harsh judgment.

"None of you grew up like that. None of you grew up being called a stupid little son of a bitch and a goddamned motherfucker every single day of his life."

He said, "Thurman Martin was a nasty man. . . . When you live in a small town, you don't meddle in other people's business, even though you might want to. It's just not the way things are done in the South.

"Think about Billy Crowder. He was Thurman Martin's punching bag, his personal whipping boy. You heard about him being punched in the face and then kicked and spit on. You wouldn't treat your dog that way, and you certainly wouldn't treat your children that way.

"There were two fingers on the trigger of that rifle—there was Billy's and there was Thurman's. This is not just another homicide. It's the last act of desperate people, who didn't think they had any other way out. He kept them under his thumbnail, using the worse kind of power there is, power based on fear, absolute fear.

"You would not be wrong in finding Billy Crowder not guilty of everything," Hal Peel concluded.

John Cloy stepped up to deliver a brisk closing for John Stanton. "This case is about Thurman Martin, a wildcat. What's so sad about this case is that these are people who tried the legal route, tried to use the legal system to protect themselves.

"They could not get away; there were no choices left in these people's shattered and destroyed lives. They had no choices."

After the closings, the prosecution was allowed to have the last word with a rebuttal. Tom Durden began, "I'm not saying this didn't occur, but does it justify killing a man?"

Which was indeed the issue to be decided. Was Thurman Martin the kind who needed killing?

Durden attacked the defendants' credibility by pointing out that "Billy Crowder almost testified with pride" that he could make a silencer. As for John Stanton's debility, "he can turn this thing on and off. He's sick, but some of this demeanor is to get sympathy."

He asked, "Why do they cover up? That's an indication that they know they had committed a crime."

This was not manslaughter, Durden argued. "That's not irresistible passion; that's calculation. If the evidence shows the killing was done in the spirit of revenge, that's not manslaughter—that's murder.

"Your verdict will not stay within the four walls of this courtroom. This case has been called a 'Tomato Patch' case; I guess they're asking you to form a Ludowici defense. But they committed murder and robbery and hindered the investigation. I'm going to ask you to find a verdict which will not excuse killings like this, but will hold those responsible accountable."

He concluded, "The only reasonable truth in the case is that they are each guilty as charged. Thank you."

Now the jury charge began. Judge Russell went over the charges in the case: murder, armed robbery, hindering the apprehension of a criminal, and possession of a firearm during the commission of a crime. He explained the terms and legalities of the charges and the rules of evidence.

He said that a finding that a person suffered from battered person syndrome may be considered in a defendant's plea of self-defense. He said that a person is wrong to attack another "solely for revenge for a previous wrong, no matter how strong the previous wrong might have been, if the previous wrong has ended." But that it was the jury's duty to acquit the defendants if the use of force was necessary.

It was late in the day, and the jurors decided to save their deliberations for the next day. They were released, and court was recessed until the following morning.

On Thursday, July 16, the last day of the trial, the jurors began deliberations at 9:00 A.M. During the proceedings, they sent a note to the judge requesting a copy of explanations of all the charges, a copy of the confessions, an adjustable wrench which Hal Peel had used for demonstration purposes, not evidence [to show what kind of tools Thurman Martin had thrown at Billy]; and a floor plan which John Stanton had drawn as part of the statement he had given after his arrest.

Judge Russell said, "Well, I don't give explanations of charges, but I will read any charges over they would like to hear. The explanations aren't in evidence, and the adjustable wrench, and any floor plan, so I won't give them that. Regarding the written explanations/confessions, the confessions are not in evidence, and they don't go out. There was testimony concerning the confessions, and that's evidence."

The judge put the court in recess while the jury deliberated. At noontime, he called a lunch break. A juror became ill at lunch, and an alternate was substituted. At one P.M., deliberations resumed.

A few hours later, in mid-afternoon, all in the courtroom rose as the jurors filed out of the jury room and into the jury box.

Judge Russell addressed the jury foreperson. "Have you reached a verdict?"

"Yes, sir."

"Is this unanimous?"

"Yes, sir."

The verdict form was handed to the judge, who examined it before handing it to Court Clerk Harrell Manning. The clerk read the verdict aloud:

"On count one, defendant Billy Crowder has been found guilty of voluntary manslaughter. Defendant John Stanton has been found guilty of murder.

"On count two, both defendants have been found guilty of armed robbery.

"On count three, both defendants are found guilty of hindering the apprehension of a criminal.

"On count four, both defendants are found guilty of possession of a firearm in the commission of a felony."

It was immediately noted that there had been a mistake in the reading of the verdict sheet. The clerk reread count two aloud, this time with the correct verdict: that defendant John Stanton had been found not guilty of armed robbery.

The clerk polled the jurors, each of whom affirmed his or her verdict and said that it was freely made.

When the polling ended, Hal Peel said that he'd like the record to reflect that one of the jurors "was almost in tears" as she was polled. He then requested that the jurors return to the jury room for further deliberations, which brought a predictable protest from the prosecution.

Judge Russell overruled the request. He addressed the jurors, thanking and releasing them. All rose as the jurors exited.

The judge announced he was now ready to move into the sentencing hearing.

Tom Durden began the prosecution sentencing argument, speaking directly to the judge.

"This is the second time we've been in this courtroom, and I remember you saying with Jason Jordan that this was one of the most cowardly things you've ever heard. And now you've heard it all again.

"I'm recommending the maximum here, because of what the court has heard twice, of how these men saw a chance to take the life unlawfully of someone who may have been abusive to them. Even after that, they robbed the man; at least Mr. Crowder did, robbed his own grandfather after he shot him while asleep."

Making the John Stanton defense argument, Cloy asked that the court take his client's physical condition into consideration. "He has cancer. Also, take into consideration his advanced age. Basically, he's been given a death sentence, and I ask for some benefit, in light of what the family has gone through."

Arguing on behalf of Billy Crowder, Hal Peel said, "I don't think the evidence in this case can be compared to the Jason Jordan case. There's a whole different set of circumstances here. The evidence shows this family was indeed tormented, tortured, and virtually destroyed by Thurman Martin."

He asked that the court run the manslaughter and armed robbery sentences concurrently, run another concurrent time on the hindering charge, and to make the possession of a firearm consecutive probation.

The arguments had been made and now it was time to pass sentence. Judge Russell asked

John Stanton to rise, saying, "This is a complicated and hard case; the jury has made a decision. There's no discretion I have. I sentence you to life for the murder of Thurman Martin."

He also gave him five years consecutive on each of the other charges, for a grand total of life plus ten years.

Billy Crowder rose for his sentencing. The judge said, "On the voluntary manslaughter, I sentence you to five years, consecutive to any other sentence. On the armed robbery, I sentence you to life. On hindering, five years, consecutive. On possession, five years, consecutive.

"Your total is life plus ten years."

AFTERMATH

In an exclusive posttrial *Court TV* interview, Billy Crowder told of his feelings when the sentence came down. "I didn't know what was going to happen. I figured probably a hung jury. I just stood there. I didn't know what to think. I only know that he said five years and I said, well, that ain't bad."

Then the judge gave him life on the armed robbery charge.

Billy said, "I've been in prison all my life. I didn't want to spend the rest of my life in there. I've been enslaved nineteen years, I don't want to spend the next nineteen in jail.

"The night before I went to court that day,

I went to all my friends and everything and told them good-bye and everything, that I loved them."

On July 29, 1998, in what courthouse veterans described as an "extraordinary move," eight of the twelve jurors who heard the case filed a petition with the court asking Judge Russell to reconsider the harshness of Billy Crowder's sentence.

In the petition, the jurors affirmed the verdicts in the case, noting that they had no argument with the life sentence given to codefendant John Stanton. But, "we as a jury believe the judge, Robert A. Russell III, was extreme in the sentencing of Billy Crowder. . . . We all hoped Billy Crowder would serve a fair sentence. In our eyes, life plus ten years was unfair. We had hoped Billy Crowder would serve a sentence which would allow him to get psychiatric help. Though Billy Crowder did commit a crime, he is not a harsh criminal. We beg you to listen to our cry for justice."

Defense attorney Hal Peel told *Court TV,* "When they returned the verdict and they found him guilty of manslaughter, I breathed a sigh of relief, and when they found him guilty of armed robbery, I felt terrible.

"Life on the armed robbery. . . . Everybody on our side of the case was extremely disappointed and let down. I felt like somebody had stuck a needle in me and let all the air out of me. And I felt bad.

"Their whole life, everybody involved in that

case, everybody in that family's lives are basically ruined. . . . I mean they are ruined. Diane is, you know . . . she's mentally ill. Dean is in prison. Katie will have a semblance of having a fairly normal life, I think. She has a little baby now. Billy . . . hopefully when we can get all this worked out and he can get out of prison and get on with his life."

Tom Durden said, summing up the case, "It's pathetic. You cannot take the law into your own hands. Let the law take care of it. You know you do not become the judge, jury, and sentencer just because you've been abused . . . that's not the way our society works, nor the way we want it to work."

GBI Special Agent Ron Brooks said, "Thurman Martin probably wasn't Mr. Personality, but did he deserve to be shot in the back of the head, sleeping in his bed, in his house?

"I think the issue really here is the methodical planning that went in to kill Thurman Martin. The main question to me is why didn't they use all that intellect to do all that planning and the execution and cover-up of it to find a different solution? Why didn't they do that?"

Sheriff Cecil Nobles opined, "Hey, when that verdict came I felt good about it. I know the DA Tom Durden felt good. We felt good about the verdict. I feel yes, sir, they got a fair trial.

"Yeah, it's sad. Nobody gains. Everybody lost in this case. You know a murder is not good, 'cause a murder's bad, because it's bad on the victim's family, it's bad on the defendant's family.

"A lot of people go through a lot of pressure and stress. A murder's not good. Before you commit a murder, the best thing to do is just walk away and forget it, or go to the police department and report it."

After pleading guilty on the hindering charge, Diana Crowder was ordered to spend one year in prison and one year undergoing evaluation and treatment in a mental hospital. She will then be on probation for an additional three years.

Katie Crowder was sentenced to five years probation, of which six to eight months would be served in a probation center. She told *Court TV,* "What do I wish for Billy? I wish for him to be set free. To live a life that he's never had. To continue his life, to have freedom in his life."

The prosecution had the last word during rebuttal in court, but Hal Peel will have the last word here:

"It's a total tragedy and I think the tragedy more than anything is, it makes me wonder how many other people were living like this? How many other people, how many other Billies and Katies and Dianes are out there that nobody knows about and nobody has reported and the only reason they'll find out is if somebody gets killed? How many other people are out there going through the same thing?"

Delaware v. *Capano:* FATAL PASSION

DISAPPEARED

In 1976, in Wilmington, Delaware, career criminal Squeaky Saunders shot one of his associates dead, executing him gangland-style with a bullet in the brain. He then compelled his two companions to each also shoot the dead man in the head, binding the trio in a web of mutual incrimination. They dumped the body in the Delaware River, but instead of traveling out to sea and away, it washed up where the authorities found it, triggering a successful hunt for the killers.

Squeaky Saunders was found guilty of murder and sentenced to prison. One of the prosecutors in the case was Thomas Capano, a young lawyer from a prominent Wilmington family. He was making some of his fledgling moves in public service in what would prove to be an illustrious career. He stood at the opposite end of the social pyramid from the convicted killer. The Capanos were among the leading lights of the Delaware elite.

Two decades would pass before Squeaky Saunders and Tom Capano once again crossed paths, and when they did, it would be merely one more twist in the most sensational murder case in Delaware in a generation.

The Capanos were a success story, living the American Dream. The founder of the family fortune was patriarch Louis Capano, a childhood immigrant from Calabria, Italy, the birthplace of pioneer bodybuilder and professional strongman Charles Atlas. Louis Capano was a different kind of builder, a skilled stoneworker and carpenter, a master craftsman who built with Old World care and scrupulous honesty. He was a hard worker and good at what he did and he wound up building much of North Wilmington. That and hard-driving entrepreneurship helped make him a millionaire in the early 1970s. He and his wife, Marguerite, had five children: Louis Jr., Joseph, Thomas, Marian, and Gerard. The family lived the good life. They had a mansion in Wilmington, another on the beachfront of Stone Harbor, New Jersey, and a third in Boca Raton, Florida.

Tom Capano was the family scholar, the golden boy. At the exclusive private school Archmere Academy, he was voted class president and was captain of the football team. At college, he met Kay Ryan, and they married in 1972. He was admitted to the Delaware bar in 1975, the beginning of twenty years of glittering success in both public and private sectors.

The tradition of service led him to a job first as a public defender, then to the state prosecutor's office, where he successfully prosecuted Squeaky Saunders for murder. He alternated stretches of private duty partnering in legal firms with ever higher profiles, and important administrative posts in city and state government.

Delaware is a small state, comprising no more than three counties. Wilmington has a population of 70,000. The smallness of the base of the pyramid made the elite at the apex that much closer, where all the movers and shakers knew each other and the same faces were seen on the boards of directors, corporations, foundations, etc. A face that was seen more and more frequently in those circles was Tom Capano's.

In 1979, while Kay was pregnant with their first child, daughter Christy, Capano began an affair with Linda Marandola, an attractive brunette in her late twenties. He was a good-looking guy, soft-spoken, and a lot of women found him sexy. Linda Marandola was one of them and they became intimate.

She soon found that Tom Capano was a controlling, engulfing kind of lover. Smothering. She had sex with him after her bachelorette party, but she wanted to stop the affair now that she was going to be a bride. Capano was not so easily dissuaded. He made a lot of phone calls, following and harassing her. He could be very persistent when he wanted something.

When she got married, she was discomfitted to see him sitting in the church. When they danced afterward at the reception, he said that he wished she had birthed his firstborn child, instead of his wife, Kay, who had recently done so.

His marriage was no obstacle to his outside amatory interests, and he saw no reason why hers should be, either. When she proved resistant to his advances, the pressure began. Ultimately, he had her and her husband evicted from the apartment building where they lived—a Capano property.

The couple moved out of the state to New Jersey, though she continued to commute to her job in Wilmington. Now that the romance had soured, Capano wanted her gone for good. He told her, "This is my state."

Her obstinacy caused his emotions to take an ugly turn. He tried to hire a guy to have her legs broken or run her over with a car. The guy made tapes of Capano incriminating himself, tapes which wound up at the state bar's ethics committee. They let Capano off with a slap on the wrist and he reluctantly turned his attentions elsewhere. For a time.

His roving eye next fell on the wife of Dave Williams, one of his fellow young lawyers at the legal firm where he worked. She was originally Deborah MacIntyre, the MacIntyres being a fine, old, monied family in Delaware. Her affair with Capano began on Memorial Day, 1981.

Time took its toll. A year earlier, patriarch Louis Capano Sr. had died of a heart attack at age 57. Later, people would say it was a blessing he didn't live long enough to see what ultimately became of his family.

Son Louis Capano Jr., "Louie," was financially the most successful. He now headed the family business, expanding and diversifying it into real estate development deals and other lucrative projects. He had a reputation for cutting corners and greasing the right wheels in government to get his projects approved. His fancy footwork had brought him to the notice of the federal authorities. He had a business difference with his sister Marian's husband, attorney Lee Ramunno, who had Louie served with legal papers at his club. This prompted an enraged Louie to break into Ramunno's house and throttle him until police arrived to break it up.

Kid brother Gerry Capano spent his time big game hunting and shark fishing. He had problems with drugs and alcohol. Joseph Capano had had the most serious scrape, abducting and sexually abusing a former girlfriend. It took all of Tom Capano's behind-the-scenes maneuvering to manage that one and keep it from blowing up into serious business.

Through it all, Tom Capano was there for the others, keeping it together, the steady hand on the tiller. As Gerry Capano later observed, "He was *the man.*"

Capano continued his ascent toward the upper echelons of power and influence. As the years passed, he held jobs as a state prosecutor, city solicitor for the city of Wilmington, legal counsel for the governor, and a partner of a major Philadelphia law firm, Saul Ewing Remmick and Saul (known as Saul Ewing). His wife, Kay, was devoted to him, and they had four lovely daughters, Christy, Jenny, Katie, and Alex. He worked hard and played hard, enjoying the good life. He liked to dine out expensively and well. He could afford it.

He had his outside women, but he had a talent for secrecy and few if any of his intimates suspected his shadow life of clandestine affairs. He kept it quiet. Which was why, to those who knew him, and even those who didn't, it was even more shocking when it all went crazy and blew up big.

At midday on Friday, June 28, 1996, Tom Capano found himself on a boat in the middle of the Atlantic Ocean, losing a problem. With him was Gerry Capano, owner and skipper of the boat, *The Summer Wind,* named after the title of one of Sinatra's classic hit tunes.

Gerry hadn't wanted to go along, but brother Tom needed the boat. The way Tom put it, Gerry couldn't say no. Tom Capano had put plenty out there for Gerry and now it was payback time.

As Gerry later told it, back in February of that year, Tom Capano had first approached him for a loan, saying that he needed it to pay off some "extortionists" who were putting the bite on him. He spoke of a man and a woman in partnership, a blackmail team. Gerry made the loan, $8,000 in cash. If it seemed odd to him that his wealthy brother didn't have the money on hand, and much more, Gerry said nothing of it.

Tom Capano had spoken darkly of what he would do if the extortionists tried to hurt his children. He would kill them. If he did, he asked, could he use Gerry's boat to get rid of them?

Sure, Gerry told him. Family is family. Sacred.

Tom Capano had promptly paid back the loan. Around that same time, he'd also borrowed one of Gerry's guns. Capano was as unhandy with guns as he was with boats. Gerry was the one who understood guns. A sportsman and big game hunter, he collected guns and had lots of them. A short time later, Tom returned the gun, saying he felt uncomfortable having it in the house and didn't really need it.

Since that time, there hadn't been any more extortionist talk, but now the other shoe had dropped.

Early on June 28, at 5:45 A.M., Gerry Capano had emerged from his home to find Tom Capano sitting in his black Jeep Grand Cherokee parked in the driveway. Capano was reading the sports page of a newspaper. Putting it aside, he said, "I need to borrow the boat."

Gerry knew what that meant. He didn't want any part of it. But he was part of it, because this was his brother, and family is family. Tom Capano put it up front, saying, "Don't leave me flat. Don't leave me hanging. I need you, bro."

He said he would just borrow the boat; Gerry wouldn't have to know any more about it. But that wasn't possible. Capano was a landlubber, he couldn't handle the boat. Gerry had to come. They agreed to meet later, at Tom Capano's place, to do what had to be done.

Capano had then gone to his former house, the house where his wife and children still lived, but where he didn't, not since moving out in September 1995, when he had separated from Kay and taken a nearby rental house on Grant Avenue. He borrowed Kay's Suburban SUV, which was bigger than the Cherokee and had more cargo space.

Later that morning, when Gerry met Capano at his place, he saw in the back of the Suburban an oversized cooler, a 162-quart Igloo model, the kind much used by hunters and fishermen to keep their catches on ice. Gerry was an avid trophy-seeking shark fisherman and could have used it, but the cooler belonged to Tom Capano, who neither hunted nor fished.

The five-foot, eight-inch-long cooler was wrapped with a heavy chain and padlocked. Gerry told Capano to get rid of the chains before they started, to keep the cooler from rocking back and forth during the ride. Capano removed the chains. In the cooler there was some ice and icy water, Gerry could hear it rattling around. What else was inside, he didn't want to think about.

Tom Capano drove them at high speed out to Stone Harbor, New Jersey, to the marina where Gerry had his boat. There wasn't much talk during the trip. On arrival, they loaded the cooler into the *The Summer Wind*, gassed up, and headed out to sea, under the vaulting sky.

About 60 miles east of the shoreline, in a shark-infested section known as Mako Alley, they halted, Gerry stopping the engines, the boat bobbing on the briny. In the distance, comfortably remote, another fishing boat lay at anchor.

Capano and Gerry hefted the cooler over the side, into the sea. Instead of sinking, it floated. That wouldn't do. Gerry grabbed a shotgun, a Mossberg he kept as part of the standard equipment for bagging sharks and other big sport fish. He took a bead on the bobbing cooler and fired a shot into its side. Pinkish-red water came pouring out through

the hole. Gerry began to get slightly nause-
ated.

The cooler stayed afloat. Gerry took the
wheel and brought the boat around, coming
alongside the cooler, while Tom took hold of
it. The boat had two anchors. Gerry put out
one anchor in the water and got the other and
some chains and gave them to Capano. He
said something like, "You're on your own,
bro."

Then he went forward to the bow, turning
his back so he wouldn't have to watch. Waves
lapped against the sides of the boat. Chains
rattled. There was the sound of Tom Capano
getting sick, retching. Gerry felt more than a
little sick himself.

Capano finished binding the anchor chain
around whatever was inside the cooler. He
tipped the cooler over, spilling its contents into
the sea with a splash.

Gerry turned around just in time to see part
of a calf and a pale white foot slip out of sight
beneath the sea.

It shook him, but he had to maintain his
calm. He unscrewed the cooler's flat-topped
lid and left both pieces in the water to let the
sea carry them away.

He turned the boat landward and headed
in. It had been rough, but when someone
threatens your family, your children, you do
what you have to do. There were a few other
things they had to do, and once they were on
shore, they did them.

* * *

If the Capanos had thus far enjoyed the smooth side of life, the Faheys had had the rough side. There were six siblings, four brothers and two sisters: Robert, Kevin, Michael, Brian, Kathleen, and Anne Marie. Their mother had died early, and their father was an abusive drunk. They'd known want and privation. The family house had been sold for foreclosure and they'd prevailed through other tough times. They were a close, tight-knit bunch.

In 1996, the youngest, Anne Marie Fahey, 30, was the scheduling secretary of Delaware Governor Tom Carper. Almost six feet tall, she was well built and strikingly attractive, with thick dark hair and dark eyes. Despite her good looks, she was insecure about her body image and weight, and suffered from anorexia and bulimia. She'd been seeing various therapists for the past ten years. Lately, she had other causes for anxiety and occasional depression. But she had a great job that she loved, and a new boyfriend, so on balance life was good.

On Thursday, June 27, 1996, with the July Fourth holiday approaching, the legislative work cycle was nearing its end, a hectic time at the office. Anne Marie Fahey looked forward to the next day, which she planned to take off from work and devote to some quiet quality time, including getting a pedicure, manicure, and later perhaps some reading in the park.

After work that day, she had a five P.M. appointment with a psychiatrist, which she kept. The new romance in her life was Michael Scanlan, a rising young executive at MBNA, a leading credit card company. They'd been brought together in the fall of 1995 through the good offices of Governor Carper, who was playing matchmaker. They'd hit it off, and had since gone on dates to concerts, an opera, family dinners, and even to a special mass conducted by the pope in Baltimore's Camden Yards, a once-in-a-lifetime event.

Michael Scanlan called her that Thursday night. There was no answer, so he left a message on her phone machine. He called on Friday, June 27, but there was still no response. They had plans to have dinner with her brother, Robert, and his family on Saturday night.

On Saturday, she still hadn't returned his calls, which was unlike her. She was very orderly and methodical, traits needed for the exacting tasks of arranging the governor's intricate scheduling calendar. He drove by her apartment building and saw her car parked out front. He thought she was home and not returning his calls because she was upset with him for some reason, although he couldn't imagine why.

So, he and Annie didn't go to her brother's for dinner. When Robert Fahey called Michael

Scanlan later that evening to find out where
they were, Scanlan confessed his bafflement
and said he didn't know where Annie was,
either.

After this unsettling news, Robert Fahey
called his sister, Kathleen Fahey-Hosey, who
called two of Annie's close friends, Ginny Co-
lumbus and Jill Morrison. They didn't know
where she was, either. A grain of fear had now
been planted in all of them, one that would
grow steadily as the night wore on.

The two friends arrived first at the apartment on Washington Avenue, where Annie's
car was still parked out in front. Landlady
Theresa Oliver said she hadn't seen Annie for
a day or two, but that was nothing unusual.
She unlocked the door to Annie's apartment
and peeked inside, but Annie wasn't there.

Kathleen Fahey-Hosey and Michael Scanlan
soon arrived, joining the others. The landlady
let the group into the apartment. The air conditioner was on and there was the stink of rot-
ting vegetables from some groceries which had
been left out on the kitchen counter for a few
days. Some of Annie's clothes and shoes were
in disarray. There were twelve unanswered
messages on her machine; Scanlan's message
from Thursday night was the first.

Her pocketbook was out in plain sight. Her
car keys and house keys were gone, but otherwise its contents seemed intact. Later, it
would be learned that her ring and some jogging clothes were also gone. A floral-print

dress lay folded and put to one side, another
action uncharacteristic of Annie, who was com-
pulsive about making sure that everything was
put away in its proper place, just-so.

There was also a gift box from Talbot's, an
upmarket women's store, containing an expensive pantsuit which Kathleen Fahey-Hosey rec-
ognized. On a recent shopping trip with her
sister, Annie had admired the item, but passed
on buying it because it was too expensive. At
that time, the sisters had also exchanged sharp
words, prompted by Kathleen's seeing how ab-
normally thin and gaunt the diet-obsessed Annie was in the dressing room.

Everything about the scene was wrong. Annie was compulsively neat, so much so that her
friends had tagged her with the nickname
"Anal Annie." Under normal circumstances,
she would not have left the apartment in the
condition in which the searchers now found
it.

As Saturday night became Sunday morning,
not long after midnight, Kathleen Fahey-Hosey
called the Wilmington Police Department to
report that Anne Marie Fahey was missing.
Time crept by as the group waited, but the
Wilmington police didn't come. Kathleen then
called a politically connected friend of the
family, Ed Freel, Governor Carper's secretary
of state, his chief of staff. He got in touch with
the state police and some state troopers were
soon on the way.

While they were waiting, Kathleen looked

around, searching for notes, clues, something, anything. She found more than she bargained for. In a drawer, she found an envelope marked "Personal and Confidential." In it was a lengthy letter to Annie, chatty and intimate—a love letter from Thomas Capano.

She knew Capano. He was a friend of a guy she had dated, Charles "Bud" Freel, Ed Freel's brother. The family owned O'Friel's Tavern, a watering hole and meeting place popular with Wilmington political insiders.

But she hadn't known what this letter showed—Tom Capano was on an intimate basis with her little sister, Annie. She'd thought that she and Annie didn't have any secrets from each other, and it hurt to find out otherwise. But the hurt was submerged in the big fear which was gripping her.

She also found her sister's diary, which documented an intense, obsessive two-year love affair and sexual relationship between Anne Marie Fahey and Tom Capano. Shocking stuff, but far more ominous and sinister was the entry dated April 7, 1996: "I finally have brought closure to Tom Capano. What a controlling, manipulative, insecure, jealous maniac."

Meanwhile, the superintendent of the Delaware State Police had assigned Lieutenant Mark Daniels of the New Castle County Criminal Investigative Division to the case of Governor Car-

per's vanished scheduling secretary. Daniels
and fellow officer Sergeant Steve Montague of
the governor's security detail arrived at Anne
Marie Fahey's apartment at about 12:45 A.M.,
where they were joined by Wilmington Police
Department Sergeant Elmer Harris, Detective
Robert Donovan, and two uniformed officers.

Donovan had received a call at home at
12:30 A.M. from his watch commander, who
told him to go to Anne Marie Fahey's apartment because her family had reported her
missing, adding that she worked for the governor. He found it unusual for state troopers
to be assigned to a Wilmington missing persons case, later recalling, "It was the first time
I had encountered that."

When the governor's secretary vanished, it
was not an ordinary missing persons case.

The case grew more extraordinary still, with
the diary and love letters bringing Tom Capano into the investigatory net. Ironically, as
the onetime chief of staff for Wilmington
Mayor Frawley, Capano had once been in
charge of overseeing the Wilmington Police
Department.

Lieutenant Daniels was a 19-year veteran of
the state police, and Donovan was a tough,
streetwise cop who'd received the WPD's cov-
eted gold detective's shield in the last year or
so. They knew the facts of life. When an attractive young woman who's been having a secret affair with a rich and influential married

man goes missing, they had a pretty good idea where to look first.

At 3:40 A.M., Daniels, Montague, Harris, and Donovan went to Tom Capano's rented home on Grant Avenue. Capano came to the door and let them in. They asked if he knew why they were there and he said, yes, he did, because earlier that night he'd been telephoned by Kim Horstman, one of Annie's friends, who'd told him she was missing. He said, "I'm aware you're looking for her."

He told police that he had picked her up on Thursday night at about 6:30 P.M., when they had driven to Philadelphia to dine at the Panorama restaurant. After dinner, they went back to his home on Grant Avenue, where he gave her a gift of the Talbot's pantsuit and some groceries, both of which were found in her apartment. He said he then took her home, going into the apartment for a few minutes, where he set the food in her kitchen and checked the air conditioner he had recently bought her. He left at approximately 10:00 P.M., he said, and stopped at the Getty station on nearby Lovering Avenue for cigarettes.

That was the last time he'd seen her. Asked if he knew her present whereabouts, he said that she was flighty and unpredictable and had probably just gotten it into her head to go off to the Jersey shore. That's where he'd thought she was, with her friend Kim Horstman, until the latter's call tonight had proved otherwise.

He said he was sure she'd be back at work on Monday.

He volunteered the information that she'd had a "big fight" with her sister earlier that week (the tiff at Talbot's). He said that he and Anne Marie Fahey had once had a sexual relationship, but not in the last six months; now they were just very good friends. When asked if he thought she was suicidal, he said that he thought she definitely was. He admitted that he'd given her some gifts, but he was a generous guy and gave lots of people gifts.

Lieutenant Daniels said, "Mr. Capano, is Anne Marie Fahey in the house now?"

"No," he said. They asked him if they could search the house and he refused, saying his four daughters were visiting and were sleeping upstairs. They said they'd be back sometime later that day, and went away.

Further investigation at the Getty gas station on Lovering revealed that Capano couldn't have bought cigarettes on Thursday the 27th at 10 P.M., as he'd claimed, since an attendant had said that the station had closed that night at 9:30. He didn't recall seeing Capano at all that night.

A check of the phone records turned up some interesting facts. On Thursday night, at around 12:30 A.M., Capano had used the star 69 callback feature to contact Debby MacIntyre. Potentially more disturbing was a call the following morning around 8 A.M. to Keith Brady. Brady, a Capano friend, was the chief deputy attorney general, the second-most important post in the state attorney general's office, a post which Capano himself had once held. Further, Brady was the boss of State Prosecutor Ferris Wharton, the man who would be in charge of prosecuting Capano, if it should come to that. Later, questioned on the call, Brady said Capano had cancelled a golf date they had. Brady later recused himself from the case to avoid any appearance of impropriety.

The detectives returned to Grant Avenue that Sunday at ten A.M., but Tom Capano wasn't there. The investigators didn't like that so well. Was he ducking them? They went looking for him, cruising the area, finding him eventually at Kay Capano's house, where Donovan spotted Tom Capano coming out of the garage. They approached him, and it was evident that the short-lived era of good feelings was over. His demeanor was agitated and jittery, and he was not as forthcoming as he had been the previous night. He said he was upset with himself for disclosing so much information earlier that morning and violating Anne Marie Fahey's privacy by revealing their affair.

They returned to the Grant Avenue house, where Capano reluctantly gave his permission for a walk-through search. The detectives were allowed to look only in areas where Anne Marie Fahey could be hidden. They didn't find her, nor did they find any signs of a violent struggle or disturbance. He allowed them to search his vehicle, the black 1993 Jeep Grand Cherokee, which also came up negative.

Later that day, Capano retained former Delaware State Attorney General Charles M. Oberly III as his lawyer, who instructed him "to start preparing a time line of everything he could remember concerning his where-abouts on June 27, 1996, and immediately thereafter."

On Monday morning, July 1, Anne Marie Fahey failed to show up for work at Governor Carper's office. As a high-profile missing person, her story was headline news. The police continued with some good, old-fashioned investigative legwork. Detective Robert Donovan interviewed Kim Horstman, Annie's friend. She knew about the two-year affair between Annie and Capano, saying that Annie had tried to break off the relationship several times before, but Capano was obsessed with her. A particularly messy incident in the summer of 1995 had resulted from one of those breakups. Capano had stormed into her apartment and took back a television and other gifts he'd given her. Later, things were patched up and he gave back the gifts, but Annie had still found it unnerving. Kim Horstman had lunched privately with Capano twice, and he told her how much he loved

Annie and how he did not understand how she could date Michael Scanlan.

On July 1, DSP Investigator Lieutenant Mark Daniels went to the Panorama restaurant in Philadelphia, where he interviewed Jacqueline "Jackie" Dansak, the waitress who'd served Anne Marie Fahey and Tom Capano their dinner on Thursday, June 27. Yes, she remembered the couple well, identifying Anne Marie Fahey from her picture. She recalled that Annie had worn a floral-print dress that seemed slightly out of place compared to the chic, black "jet-setty" outfits favored by the eatery's regular female clientele. That sounded like the dress which had been found folded and put aside in Annie's apartment. She also said that Annie's hair was "unkempt," and that the couple had not seemed very happy during the meal, with the lady looking "solemn" and forcing a smile whenever the server approached the table. Capano had done all the ordering for both of them, but they hadn't touched much of their food, which was packed away in oversize "doggie bag" containers (which had been found in Annie's refrigerator). Daniels took Capano's signed credit card receipt with him.

Also on that day, Charles Bud Freel learned that his friend of over 20 years, Tom Capano, was implicated in Anne Marie Fahey's disappearance, and that he was not being entirely forthcoming. A physically large man who was an officeholder in city and state politics, Freel was also a close friend and confidante of the Fahey family, and had once dated Kathleen Fahey-Hosey when she was single. When he finally reached Capano on the phone that day to find out what the hell was going on, Capano told him it was a lot of "shit" and asked for his support.

On Tuesday, July 2, Lieutenant Daniels was contacted by Lisa D'Amico, Anne Marie Fahey's hairdresser, who'd seen the news and knew that she was missing. Annie had confided to her about her stormy relationship with Tom Capano, calling him "crazy." Annie was scared of him. The hairdresser said that she was scared of him, too. Annie told her that she and Capano argued constantly, that he besieged her with phone calls, letters, and e-mails at work, that she'd seen him waiting outside her building a number of times, and that she wouldn't let him inside her apartment.

During a May hair appointment, Annie told her that he had recently "gone crazy" and grabbed her. He'd then told her that she'd ruined his life because he had left his wife for her and now she was rejecting him. Annie said that she planned to tell him the relationship was over. She was nervous and frightened that he might harm her.

Also on July 2, another key player learned for the first time that she was actively involved in the case.

After divorcing Dave Williams, Debby MacIntyre had raised her two children by herself.

She was employed by the exclusive Tatnall private school as an administrator, the school she had attended for 15 years in her youth. She had never remarried and was still single.

For the last 15 years, she'd been having an affair with Tom Capano, living a kind of soap-opera existence as the Other Woman, Capano's loyal mistress, always available to him, grateful for any crumbs of affection. Unable to walk publicly and in the open with him, it was a backstreet affair, punctuated with trysts at the Motel 6 below the Delaware Memorial Bridge and meals at unprepossessing restaurants in Philadelphia, far from their usual haunts.

Capano advised her closely, taking a real interest. He had strong opinions on just about every aspect of her existence, from her clothes to finances to how much overtime she put in at her job. A few times they had come close to breaking up, or of him leaving her, really. But it had never come to a complete break. She was the one who came back to him.

She accepted her status uncomplainingly, knowing he could never leave his wife because of his daughters. He "worshipped" them. Family was all-important to him. Besides, if he was crowded, he was quick to lash out. He could be ice cold, chilling in his stony disdain.

She couldn't bear to lose him. A life in the shadows with him was infinitely preferable to one without him. He knew it, too.

Then, in September 1995, came the unthinkable. Something she had never dared dream, had happened. Capano had separated from Kay, moving out of the family house and into his own place on Grant Avenue, located conveniently close to both Kay Capano's house and to Debby MacIntyre's, too. (It was also about five minutes' drive away from Anne Marie Fahey's apartment, but Debby didn't know about that yet.)

Wednesdays were "their" nights. Capano told her that he needed 18 months time to pass after the breakup, out of respect for Kay, before he and Debby could be wed. They would have a life together.

On July 2, while she was at work at the Tatnall School, Tom Capano phoned her, telling her that he had some shocking news. In the story of the day, the continuing disappearance of Anne Marie Fahey, mention had been made in the newspapers that she was last seen dining in the company of a prominent but as yet unnamed Wilmington attorney.

Capano told Debby MacIntyre that he was that man. What was really shocking to her was not so much his presence in a missing persons case, but his relationship with the missing woman. Who was this Anne Marie Fahey, anyway?

Capano said he'd retained an attorney to represent him. He said he was getting out of town for a few days, taking his family to Stone Harbor for the Fourth of July extended weekend. He'd call her later that night so they could talk.

That gave Debby plenty of time to stew over the matter of Anne Marie Fahey. The newspaper photos showed an attractive and vital young woman, some 15 years Debby's junior. How many times had Capano been with her? Debby's relationship with him wasn't exclusive on either side, but he'd kept a part of his life a secret, even to her, and that hurt.

At about 5:30 P.M., at home, she took a call from Capano's lawyer, Charles Oberly, who asked her questions about the time line for June 27 to 28. She said that she'd called Capano a couple of times on Thursday night, starting after 10:30, and that she'd been with him on Friday night.

Later, at 9:30 on Tuesday night, she received a phone call from Capano in Stone Harbor. He opened up to her about Anne Marie Fahey. He'd been involved with her—he'd even been in love with her for a time. But that ended long ago, when he'd first left Kay in September 1995, so he and Debby could at last be together as soul mates. Of course, after they'd ceased to be intimate, he was still the girl's friend, advisor, and confidante. She needed looking after, she was "ditsy," an "airhead." No doubt she'd be back at work in the governor's office come Monday.

Oh, yes, there'd been another woman in his life, too, but that was unimportant. What was important was that he promised he'd never lie to her again.

Debby MacIntyre bought it. She had to. To say "no" to Tom Capano was to risk losing him forever.

On Wednesday, July 3, the papers stopped being so circumspect about the identity of the "prominent Wilmington attorney" who'd dined with Anne Marie Fahey right before she disappeared. They named Tom Capano as that individual, although they noted that the police did not consider him a suspect.

Capano knew that you can't believe everything you read in the papers. So did Bud Freel, who drove out to Stone Harbor that day for a talk with Tom Capano. Earlier, he'd had a meeting with his old friends the Faheys, experiencing at firsthand their pain and fear for their missing sibling. He was hurting himself. He'd known Annie since she was a kid and he thought of her as family.

Freel's arrival at the Capano compound at the Jersey shore was greeted with no great enthusiasm by Capano. Freel urged him to cooperate with the police. Capano talked about how good he'd been to Annie. A few hours later, Freel left without any solid commitments from Capano.

The next day, the Fourth of July, Capano called up Freel and asked him if he'd been wearing a wire (i.e., a recording device) during the previous day's meeting. Freel got steamed, saying that was a hell of a thing to say to a friend, and warning that his attitude was doing a lot of damage to his family and himself back in Wilmington.

During the holiday weekend, President Clinton called Governor Carper, a fellow Democrat, offering U.S. government assistance in investigating Anne Marie Fahey's disappearance.

Also that weekend, about ten miles off the Delaware coast near Indian River, fisherman Ken Chubb made an interesting catch. Out in a boat with his son, they spotted something white bobbing in the water and hauled it in. It was a cooler, minus a lid and with a couple of what looked like bullet holes in it. Apart from that, it was in good shape, almost like new. Chubb took it home and kept it.

On Monday, July 8, with Anne Marie Fahey still missing, the investigation moved to a higher level of law enforcement, as the federal government became involved. Ferris Wharton, Mark Daniels, and Robert Donovan had already had some help from FBI Special Agent Eric J. Alpert. Now, the U.S. Attorney's Office assigned Assistant U.S. Attorney Colm Connolly, 32, to spearhead the federal part of the investigation. The probe would not only have the full force and resources of federal law enforcement behind it, but would also be more impervious to the kind of counterpressures that someone as well placed as Tom Capano could exert on a city and even state level.

That night, Capano called Bud Freel to tell him that, on the advice of his lawyers, he'd decided not to talk to the police. They wanted to crucify him and were only interested in the salacious stuff about his relationship with Anne Marie Fahey and he wasn't going to give it to them.

Freel gave him the bottom line: the Faheys were hurting, Capano might know something, some small fact whose significance he was unaware of, but that would give investigators a lead, and if Capano wasn't willing to do that, there was nothing more to say.

There was nothing more to say, and they never talked after that.

But Capano was making moves. On July 9, he met with public relations expert and old friend J. Brian Murphy, who helped him draw up a press release in which Capano would be quoted as expressing his shock and anguish at the mysterious disappearance of Anne Marie Fahey, denying any involvement in same, and stating that he had and would continue to fully cooperate with investigators. Capano said the press release was accurate, and told Murphy he would review it with his attorney and get back to him. Ultimately, Capano decided not to release the statement, and it would not have its first public airing until two and a half years later, when it was entered into evidence as a prosecution exhibit.

The next day, July 10, Capano and his attorneys met with J. Clayton Undercofler, Esq., the chairman of Saul Ewing, Capano's law firm. The chairman told them that since the firm did not represent Capano, any communications he had made in that context were not privileged or otherwise covered by an attorney-client relationship.

The investigative triumvirate of Assistant U.S. Attorney Colm Connolly, FBI SA Eric Alpert, and Wilmington Police Department Detective Robert Donovan worked in a tight-knit harness with each other, gathering a mosaic of information piece by piece.

Meanwhile, as Capano withheld his press release, on July 24 Robert Fahey wrote a letter on behalf of all the Faheys and sent it to Capano, urging him to come forward and "do the right thing" by telling police all he knew about Anne Marie Fahey's disappearance, instead of using his attorneys to fend off investigators as he'd been doing successfully up to now. They asked him to imagine it was one of his own daughters who was missing.

Again, Capano had nothing to say, officially. Later, the letter was made public, getting a big play in the press and, ultimately, in court.

A few days later, Robert Donovan interviewed Al Franke, one of Anne Marie Fahey's friends. She'd told him of a frightening incident that had taken place some six to eight weeks before Anne Marie disappeared. Tom Capano had climbed the fire escape, broken into her apartment, yelled and screamed at her in a rage, and taken back his gifts to her. It was an eerie echo of what he'd done when they'd broken up in the summer of 1995.

Colm Connolly and Eric Alpert had been looking into some of Capano's financial records. On July 26, while examining some of his credit card receipts, they discovered one for a sum of about $300 from Wallpaper Warehouse on July 29. Further investigation revealed that the store also did business as Air Base Carpet, and that on that date Capano had purchased a new rug and padding from them. Agent Alpert thought the $249 rug was inconsistent with Capano's spending habits and lifestyle. The investigators also thought that Capano might have used the rug to wrap up Anne Marie Fahey's body while he got rid of it.

Connolly then interviewed Ruth Boylan, Capano's house cleaner. She said that she had last cleaned the Grant Avenue house on June 24, and had been scheduled to clean it on July 8, but Capano had called her a few days before, canceling the cleaning session.

When she next went to clean the house on July 22, she was immediately aware that there had been some changes made since her last visit. In the den, which Capano called his "great room," a maroon sofa and the wall-to-wall carpet which had been there on her last visit were gone, replaced by a rug and two new chairs.

On July 29, during the course of a follow-up interview, hairdresser Lisa D'Amico told Detective Robert Donovan that Anne Marie Fahey told her that on one occasion in May 1996, while she and Tom Capano had been sitting in his car and she'd told him that she wanted to end their affair, he started screaming and yelling at her and called her a slut and a bitch. He grabbed her by the neck and she jumped out of the car and ran into her apartment.

That same day, Eric Alpert interviewed Michelle Sullivan, a psychologist who'd been treating Anne Marie Fahey. She'd told Sullivan that Tom Capano was stalking her and that she was frightened of him. Sullivan was working with Annie to help her end the relationship, and had urged her to make a complaint to the attorney general's office to get him to cease and desist harassing her.

The psychologist thought that the only reason Annie would have accompanied Capano to Philadelphia for dinner on June 27 would be to break off the relationship. That agreed with what investigators had learned from waitress Jackie Dansak about the strained, uncomfortable demeanor of Capano and Anne Marie Fahey while dining at the Panorama. Sullivan also said that she did not believe that Annie would have gone willingly to Capano's house that night, that she was not suicidal, but was looking forward to the future.

Investigators learned that Capano had borrowed Kay Capano's Suburban right around the time Anne Marie Fahey had vanished. A neighbor reported seeing Capano washing out the vehicle on Sunday, June 30.

On July 30, Detective Robert Donovan spoke to Anne Marie Fahey's friend, Jill Morrison. She said that Annie had told her of her affair with Capano and that he was possessive, controlling, psychotic, and needed counseling. She related that sometime in 1996, Capano had picked Annie up in his car for a drive, and that he'd locked the doors of the car and refused to let her out. He'd driven to his house without her consent, driven the car into the garage, locked the garage doors and refused to let her out of the garage until she had listened to what he had to say about her attempts to dissolve their relationship.

FBI SA Alpert went before federal U.S. Magistrate Mary Trostle with an affidavit listing the reasons why a search warrant should be issued, allowing investigators to examine Capano's Grant Avenue house and vehicles. In that affidavit, Alpert stated, "I believe that there is probable cause to believe that Tom Capano took Anne Marie Fahey without her consent from the Panorama Restaurant in Philadelphia to his home at [ ] Grant Ave. in Wilmington, Delaware, and that he killed her at his residence." He also stated that he believed that a search of that residence would reveal evidence of the federal offense of kidnapping. The magistrate authorized the warrant.

On July 31, crack FBI search teams of crime-scene technicians and evidence collectors moved on Capano, thoroughly searching Kay Capano's Suburban and Capano's house and Jeep Grand Cherokee. Among other things, searchers found Capano's unreleased press release and took custody of it. More important, they located two tiny drops of blood, each about the size of a pencil eraser, in the den— one on the baseboard and another on a radiator. No mean feat, considering that the room had recently been repainted. They collected the specimens and took them to be analyzed. They might be able to match them up with Anne Marie Fahey's DNA, but first they needed a sample of her blood.

As it turned out, she'd been a blood donor at the Blood Bank of Delaware in April, and after exacting efforts, her plasma was located in the cargo hold of a ship bound for Europe, and retrieved for analysis at the crime lab. But that came later.

Around the same time as the search, detectives discovered a suspicious circumstance. On July 1, by special order from brother Louis Capano, the Dumpsters at a Capano development site had been ordered to be picked up and delivered to a landfill for their contents to be pulverized. It was strange because the Dumpsters were only half full, and it wasn't cost efficient to have them emptied before they were completely filled. But it had been important enough for Louie to personally see that it got done.

Was Anne Marie Fahey's body in one of those Dumpsters, and had it been crushed into landfill? Probers searched the dump site in the heat of August for days, coming up blank.

Also provocative was information which surfaced about Gerry Capano having sold his boat, *The Summer Wind*, minus one anchor.

Tom Capano wasn't taking it lying down. He was still making moves, once more involving the prestigious law firm of Saul Ewing. The moves revolved around the time line which his attorney Charles Oberly had told him to make back on June 30, when he was first retained. Capano wrote out the time line on several sheets of paper, detailing a chronology of what he had done and whom he'd seen on June 27-28. For security, he placed some of these documents in a file at his law firm.

Not in his office, though. He placed the file in the office of Timothy A. Frey, a law partner, without telling Frey he'd put it there, among the files on his shelves. As he later stated, he did tell Frey that if he "saw in his office a file which he did not recognize, he was not to destroy the file or throw it out."

As Frey later recalled it, "I gave Capano a quizzical look to suggest I found his statement odd. In response to my facial expression, he said that he was concerned that the media could look at the contents of the file. He did not tell me what was in the file; nor did he tell me that the file contained confidential or privileged information. He never told me not to look at the contents of the file."

Sometime in July or August 1996, Frey saw a file on a bookshelf in his office. He read through the notes, placed them back in the file, and returned it to the shelf. He assumed Capano had made the notes. They remained in his office until November 1996, when they came into the possession of investigators.

On August 5, U.S. Attorney Colm Connolly made formal notification to Capano and his lawyer, Charles Oberly, that Capano was the subject of a federal grand jury investigation.

The investigation's pace quickened, increasing the pressure on Capano. On August 16, 1996, Agent Alpert submitted a second affidavit to the U.S. magistrate, seeking a warrant to compel Capano to produce blood and hair samples. This affidavit stated that the searches of the suspect's house and vehicles on July 31 had found bloodstains in the house and an apparent bloodstain in the backseat of his Jeep Cherokee. They also found hairs and fibers in the vehicle and house.

Alpert then stated: "I believe there is probable cause to believe . . . that Tom Capano killed Anne Marie Fahey at his residence and then attempted to clean evidence relating to the cause of her death in his laundry room and then removed at least some of that evidence from the residence in his black Jeep Grand Cherokee. I also believe that comparison of blood and hair samples found in the defendant's residence and jeep with the defendant's blood and head and pubic hair will result in evidence of [the] federal offense of kidnapping."

The magistrate issued the warrant. Capano was now compelled by law to appear at the hospital with his lawyer so an FBI technician could take those samples and deliver them to the lab. He didn't like it, but he had no choice but to obey.

More problematic was the fact that his daughters, who frequently visited the Grant Avenue house for overnight stays, might also have to have their blood tested to eliminate the possibility of one of them having been the source of the blood droplets. On that point, Capano was intractable, ferociously guarding their privacy and refusing to allow them to be tested. He also rejected all proposed compromise solutions by the prosecutor's office, which would have involved his swearing in an affidavit that the blood was not theirs, and that they would not later appear as alibi witnesses for him. The alibi witness clause was a sticking point, too. Capano wouldn't budge, leading investigators to wonder if he might try to get the girls to perjure themselves as to his and their whereabouts on the night of Thursday, June 27.

The request to test the blood of his daughters would fester in Capano's mind for the next two and a half years, finally erupting in what would be the most scaldingly explosive moment in Delaware's most sensational murder trial in decades.

The investigative strategy was a standard one used for prosecuting criminal conspiracies: catch the small fish first, and use them to catch the big fish. In this case, the small fish were Louis Capano and Gerry Capano, both of whom were implicated in at least the cover-up if not the crime. And they both had handles sticking out of them. Louis Capano's was his fast and loose financial dealings, which probers were already scrutinizing. With Gerry Capano, it was drug abuse and a pseudo-wise-guy lifestyle.

Then there was the matter of the time line and notes which Capano had hidden in Frey's office in July. Colm Connolly found out about them and on November 4, 1996, sent FBI SA Kevin Shannon to the Saul Ewing law firm with a subpoena for the file. Timothy Frey placed it in an envelope and sealed it. Agent Shannon delivered it to the U.S. Attorney's Office, where on the following day it was delivered to Connolly.

The time line for Friday, June 28 showed a lot of hours spent with Gerry Capano, which tended to throw a spotlight on him and his role in the proceedings. The detailed notes described Capano's relationship with Anne Marie Fahey, naturally weighted from his point of view, depicting him as a caring friend and lover, and her as troubled and seriously disturbed.

A few months later, Capano's attorneys contended in an evidence admissibility hearing that the file and its contents were privileged information. The judge ruled otherwise, noting that Frey's "unlocked and easily accessible office, where an adversary might obtain the file, meant that the defendant [Thomas Capano] had waived the right to assert the doctrine." The court also found that Capano had acted unreasonably by waiting four months before filing a complaint.

The investigation had now stretched into the first quarter of 1997. But it was early yet. The one-year anniversary of Anne Marie Fahey's disappearance came and went. The summer was enlivened when, on August 13, 1997, FBI SA Ron Poplas delivered a subpoena to Capano's mother, Marguerite Capano, in Stone Harbor. The agent just handed her the papers, and went away without questioning her, but the incident infuriated the family.

In an affidavit dated September 4, 1997, Agent Eric Alpert sought a search warrant for the law firm of Saul Ewing for specified e-mail and voice mail. In it, he set out the facts "concerning a relationship between [Thomas Capano] and another woman in the early 1980s, where he allegedly committed various crimes to retaliate against that woman for ending a relationship with him." The harassment of Linda Marandola had come home to roost.

What's more, Alpert went on to develop a startling chain of events bearing on the case. In the spring of 1996, at the same time Capano was obsessing about Anne Marie Fahey and conducting an affair with Debby MacIntyre and another woman, Susan Louth, he had also initiated contact with Linda Marandola, whom he had not seen or spoken to in years. Amazingly, he'd even arranged for her to obtain a job in his firm. At the last minute, she got cold feet, rejecting the job on the day she was to begin to work. Capano then sued her for money she owed him, a $3,000 "loan" which he'd made to her in anticipation of her taking the job. The legal action had taken place on June 14, 1996, 13 days before Anne Marie Fahey was last seen alive.

Alpert argued, "I believe that [Linda Marandola's] rejection of Tom Capano contributed to his reaction to Anne Marie Fahey's attempt to end her relationship with him on June 27, 1996.

"I also believe that any e-mail and voice-mail messages between Tom Capano and Anne Marie Fahey may provide evidence of an affair between them and the fact that she was attempting to end the affair and being harassed and intimidated by Capano. Such evidence would be relevant to Capano's motive and intent to harm her."

He maintained that the facts supported the theory that Capano "knew Anne Marie Fahey was attempting to end the relationship, he formed an intent to kill her, he took her to dinner knowing he planned to kill her, and he crossed the Pennsylvania/Delaware border after forming this intent."

The warrant was issued and the FBI secured Capano's e-mail at Saul Ewing. Shortly after, Capano resigned from the firm.

The prosecution was ready to land one of the small fish. Federal law enforcement agencies, such as the DEA and ATF, had been investigating Gerry Capano for drug and weapons offenses. There may have been a few informants in the picture, too. On Wednesday, October 8, 1997, they tightened the net in a massive night raid on Gerry's Brandywine Hundred mansion, storming inside with drawn guns, putting a gun to the back of his head as they searched the house. It was overkill and was meant to be. The feds were sending a message not only to Gerry, but beyond him to Tom Capano and the rest of the family, that they were playing hardball. The raid yielded 21 guns, plus small amounts of marijuana and cocaine, leaving Gerry vulnerable to federal charges of possession of weapons by a drug user.

More damaging was another raid, this one on the home of his best friend, which produced a gun registered to Gerry, thus nailing him on the illegal transfer of a weapon. That was good for a three-year federal prison term.

Visits by caseworkers for a children's welfare agency investigating whether the possession of guns and drugs in the home rendered Gerry and his wife "unfit parents," whose kids should be taken away for their own good, also turned up the pressure.

Gerry was really in a quandry. Family was family, but to which one did he owe his ultimate loyalty: to his wife and kids, or to brother Tom? Not to mention any concerns he might have had himself about staying out of federal prison, or any prison.

Gerry Capano and his lawyer made an agreement with the government, in which he agreed to testify as a witness in the case, providing information about an "alleged disposal of a body in the Atlantic Ocean." He stated that several months before the raid, he'd told his attorney, Edmund D. Lyons Jr., about the "sea burial." He also told of his extensive drug use before and after that disposal. He was allowed to plead guilty to a misdemeanor misprision of a felony (knowing about a felony and failing to report it) and would get three years probation, if he continued to tell the whole truth and nothing but.

Gerry was cooperating. On November 10, Louis Capano came in, telling what he knew to the prosecution. It was only a matter of time now before the investigation netted the big fish.

On November 12, 1997, Tom Capano was arrested and held in Wilmington's Gander Hill prison.

The next day, the 13th, a man named Ron

Smith contacted FBI SA Eric Alpert. He said
his friend, fisherman Ken Chubb, had found
a cooler bobbing in the sea several miles off
the Indian River inlet during the Fourth of
July weekend in 1996, a white cooler with no
lid and two holes in it.

Detective Robert Donovan went out and secured the cooler. There weren't any traces of
blood inside it for a DNA match with the victim, but the cooler's ID numbers marked it as
the one which Capano had bought in April
1996.

Capano was a problem prisoner. As a former
prosecutor, he was a target for vengeful con-
victs, or for anybody seeking to make an in-
stant reputation as a big man by sticking him
with a shiv. For his own safety, he had to be
put in administrative segregation, away from
the general prison population. In reality, this
meant that he spent almost all of his hours
locked down in solitary confinement in his cell
in Pod 1F. He was allowed phone and letter-
writing privileges, and he worked both as hard
as he could.

On January 8, 1998, Capano pleaded not
guilty and asked for bail. The prosecution opposed bail on the grounds that this was a
death penalty case. Now the defense knew that
the prosecution was going to demand the
death penalty.

Debby MacIntyre was in deeper than she
knew. Capano's phone calls to her during the
critical time period of June 27–28, 1996, had

already attracted investigators' interest in her, but what really grabbed them was the discovery that on May 13, 1996, just about five weeks before Anne Marie Fahey's disappearance, Debby had bought a gun, a .22-caliber Beretta.

The time was fast approaching when she would have to answer the hard questions. Capano had already told her how to answer them, but the question was whether or not she'd stick to his script.

While Capano was locked up in Gander Hill, he continued to communicate extensively with MacIntyre through letters and telephone calls. He was eagerly awaiting a hearing ("proof positive hearing") in an attempt to obtain bail. He was counting on Debby to testify on his behalf. She was having problems with the government in connection with her story regarding her purchase and disposal of the gun before Anne Marie Fahey's alleged murder.

On Wednesday, January 28, 1998, Debby MacIntyre was interviewed under oath at the state attorney general's office, where she was represented by Adam Balick, a lawyer Capano had gotten for her. She answered various questions regarding her purchase of the gun in May 1996.

Colm Connolly first just asked general questions about whether or not she owned a gun, and when she had purchased it. Debby floundered, saying she'd bought it in 1994 or 1995, well, maybe 1996. Did she still have it? No, she stumbled into saying that she'd gotten rid of it in mid-June 1996, about two weeks before Anne Marie Fahey disappeared. She said she threw it in the trash. Using some psychological tactics, Eric Alpert showed her a gun, a .22 Beretta that looked identical to the one she'd bought. Since she'd given the gun to Capano, she had no way of knowing if investigators had recovered it, thus catching her out in a lie. Then Connolly confronted her with the federal firearms form she'd filled out on May 13, 1996, showing that she'd bought a Beretta.

She was asked what she'd say if she learned that Capano's fingerprints had been found on the gun. They hadn't. This wasn't the gun, but again, she didn't know that. She could feel the walls closing in on her. She came up with the unsatisfying answer that Capano might have picked it up out of the trash after she'd thrown it away.

That was the breaking point for Debby MacIntyre. Now it wasn't just Capano's neck that was in the noose, it was her own. After the hearing, Adam Balick contacted Charles Oberly to give him the bad news about how her testimony had gone.

Capano was furious. He'd been counting on her to say that she'd bought the gun herself, for self-protection, but that she'd been uncomfortable with having a gun in the house where her children were living, and so she'd thrown it out. That version kept him out of it all the way. Now Debby had tied him to the gun.

That night, he wrote her yet another letter,

abusing her for her incredible stupidity in linking him with the gun. He also trashed Adam Balick for not being able to forestall Colm Connolly during the questioning. He went on to say how much he needed her to testify on his behalf at the proof positive hearing, which was coming up in a few days. He really wanted to get out of jail and was confident that he would. He told her how important his lawyers thought her testimony would be for him, that she would be a very powerful and convincing witness.

In the letter, he reiterated the story he wanted her to tell, stating it in such terms as, "Of course you remember that . . .," "as we discussed," and other circumlocutions. He also discussed the cooler, "reminding" her of how she'd seen it back in April at his Grant Avenue house, where he'd said he bought it as a gift for Gerry Capano. This went to the heart of the premeditation issue and, ultimately, the charges of first-degree murder.

What he didn't know was that right around that time, Debby had gotten in touch with her ex-husband Dave Williams, Capano's onetime associate at the law firm so long ago. Williams set about helping her to get a new lawyer.

The proof positive bail hearing was scheduled to begin on February 2, 1998. On that day, Adam Balick notified Capano's defense lawyers that Debby MacIntyre would assert her Fifth Amendment privilege against self-incrimination if called to testify. Capano wrote her a letter that night expressing surprise at her intention to assert her rights because she had not "done anything wrong." He also gave her "advice" on obtaining immunity from the State because that "snake" Colm Connolly and "the hangman" Ferris Wharton would twist her words, particularly with regard to the gun.

On February 4, Capano learned that Debby MacIntyre would not testify at the bail hearing. That was a severe blow. He'd been certain of his release on bail. He also learned that certain testimony at the hearing from FBI SA Alpert indicated that if MacIntyre wasn't yet actively cooperating with the prosecution, she certainly wasn't cooperating with the defense.

That same day, Capano belatedly received a letter from Debby explaining her decision not to testify at the hearing. She'd written it before the hearing had started, but he'd only now received it. He wrote back, venting his complaints and his disgust, ripping into her for her decision and criticizing her attorney. He further commented upon the gun which she'd purchased, slanting the text to support his own line of defense.

The proof positive hearing ran from February 2 to 6, 1998, an unusually lengthy hearing for such a procedure. At its conclusion, Capano's request for bail was denied.

His unhappiness only increased when he learned that on February 10, Debby MacIntyre had hired a new attorney, Thomas Bergstrom, of Malvern, Pennsylvania, a smart and vigorous lawyer who'd recently been in the headlines for defending millionaire client John DuPont, charged with the murder of Olympic wrestler David Schultz. Adam Balick had been Capano's choice for Debby's lawyer, and Capano hadn't thought much of his efforts, but Thomas Bergstrom was Debby's choice. Capano called him, "that loathsome attorney" and "the Malvern malefactor."

Worse was the fact that her ex-husband Dave Williams had helped broker the change in legal counsel. Capano was losing control. He didn't want Debby's lawyer looking after her best interests because that wouldn't suit his own best interests. Not that Balick hadn't tried. He'd grown frustrated by his client's steadfast adherence to Capano's line of defense.

Adding to Debby MacIntyre's woes in the last weeks of February was her dismissal from her job at the Tatnall School. The involvement of one of its administrators in a scandalous murder probe was not the image that the high-status facility wished to present. She'd been employed there for twelve years, and had attended Tatnall as a student for fifteen years, an involvement with the institution that covered more than half her life.

Capano wrote to her, urging her to fight the decision. He had to know the termination wouldn't make her any easier to control.

On February 27, Debby MacIntyre and her attorney met with Ferris Wharton, Detective Robert Donovan, and Colm Connolly. At the start, MacIntyre signed an immunity agreement, agreeing "to cooperate fully in the investigation of Anne Marie Fahey's death" in exchange for freedom from prosecution for false statements she'd made to federal investigators, false testimony before a federal grand jury on September 10, 1996, false statements made on an ATF form when buying the gun on May 13, 1996, and the false statements she'd made under oath on January 28, 1998.

She told how Capano had called her on numerous occasions from Gander Hill prison, and that he'd slammed her for not testifying at the bail hearing and for hiring Thomas Bergstrom. She further told them that his statements in the February 3 letter regarding the cooler were not true, and that she'd never seen the cooler nor discussed it with him.

She "loved" Tom Capano, she said, and despite her attorney's instructions not to communicate with him, she claimed she could not ignore his phone calls. She was "emotionally dependent" upon him, and he was well aware of this dependency, and sought to use it to control her.

Wharton and Connolly thought they could not prevent MacIntyre from speaking to Capano, and feared if her phone conversations with him were not monitored, then he later could misrepresent what she said. They were of the opinion that his actions toward her constituted tampering with a witness, making criminal solicitations, and suborning perjury.

They asked her to place a recorder on her phone and to record any conversations she had with him.

She agreed. Robert Donovan installed the recorder and showed her how to operate it. She was told not to try to obtain any incriminating statements from Capano. Capano knew she'd met with prosecutors on February 27. In a letter dated the same day, he noted that his attorney had instructed him not to call or write her, but that he was "going to ignore him without a second thought." He also noted that a fellow prisoner ordered "me not to write or call because you obviously don't love me and cannot be trusted."

On February 28, he called Debby MacIntyre twice. She recorded the first call, but not the second; she claimed she was unsure how to work the recorder properly and failed to activate it for the second call. He also called on March 1, 2, and 3, and all these calls were recorded.

The condensed transcripts of the calls give a clear picture of the dynamic between Tom Capano and Debby MacIntyre.

2/28/98: TRANSCRIPT of Recorded Telephone Conversation between Debby MacIntyre and Tom Capano:
MacIntyre: Hello?
OPERATOR: Bell Atlantic has a collect call from inmate at the Gander Hill State Correctional Facility. To refuse this call,

hang up. If you accept this call, do not use three-way or call-waiting features or you will be disconnected. To accept this call, dial one now. *[beep]* Thank you.

Capano: Hello?

MacIntyre: Hi.

Capano: Where were you? It took you a while to answer the phone.

MacIntyre: Oh, I check to see who was calling me. You know I had to get a caller ID thing.

Capano: Why?

MacIntyre: I always check my calls. I don't answer anything unless I know who it is. It tells me who it is.

Capano: Would you, would you please tell me what's happening?

MacIntyre: I will tell you. I told the truth.

Capano: How did you get this new lawyer?

MacIntyre: [sigh] It was recommended by [ex-husband] Dave Williams.

Capano: So you listened to Dave and you went to this new lawyer and then what?

MacIntyre: I saw him . . . and I liked him, I really did and he seemed very competent and very self-confident. . . .

Capano: We only have fifteen minutes.

MacIntyre: I know. So I said I'm gonna meet with these people and he went and he met with the government and then he said, we need to go back and talk to them. . . . And, of course, we went in on

Friday and it was like an event. So, I went in there and I talked to them.

Capano: What did you . . . ?

MacIntyre: I told them the truth. I told them everything that I had told them before which is exactly the truth, except at the end, they asked me about this gun and I . . .

Capano: What did you say?

MacIntyre: I was truthful about it, I said—

Capano: Don't say that, just tell me what you said.

MacIntyre: I told them that, uh, I bought it and I gave it to you. You wanted it and I gave it to you.

Capano: Why did you say such a thing?

MacIntyre: Because you did.

Capano: Why did you, why did you go in there and . . . ?

MacIntyre: I told the truth.

Capano: Say that?

MacIntyre: Darling. I told the truth. It's so obvious when I was in the interview, that I can't lie. If I'd gone to that bail hearing and said what I was, you know, thinking of saying, it would have been— terrible.

Capano: [intense] Do you know what you've done?

MacIntyre: I've told the truth.

Capano: No, no, excuse me, do you know what you've done to me? Do you know

what you've done to me? Do you know
what you've done to us?

MacIntyre: [sigh] Look, I told the truth—

Capano: What, will you stop that?

MacIntyre: I told the truth and that—

Capano: One more time, I'm gonna hang
up. What did you, what do you mean . . .
do you know what this has done to us?

MacIntyre: Well, I still love you.

Capano: How could you?

MacIntyre: How could I not?

Capano: How could you, how could you
love me and then betray me?

MacIntyre: I told the truth.

Capano: Yes, and Debby, don't say that
one more time. Debby, how could you do
something like that without even talking
to me? We have made promises to each
other. . . . We have made vows and
promises to each other.

MacIntyre: I know, darling.

[He then warns her about not giving his letters
to her attorney, but she already has, the recent
ones.]

MacIntyre: Do you know what you did in
the letter that you just wrote to me?

Capano: What?

MacIntyre: You spelled my name wrong.

Capano: Where?

MacIntyre: You spelled my name *D-E-B-B-
I-E.* You addressed me "Dear Debbie" *I E.*

Capano: . . . Can we not talk about such trivia?

[Later.]

Capano: Are you recording this conversation?

MacIntyre: Yeah, right.

Capano: Are you?

MacIntyre: No, I am not.

Capano: And you gave personal letters, emotional heartrending letters that were from my heart to your heart, you gave them to some stranger.

[Later.]

Capano: You abandoned me when I needed you and now, more than abandoning me, you're destroying me.

MacIntyre: I'm not destroying you.

Capano: You're destroying me, Debby. Do you know what they're gonna do with this? Do you know how they're gonna try to make this look? Do you understand?

MacIntyre: I don't know what this means.

Capano: You think that what? You think that I'm gonna be here for the rest of my life?

[Later.]

Capano: This is all your doing. Nobody made you do this. Nobody made you listen to Dave Williams. Nobody, I can't believe this.

MacIntyre: [flustered, agitated] Nobody, but wait a minute— Whoa, whoa, whoa,

whoa, whoa, now wait a minute. Let's go
back to this gun. Hah.

Capano: No, no, no, no, no . . .

MacIntyre: Hehh. Who made me get, give
you . . . the gun?

Capano: . . . no, no, no, no, no, no, no,
no, no, no, no, no.

MacIntyre: Who made me give you the
gun?

Capano: No, no, no, etc.

[That "You think that I'm gonna be here
for the rest of my life?" could be taken as a
threat or warning, the implication being, I'm
not going to be here forever, and when I get
out, watch out.]

3/1/98: TRANSCRIPT of Recorded Telephone
Conversation between Debby MacIntyre and
Tom Capano:

Capano: Do you love me?

MacIntyre: I do love you.

Capano: Okay. So let's not fight, okay?

MacIntyre: Okay.

Capano: Do you love me enough to fight
for me?

MacIntyre: Sure, I'll fight for you.

Capano: Do you love me enough to
switch lawyers like I asked you to?

MacIntyre: I don't know why I want to
switch lawyers.

Capano: because I'm asking you to.

MacIntyre: I like my lawyer [Bergstrom].

Capano: But I'm asking you to, it's important to me. Last night you said you'd do it.

MacIntyre: I'll think about it.

Capano: Well, last night you said "yes."

MacIntyre: I don't remember you asking me that last night.

Capano: Well I did, I did—

MacIntyre: Okay.

Capano: —and you said "yes." I mean, why do you even have to think about it . . . ?

MacIntyre: I like him, well, okay, yes.

Capano: Will you?

MacIntyre: I will.

Capano: Thank you. It means all the world to me.

MacIntyre: Why?

Capano: Because he doesn't care about me. He doesn't care about us. . . . He's a former prosecutor and all he wants to do is cooperate with the gov.

MacIntyre: He's looking out for my best interests, is all.

Capano: Debby, I tried to tell you, you're destroying me.

MacIntyre: No, I'm not.

Capano: Debby, don't argue with me, you're destroying me, partly because of him. Okay? Now, this guy should not be important to you. I guess I need to know, who's more important, this guy or me?

MacIntyre: Well, that's not a fair question, I mean, this guy is good.

Capano: What are you talking about?

MacIntyre: I mean, he's good, I got myself in a jam.

Capano: You did not, that's just it. You did not get yourself in a jam, Debby. You are so confused. I think you've been a mess since February fourth. I don't think you've been thinking clearly.

MacIntyre: That's right, I've been a mess since January twenty-eighth.

Capano: I think you've made a lot of bad judgment calls, a lot of 'em, Deb. And I got to ask you to do things for me just on the basis of the fact that you love me and if you're not willing to do 'em, then I have to interpret it that you don't love me because I'm not asking you to do anything significant.

MacIntyre: Well, then I don't know why you want me to do it then.

Capano: Because it's insignificant to you but it's very important to me.

MacIntyre: Well, I like my lawyer though. I like him.

Capano: So what? Lawyers are a dime a dozen.

MacIntyre: Oh. Is there another question?

Capano: [sigh] Well, I'd like the answer to that one. You told me you would do it.

MacIntyre: I'll think about it.

Capano: No, you told me a minute ago

you would do it. Now you're telling me you're not going to do it?

MacIntyre: I mean I'm struggling with that question.

Capano: Why would you struggle, this is—

MacIntyre: Because I like the guy and he's doing a—

Capano: —killing me, this is killing me, Deb.

MacIntyre: [sigh]

Capano: This is killing me, I mean so what if you like this guy, he's a stranger. . . .

MacIntyre: He's not a stranger to me.

Capano: Don't interrupt me, I'm telling ya. He's a nobody to you, you've only known him for a month.

MacIntyre: Okay, what, okay, I say yes. So what's the next question?

Capano: Get the letters back from him.
[Later.]

Capano: Deb, do you want to help me?

MacIntyre: I do. You're mad at me though. You're mad at me, for what I've done.

Capano: Yeah, I am but I think we can get over this.

MacIntyre: Good. Good.

Capano: I think we can get over this but you're gonna have to help me. I'm not yelling at ya, you've really, really hurt me. And this thing with this lawyer hurts me

immensely and I can't believe that you
would even think for two seconds. You
have to understand about love, I mean,
making a little sacrifice and I'm not asking you to do much.

MacIntyre: Oh God.

Capano: All right honey? You promise me
you're gonna do this?

MacIntyre: Yes.

[Later.]

Capano: Deb, tell me you'll do it.

MacIntyre: [sigh] Stop it, I'll talk to the
guy.

Capano: Talking to him won't help, Deb.
Please say yes.

Debby MacIntyre had made it clear she
would not be following Capano's instructions.
He wanted to send her a message, and turned
to Nick Perillo.

Nick Perillo was a small-time career criminal,
thief, con artist, and drug dealer. A habitual
offender, he'd been on parole when he was
arrested in January 1998, for trying to sell his
mother's stolen refrigerator. He was locked up
in Gander Hill prison, where he scammed his
way into a private cell by lying that he was going to testify against an accomplice who was
in the general prison population and had to
be protected from him. By doing so, he
avoided having to sleep on the floor and wan-
gled himself a bed in a cell.

On March 3, 1998, while meeting with his

attorney, Thomas A. Foley, at Gander Hill, Perillo stated that Capano was soliciting him to arrange for someone on the outside to burglarize Debby MacIntyre's house. He also said that Capano was going to give him a diagram of the house later that same day. Foley was doubtful that Capano would come through with the incriminating diagram, but he communicated his information to Ferris Wharton.

However, Capano did just that, furnishing Perillo with an elaborate floor plan of MacIntyre's house showing the location where valuables were hidden, and even including the security alarm number code that would neutralize the burglar alarm. There were also explicit written instructions about what things to take and what to destroy, including the demand that the intruder shatter a wall-length mirror in Debby's bedroom. This would be significant to Debby, since she and Capano used to watch themselves in the mirror while having sex.

Foley contacted Colm Connolly at his residence, furnishing him with the information and evidence. He also gave Connolly the standard disclaimer that Perillo had been informed that neither the State nor the U.S. Government would promise him any deals in exchange for his cooperation.

On March 11, 1998, Nick Perillo was brought to the courthouse to meet Wharton, Connolly, and Donovan, at which time he turned over the diagram and written instructions.

There was also convicted cocaine dealer Wilfredo Rosa aka "Tito." Imprisoned on federal drug charges, he was transferred to the cell next to Tom Capano's in late November 1997. The State Attorney General's Office would later allege that during this time, Capano and Rosa planned the murder of Gerry Capano. In late December, Rosa was transferred out to a federal correctional institution in Fairton in southern New Jersey. March 1998 saw Rosa once again returning to Gander Hill and once more lodged in the cell next to Capano's. The sequence might have seemed suspiciously fortuitous, but the attorney general's office and the law enforcement officers on the case all denied any knowledge of or control over Rosa's transfers and cell placements.

Once more, Capano began plotting with Rosa, only this time he not only wanted to have Gerry Capano hit, he wanted to have Debby MacIntyre killed, too. Or so Rosa said, as he came forward and passed along the information to the authorities.

But it was Nick Perillo who'd obtained the diagram and instructions written in Capano's own hand, and on May 26, 1998, he was allowed to enter a plea to his charges that resulted in only one year of incarceration, despite the fact he was a habitual offender according to Delaware law. In addition, the State did not pursue a parole violation that would

have mandated several years of additional jail
time.

Earlier that month, on May 1, Capano's lawyers made a motion asking the court to suppress
all the evidence seized from his residence and
motor vehicles during the search of them on
July 31, 1996. Judge William Swain Lee ruled
against that motion. On August 18, 1998, the
court held a hearing on Capano's lawyers motion "to suppress the contents of all telephonic
conversations occurring between the defendant
and one Deborah MacIntyre between 2/28–
3/3/98." The judge ruled against that motion,
opening the way for those conversations to be
entered into evidence at Tom Capano's trial for
murder in the first degree.

TRIAL

The trial would be held at Wilmington's
Daniel J. Herrmann Courthouse, in Courtroom 302, with Superior Court Judge William
Swain Lee presiding. Appearing for the prosecution were Assistant U.S. Attorney Colm Connolly and State Prosecutor Ferris Wharton. For
the defense were attorneys Charles Oberly,
Eugene Maurer, John F. O'Donnell, and
Joseph Oteri. The defense was a million-dollar
lineup of legal heavy hitters—both in expertise
and cost. A fifth attorney who'd been repre-
senting Capano, high-profile defense lawyer
Joe Hurley, had left the case back in April,

making the cryptic comment that the reason he'd left was a secret that he'd "take to the grave."

Jury selection began on October 6, 1998. A jury made up of six men and six women was impaneled.

The trial began at Monday, October 26, 1998, playing to a packed courthouse. Seated at the defense table with his quartet of high-priced lawyers, Tom Capano showed the effects of his incarceration and the strain of being on trial for his life. He'd lost weight, his eyes and cheeks were sunken and hollow.

On the scene to support him, seated behind him at the defense table were two rows of Capanos, including his wheelchair-bound mother, Marguerite, three of his daughters, other family members, and friends.

Across from them, on the other side of the aisle, sat the Faheys. Members of the two contending families cast some hard looks at each other, but no words were exchanged.

The jurors were sworn in, and the prosecution began its opening statement, a 90-minute summation of what the State hoped to prove. Ferris Wharton methodically outlined the State's case, complete with charts and time lines, photos, phone records, credit card receipts, etc., showing who did what when.

He began by reading from the entry from Anne Marie Fahey's diary that labeled Tom Capano a "controlling, manipulative, insecure, jealous maniac." He then made the point that two weeks after she made that entry stating that she had brought "closure" to Capano, he bought the cooler. Wharton called the cooler "Anne Marie's coffin." Laying out the time line, he stated that, a month after that, Capano had Debby MacIntyre buy the gun, and that he then killed Anne Marie Fahey on June 27, 1996.

He said, "Tom Capano had determined that if Anne Marie Fahey could not be manipulated into being with him, she would be with no one else forever. The evidence will show you that Tom Capano murdered Anne Marie Fahey."

He went on to describe how, on the morning of June 28, in the driveway of Gerry Capano's house, Tom Capano had nodded when Gerry asked if he had killed the "two extortionists" that Tom had first made mention of to him in February, when he originally asked if he could use his brother's boat in case of such an eventuality. He said that Gerry Capano would testify that he helped his brother dump a body at sea and that Louis Capano Jr. would tell how Tom Capano used Louis's construction Dumpster to dispose of evidence.

Ferris Wharton told the jury that the State was seeking the death penalty in the case.

At the defense table, pointman for the legal team was Boston-based attorney Joe Oteri, 67, a flamboyant spellbinder with a reputation for tackling tough federal prosecutions in high-profile drug cases and winning. He was white haired and bearded, canny, tough, and street-wise.

He delivered the opening statement for the defense. It was no surprise when he slammed the prosecution's star witnesses, calling Louis Capano and Gerry Capano "two boobs who cut a deal" and a pair of "admitted liars." Then came the real shocker. Oteri told the jury, "You are going to hear testimony that Tom Capano did not murder Anne Marie Fahey. She died as the result of an outrageous, horrible, tragic accident."

After two and a half years of stonewalling, Capano had finally admitted to disposing of Anne Marie Fahey's body.

Oteri said that the defendant "was scared he was going to lose everything he had, his social position, his political position. Tom Capano lied to everybody except one person who knows the horrible truth."

But Capano hadn't murdered Anne Marie Fahey, Oteri said. Her death was a "horrible accident," though he wouldn't say what kind, but there was that one other person besides Capano who knew the truth, that as-yet un-identified mystery witness. Oteri's phraseology was deliberately ambiguous and elastic, leaving room to maneuver as the trial proceeded.

He continued, "My client and his brother took the body out to sea. Another person is fully cognizant of everything." He hastened to reassure the jurors that the defendant was "not the least bit proud" about what he had done in covering up Anne Marie Fahey's accidental death, but he was no killer.

There was nothing sinister in Capano's buying the cooler, not when he'd bought it with his own credit card. In fact, the act proved the innocence of his intentions: "He wouldn't buy it at a Wilmington store using a credit card. Tom Capano's a bright guy. That's insanity."

Oteri heaped rhetorical hot coals on the head of Gerry Capano, who he said "had a brain like a fried egg because he was a boozer and a druggie. He was a typical screwed-up rich kid who never had to earn anything. He's a poster boy for the 'Me Generation.'"

He went on to explain that Gerry suffered from a condition called "confabulation," a mental disorder that drug users were particularly susceptible to, that left "black holes in the mind" and prompted sufferers to make up stories.

The defense had essentially conceded that Gerry Capano's account of the body dumping at sea was true, but now mocked and discredited what he'd said about the defendant's remarks in February 1996, about having to do away with "extortionists."

Oteri said that the victim was no innocent babe in the woods, but knew the score. "We have no intention of besmirching Anne Marie Fahey, but she was not an 18-year-old kid just out of high school." She was a 30-year-old woman who knew what she was getting into when she began a relationship with Capano, who was a concerned, caring lover and friend, who gave her gifts and tried to help her get treatment for her eating disorder. She was psychologically unstable, depressed, and suicidal.

Oteri reserved some of his scorn for Debby MacIntyre, who'd lied five times to investigators before striking her own deal for immunity. He finished his opening statement by wrapping himself in the flag, lecturing the jury that the presumption of innocence is one of the foundations of American democracy, concluding, "Please, I beg of you. Don't forget that."

The opening statements encapsulated the respective trial strategies of the prosecution and the defense. The prosecution went in handicapped by the lack of a body and the forensic evidence it would yield as to cause of death. No witness had come forward to say how Anne Marie Fahey died. The State of Delaware had only prosecuted one murder trial with no body before. They lost.

The prosecution had the cooler, a gift from the sea-gods. There were a few of Anne Marie Fahey's blood droplets from the house, which the defense would do its damnedest to minimize. The sofa and carpet were gone, ground into powder and paste at the dump. There was no murder weapon. The prosecution's key witnesses—Gerry Capano, Louis Capano and Debby MacIntyre—all had credibility problems. Joe Oteri's opening statement had provided a foretaste of how the defense would handle Gerry Capano. They relished the prospect of getting him under oath on the witness stand. In a pretrial press statement, Oteri had already tagged Gerry as "a liar, a junkie, and a stone-cold bum."

The defense strategy was complex. They'd admitted that Tom Capano had disposed of Anne Marie Fahey's body, but not that he'd killed her. By maintaining that her death was "accidental," they might save their client from conviction on murder one charges and spare him from the death penalty. Oteri's opening statement had been phrased to leave them a lot of room to move as the trial developed. His remarks about Fahey being "depressed and suicidal" left open the possible interpretation that she'd killed herself. (In fact, Capano had told Louis Capano early on that she'd slit her wrists while at his house, staining the sofa and carpet, compelling him to get rid of them when she'd gone missing shortly thereafter.) Or, the "horrible accident" which took her life could have come about due to some action by the mysterious "other person who knew the truth."

The identity of that mystery witness was no mystery at all to the prosecution. For months now, Thomas Bergstrom, Debby MacIntyre's lawyer, had said he expected Capano to blame her for Anne Marie Fahey's death. A month before going to trial, the prosecution had filed court papers on that same subject, saying that Capano's recent letters to Debby had implied her involvement. She'd sworn to a signed affadavit denying any part in Anne Marie Fahey's death and disappearance, and her immunity deal was predicated on her telling the whole truth to prosecutors. If she'd lied, the deal went out the window and she was subject to prosecution on the earlier charges, in addition to any new charges that might result from the revelations.

Joe Oteri's provocative opening was the courtroom equivalent of bringing a gun out on stage at the start of the first act. Before the final curtain, someone must fire that gun. The defense had made some tall talk, and now the jury would be expecting them to back it up. It was the first indication that Capano himself might eventually take the stand, since who could better detail the circumstances of that "horrible accident"?

After opening statements, the prosecution began presenting its case, first calling Brian Fahey, Anne Marie Fahey's 37-year-old brother, who testified about their family background, the hard times and good times. He said he'd once cautioned Annie to "be careful" about getting involved with Tom Capano.

On cross-examination, the defense said that Anne Marie Fahey had something of a temper, asking the witness about an incident in her youth where she'd once hit their alcoholic father with a hockey stick (after he'd stolen money from her). The witness also said that he hadn't known about her relationship with Capano, and admitted that the Faheys were suing all four Capano brothers in a civil action. He said, "They were responsible for causing my family a great deal of pain . . . killing my sister. I didn't believe they should be able to get away with it without putting up a fight."

Next called were two of Anne Marie Fahey's coworkers, Susan Campbell Mast, who'd been Governor Carper's secretary in 1996, and Diane Hastings, the governor's office manager. In succession they testified that on June 27, 1996, Annie had been in an upbeat mood, that at this end of the legislative session, when things got really crazy, she was looking forward to taking Friday off for a manicure, pedicure, and reading in the park. On cross-examination, both said they were unaware that Annie and Capano were going to dinner that night, and said they didn't know whether that was why she seemed happy.

Next called was Jacqueline "Jackie" Dansak, the waitress who'd served the couple at the Ristorante Panorama in Philadelphia. She recalled that Annie wore a floral-print dress, and that Capano wore tinted eyeglasses. She said the two were somber, quiet, and that Fahey looked "sad," distracted. Capano had done the ordering for both of them. Fahey had eaten little of her food, and the witness had made up an oversized "doggie bag" for them.

On cross-examination, trying to undercut Capano's image as manipulative and controlling, Oteri made the point that there was nothing unusual about a "gentleman" and host doing the ordering for a dinner guest. The witness admitted that she'd only seen the two while serving their food and drinks, and was not present for the rest of the meal to observe their demeanor.

As to Fahey's appearance, the witness maintained that her hair "wasn't kempt by any standards," buttressing the prosecution's contention that the unhappy circumstances of the meal had caused her to be neglectful of her looks.

On Tuesday, October 27, Dr. Neil S. Kaye took the stand, for Ferris Wharton's direct. A psychologist who'd been treating Anne Marie Fahey, he'd had an appointment with her on the day of her disappearance. Wharton had Kaye detail Fahey's background regarding her treatment and psychological history. The witness said that she'd first begun treatment at age 20 in 1986, and that at the time of her death, she was suffering from anorexia, depression, anxiety attacks, and co-dependency; and that her negative body image caused her to take 15 laxatives daily for weight loss. He said that her family background had caused her to be attracted to a "father figure" like Capano, who lavished her with attention and expensive gifts, including a big-screen TV, clothes, concert and play tickets, etc. He said she felt guilty over her affair with a married man with four children, and that by June 1996 she knew she had to end the relationship.

Wharton brought the questioning around to the day of her disappearance. Dr. Kaye testified that when Fahey had a session with him around five P.M. on June 27, hours before she vanished after dining with Tom Capano, she'd said she was "genuinely fearful" of him, that she was trying to let him down easily as she extricated herself from him, and that he harassed her with numerous telephone calls and e-mail messages.

On cross-examination, Oteri began by calling attention to the distinctive wide-brimmed cowboy hat which the witness had worn that day, and which he'd brought with him to the stand, prompting Kaye to state that the unusual headgear had been carved (or actually, lathe-turned) by a Vermont artist from a single block of wood.

"Interesting," Oteri said. Kaye went on to say that his hobby was collecting such turned-wood objects, having over 300 such items in his home. In his sly way, by pointing up the witness's eccentricity, the defense implied a lack of credibility on his part. Although he was cordial and polite to him while he was on the stand, throughout the rest of the trial, whenever Oteri referred to Kaye, he would call him "Dr. Wooden Hat."

Oteri then forced Kaye to admit that he had met with Anne Marie Fahey little more than a half dozen times, or about a total of three

hours. Oteri said, "You didn't know her well."
He also challenged the witness to show any
threatening content in Capano's voluminous e-
mails to Fahey, which the witness couldn't do.

Next called was Connie Blake, who lived in
the apartment below Fahey's. She testified that
on the night of June 27, at about 9:45 P.M.,
she'd heard the sound of someone walking on
the floor above her. She'd heard only one set
of footsteps and no conversation.

Toward the close of the day's session, Michael Scanlan took the stand, under Colm
Connolly's direct examination. He told of how
Governor Carper had arranged for the two to
meet, how they'd gone on their first date in
September 1995, and how their romance had
blossomed in the following nine months. He
said that Annie had told him of her past relationship with Capano.

On Wednesday, Joe Oteri cross-examined
Scanlan, the thrust of his questions seeking to
minimize the importance of the romance between the witness and the deceased. Underlying it was the idea that if their relationship
had been a casual thing, Capano would hardly
have felt threatened and angry enough to take
action. Oteri asked if it was true that the relationship was not sexual.

Scanlan said, "Correct."

Oteri asked if Scanlan had offered her
money to fix a small ding in her windshield
or to replace her broken air conditioner, as

the "caring" defendant had done. Scanlan said he hadn't.

Later, under Colm Connolly's redirect, Scanlan said Annie had told him she didn't approve of premarital sex and he'd assumed she was a virgin. Also, he said he'd bought her modest gifts. "I never bought a girlfriend, and I never intend on buying a girlfriend."

Kathleen Fahey-Hosey took the stand, with Connolly on direct examination. She testified that she knew Capano through her former boyfriend, Bud Freel, but she'd been unaware that he'd been having an affair with her sister. She told of how she'd gone to Annie's apartment on the night of Saturday, June 29, 1996, and of how she hadn't found Annie, but had found her diary. It was admitted into evidence, as she read aloud from it to the jury and rapt courtroom spectators.

The entry from March 2, 1994 said, "I have fallen in love with a very special person whose name I choose to leave anonymous. We have built an everlasting friendship. I feel free around him, and like he says, 'He makes my heart smile.' "

In the entry of March 5, 1994, Annie, who was fluent in Spanish, named her secret love as "Tomas," but agonized, "We have problems because he has a wife and children also. I don't want to be in love, but I can't help it. By God, please don't judge me."

On March 24, after writing that he'd offered to pay her rent, "I need to think. I love him but he has four children (girls) and a wife. I will be a silent girlfriend. Oh my God."

In April, she wrote of her pain after Capano told her she'd be better off with an unmarried man, but the next day he called, told her he loved her and they could still keep dating. "All morning I wondered if he would [call]. I prayed he would. However, I vowed to myself I would not call him."

For the next ten months after that, the diary contained no mention of "Tomas," who reappeared in her entry of February 25, 1995, when she said she was "madly in love" with him, after she'd seen him at a restaurant with his wife. "I then realized the fact that he will never be mine. . . . The day after, I thought about Tomas every minute of the day."

When he didn't return her calls, she became frantic. "Why won't he talk to me? What did I do? God, please tell me. What the [deleted] is going on."

Later, after things had apparently been patched up, she wrote, "Tomas is kind, caring, responsive, loving, has a beautiful heart, extremely handsome and was kind and gentle to me."

She said he asked her how she wanted to spend the last day of her life. "I told him by playing hookie from work, making marinara sauce together, making loving while it was cooking, drinking red wine, eating bread and watching all the movies we have talked about watching together."

On March 1, 1995, the final diary entry for that year, she wrote of chatting briefly with him and calling him later that day. "But I never received a call back."

There were no further entries in the diary until April 7, 1996, the "closure" entry in which she'd named her secret lover as Tom Capano and literally wrote him off as a controlling, jealous "maniac."

Apart from the emotional impact of Kathleen Fahey-Hosey reading her dead sister's diary aloud in the courtroom, there were some interesting details for the jurors to mull over. One was the curious gap in the entries from March 1995 until April 1996. Another was the fact that there was no mention of harassment in the diary. The third, which had the most sinister implications, was Annie's response to Capano's question about how she'd like to spend her final day on earth. For, indeed, she had spent the last day of her life with Capano, she'd planned on playing "hookie" by taking off from work on Friday, and they'd shared a meal together where she'd drank red wine. If he had murdered her, had her remarks served as a kind of template or model which he'd carried out?

On Thursday, Detective Robert Donovan took the stand for the first of what would be many appearances during the trial, where he'd be called by both the prosecution and defense. Now, as a State witness, he told of how he'd become involved in the case, of going first to

Anne Marie Fahey's apartment and then to
Tom Capano's Grant Avenue house at 3:40
A.M. Sunday morning, and of returning later
that day. When Capano had been located that
day at Kay Capano's house, Donovan said the
defendant "was very agitated and not as forthcoming. He said he was upset with himself for
disclosing so much info earlier that morning."
He told how the walk-through search of the
house and a search of Capano's car had failed
to locate Anne Marie Fahey.

On cross-examination, the defense got into
the record that Anne Marie Fahey's apartment
had neither been secured nor fingerprinted.

Following the detective to the witness stand
were Gary M. Johnson and Michelle Sullivan,
two psychologists who'd been treating Anne
Marie Fahey. Johnson testified that Fahey had
told him of an unnamed lover who'd once
held her captive in her apartment for three to
four hours, threatening to tell Michael Scanlan
of their relationship.

Fahey had not been so circumspect with
Michelle Sullivan, who'd been treating the patient from February 28, 1996 until her death.
The witness said Annie was afraid of Tom Capano and named him to her in March 1996.
She'd encouraged her to report him to the
attorney general's office, but Annie hadn't.
She said Fahey had feared that Capano might
hire a third party to kidnap her.

* * *

This testimony and others occupied the first two weeks of the trial. Now, on November 9, 1998, the State called as its next witness Gerry Capano. He was under pressure, truly the man in the middle. He didn't want to testify against his brother, but he didn't want to go to jail on federal gun and drug charges, either. To the rest of the family, including his own mother, he was an outcast. Seeing him, courtroom observers agreed that here was a man in pain.

Colm Connolly took the direct, asking him what Capano had said to him back in February 1996, about the boat.

Gerry testified, "He said that if either one of these persons [the supposed male-female team of 'extortionists'] that was threatening to hurt his kids were to hurt one of his kids and he was to do something to them, could he use the boat."

Connolly asked, "What was this 'to do something'?"

"If they had hurt his kids and was to kill them, could he use the boat."

Connolly then took him through the events of Friday, June 28, the day they got rid of the body. Gerry was hurting up on the stand as he told how Tom Capano had said, "Don't leave me flat. Don't leave me hanging. I need you, bro." He told of the cooler, the trip to Stone Harbor, the boat ride out to sea, and how they got rid of the body and cooler.

Then he told of returning to the Grant Ave-

nue home to dispose of a "love seat" sofa
and rug. He said the maroon sofa had had a
"basketball-sized" bloodstain on the right side
at shoulder height. He'd used a pen knife to
cut out the bloodstained fabric, and knocked
a leg off the sofa so it would look like derelict
junk that was being thrown out. He and Capano had loaded the sofa and the rolled-up,
bloodstained carpet into the SUV and un-
loaded it into a Capano construction-site
Dumpster in North Wilmington.

He went on to detail the stages of his path
to becoming a prosecution witness. He admitted to his drug use, but said he was clean and
sober on the day he helped his brother. Afterward, he said, he really started using drugs
heavily.

While testifying about talks he had had with
his lawyer, Dan Lyons, whom he'd told about
the "sea burial" months before being arrested,
he started to blurt out something about having
taken a lie detector test, causing the defense
to leap up, object, and call for a mistrial.

Delaware law does not allow the use of polygraph tests as admissible evidence, due to their
perceived unreliability. Now the defense objected, arguing that the mention of the test
required a mistrial.

Was it an honest mistake, or was Gerry playing both ends against the middle, trying to do
a favor for brother Tom by provoking a mistrial? While preparing him to testify at the
trial, the prosecution had carefullly instructed

him not to mention the polygraph test. Had
he done so deliberately, as a way to get back
in the family's good graces, while still preserv-
ing his immunity deal? Or was it just an honest
mistake?

One can only wonder. The question is academic, since Judge Lee denied the motion, in-
structing the jurors to disregard the testimony
that they had heard.

In late afternoon, Joe Oteri began his cross-
examination with deceptive mildness, killing
Gerry Capano with kindness as he started.
Oteri said, "They told you I was going to be
a bastard, didn't they?"

Gerry said, "No."

"Told you I was going to rip you apart,
didn't they?"

"They may have hinted toward that."

"I'm not doing that. I'm a nice guy, right?"

Oteri established Gerry Capano's various
substance-abuse problems, including the fact
that he had been doing drugs since his arrest,
and that the prosecution knew it and hadn't
done anything about it.

The next day, Oteri resumed his questioning, outlining how Gerry and Tom Capano
would drink potent red wine, and in Gerry's
case, at least, do some lines of coke, while
hanging out together playing pool, and that it
could have been the drugs talking when they
spoke of "doing something" to the alleged

"extortionists." Gerry conceded he was unsure whether he had first broached the topic of loaning a gun to Tom Capano to handle the man-woman shakedown team.

Oteri moved on to the events of Gerry's October drug bust, when 20 or so federal agents had burst into his home and put a gun to the back of his head. Oteri then addressed the pressure applied against Gerry Capano and his wife to have them declared "unfit parents" by a state child-welfare agency to begin proceedings to take the children away.

Gerry Capano squirmed some more as Oteri took him over the contents of a taped phone-answering machine call which Gerry had allegedly made on February 9, 1998. He did not produce the tapes in evidence, but phrased his remarks in the format of, "What if I were to tell you that the tapes have you saying," and then go on to read what he implied were the transcripts. The transcripts seemed real enough, and in any case, Gerry Capano seemed to know what Oteri was talking about, nor did the prosecution raise any objections to this line of questioning.

According to the defense, Gerry Capano, had called his mother, Marguerite, and, angry at his isolation from the family, had told her to "go fuck herself." Mention was made of a second call, where the answering machine caught Gerry saying that when he testified against Tom Capano, he would even "make up shit" to "keep his ass out of jail."

It was raw and ugly stuff. It had an impact on the courtroom spectators, causing visceral reactions, gasps. His mother and family were in the courtroom to hear it, too. Marguerite Capano sat there in her wheelchair, sobbing. Gerry never denied that he'd said any of it.

Kay Capano then took the stand, testifying with stoic dignity, telling how Tom Capano had borrowed her Suburban on June 28, 1996, and noting that at that time he'd appeared "normal." The next night, when he came to pick up their daughters for a visit, he seemed "agitated." She said she had sent money orders to several prisoners at Gander Hill, part of the network which Tom Capano had arranged to circumvent limits on his phone calls and letters, and extend his reach outside jail.

On November 13, she reached a significant milestone as she legally became Kay Ryan, her divorce having become finalized.

It was proving to be some Friday the 13th, as on that same day the family feud continued as Louis Capano took the stand. Like his brother Gerry, he, too, was in the family doghouse for testifying against Tom Capano. He'd made a plea agreement to avoid prosecution for lying to the grand jury and other crimes.

He stated that his involvement in the case began after Anne Marie Fahey's disappearance, when the defendant had first told him that she'd slit her wrists while on the couch in a dramatic suicidal acting-out. Now that she'd disappeared and the cops were sniffing around, he wanted to get rid of the couch and rug and begged for Louie's help to do it. Louie had personally arranged for the emptying of the Capano job-site Dumpster which held the couch and rug. The Dumpsters were only half full and not due to be emptied and the deviation from the pattern struck the Capano employees who handled it as strange and puzzling. The Dumpsters were dumped and their contents crushed into landfill, never to be recovered.

Louis Capano told how he had begged Tom Capano to confess, saying that Gerry Capano was cracking from the pressure. The defendant had said that he should tell Gerry to grow up and "be a man."

Tom Capano wasn't the only Capano with an active social life outside his marriage, as the defense's Gene Maurer brought out on cross-examination. Louis Capano was married to women's golf champion Lauri Merton, who'd been taping his phone calls, not because of the Anne Marie Fahey business, but because she was suspicious of his extracurricular activities. So was his lady friend Kristi Pepper, who'd also been taping him. But the tapes had caught him pressuring Kristi Pepper to "remember" things about the case that he wanted her to remember. Louie admitted in court that he'd been concerned about what she might say to investigators.

But what was on the tapes wasn't as important to Gene Maurer as establishing Louis Ca-

pano's amours and marital troubles, to help
discredit his testimony. A veiled reference by
the defense to an insurance claim he'd put in
on his BMW was understood by insiders to al-
lude to the fact that his expensive luxury car
had recently sustained serious damage, not unlike that which could have been inflicted by a
golf club in the hands of someone who knew
how to use it.

On Wednesday, November 18, the State
called Keith Brady, the number two man in
the attorney general's office and Tom Capano's friend. Brady's demeanor was that of
the condemned waiting for the ax to fall.

On direct, Colm Connolly asked Brady
about his association with Tom Capano. The
witness said that Capano had told him in confidence that he was in a "relationship" with
Anne Marie Fahey, that he'd gone on a four-
day Virginia resort trip in the summer of 1995,
and that he was unhappy when she'd broken
up with him shortly after that trip.

Connolly then asked him about the phone
call he'd received from Capano at eight A.M.
on June 28, 1996. Brady said that on June 24,
Capano had called him to set up a golf date.
Capano had then cancelled, later making that
eight A.M. call to Brady's office on Friday the
28th, but Brady had been at another location.
On Sunday, June 30, he'd first learned from
his subordinate Ferris Wharton that Anne

Marie Fahey was missing and Capano was the last to see her alive.

Not until July 2 had he been able to reach Capano on the phone, at which time he'd taken notes of their conversation. Capano said he was "blown away" by what had happened and that the cops had been treating him badly. He said that he and Anne Marie Fahey had had dinner and that was all. He said that he'd told Kim Horstman that if Annie didn't show up for work Monday morning, "I'd die." He described Annie as a "serious head case under psychiatric care."

Following the legal strategy of airing a witness's dirty linen before the other side does, Colm Connolly asked, "Did Tom Capano ever arrange a sexual encounter with you and Debby MacIntyre?"

"Within the context of his relationship with her," Brady said, squirming.

On cross-examination, Joe Oteri jumped headfirst through the door opened by the prosecution. The aim was to discredit the witness, and if anything reflected badly on Debby MacIntyre, so much the better for the defense. Oteri got Brady to admit that he had committed adultery with three different women on various occasions. Brady said he considered Capano his "mentor," but the menage with him and Debby MacIntyre had had something of a chilling effect on the friendship.

Dully and stiff-faced, the witness described how a few years earlier, after a game of golf, he, Capano, and Debby MacIntyre had all gone back to her house. Capano then had sex with her in one room while Brady waited naked in another. Capano finished with Debby and watched porno movies while Debby tried to perform oral sex on Brady. "Debby MacIntyre tried to arouse me by performing oral sex, but I could not achieve erection," Keith Brady said.

On redirect, he said, "I'm ashamed. It has been a profoundly agonizing experience and I'm dealing with it with God's help. I'm extremely remorseful."

When Keith Brady's testimony was finished, so was he, professionally and personally. That same day, he took an unpaid personal leave of absence. Soon after, his wife left him. The juggernaut of the Capano murder case had claimed another victim.

Keith Brady had paved the way for the State's next witness, Debby MacIntyre, who on that same day took the stand, with Ferris Wharton on direct. He established her 15-year adulterous relationship with Tom Capano and his manipulative, controlling ways.

Then the questioning zeroed in on the gun. Debby said that in April 1996, Capano had asked her to buy a gun for him. She'd told the store clerk that she was buying the weapon for someone else, and he'd refused to sell it to her, citing it as a violation of federal gun laws to buy a gun for someone else. Capano had dropped the subject for a month, broach-

ing it again on May 12, 1996—Mother's Day.
The next day, he picked her up at Tatnall
School, driving her to Wilmington's Miller's
gun shop. He'd waited in the car while she
went inside, filled out the federal gun forms,
and bought a .22 Beretta pistol. She said that
after she gave it to him, she never saw it again.

Wharton moved on to the chronology of the
phone calls exchanged between MacIntyre and
Capano in the June 27–28 time frame. She
said that on Thursday the 27th, at about 10:30
P.M., when the TV show *ER* was on, she'd called
him for the first time. There was no answer
and she'd left a brief message on his machine,
saying that if he didn't come in too late, she'd
love to hear from him. She'd dozed off, but
about an hour later, when Letterman was on,
she was awakened by a call from Capano. He
was irritated and told her never to leave a message on his answering machine, which surprised her, since she'd done it before and it
had never been a problem. He said that he
might need her help to do something on Friday morning, and when she refused, saying
that she had to go in early to Tatnall to take
care of the paychecks, he grew angry. The call
ended soon after that.

About 45 minutes later, she called him back,
but hung up after a few rings, before his answering machine picked up. She got a quick
callback, as he used the star-69 feature. The
call was somehow disconnected, and Capano
immediately called back, his mood much im-

proved, and they had a nice little chat before she went to sleep.

On Friday at 6:45 A.M., she called him, but he said that he wouldn't be needing her help after all. She saw him an hour or so later at the jogging track as she was driving back to Tatnall, a meeting which she described as accidental. At 10:00 A.M. he'd called her at work, not saying that he was in Stone Harbor. That night, sometime after 11, he'd let himself into her house (he had a key), gone to her bedroom, undressed, climbed into bed with her, and fallen asleep.

On Thursday the 19th, MacIntyre read aloud from some of the letters Capano had written her in prison, a dreary and lengthy stretch of testimony. It was obvious that from the extensive use he made of letters and e-mail, Capano was a great believer in the power of the written word. His own written word.

In his letter of February 2, 1998, urging her to testify at his proof positive bail hearing, Capano wrote, "You didn't do anything wrong and you have nothing to be ashamed of, so don't let your obsession with privacy distract you from what matters."

On February 20, after she'd gotten a new lawyer and was moving toward dealing with the prosecution, Capano wrote, "Do I now have to worry about you? I can now feel myself getting angry and again feeling the sense of betrayal I felt when you abandoned me at the bail hearing. Do you love me or not? You must now prove your love to me."

Then Wharton showed her the diagram of her house, which Capano had drawn for Nick Perillo in March. She shuddered, hands shaking as she said, "It is very accurate."

Wharton said, "Did Tom Capano ever say you were soul mates? That you were the love of his life? That he would give his life for you?"

"Yes, he did."

"Did he ever tell you Anne Marie Fahey's body was dumped in the Atlantic Ocean?"

"No, he did not."

"Did he tell you she died as a result of an accident?"

"No, he did not."

That was the end of the direct examination, and the prosecution's friendly questions. On cross-examination, Gene Maurer began laying the foundation for the defense. "You have not told the truth many, many, many times."

Debby said, "Correct."

Taking a phrase from her January 24, 1998, letter to Capano, Gene Maurer then wrote in big letters on an easel, "The truth is all I know." Maurer pointed out that that was written a month before she said she'd stopped lying about the case. The easel with its bold-lettered message stood where the jurors could see it for the rest of the afternoon's cross-examination.

Maurer noted that she'd told the grand jury that she and Capano did not begin their affair until September 1995, when he separated from Kay Capano. During an August hearing, she'd said that was "an unintentional lie."

"That was a poor choice of words," she now said, admitting that she'd lied because "I was embarrassed for myself."

Maurer said, "You were lying to protect yourself."

"Yes, and Tom Capano."

Maurer took her back to the roots of the affair, when she'd first met Capano back in 1977, when he and her then-husband, attorney Dave Williams, worked at the same law firm. The affair itself had begun on Memorial Day weekend 1981.

Maurer said, "You and Kay Capano were very good friends. You did things together. You socialized together. She considered you a trusted friend."

MacIntyre said, "Yes."

The tactic was to impugn the witness as a liar and betrayer.

Maurer took MacIntyre through her many lies. He also rehashed the high school lover tryst and the Keith Brady encounter, trying to get her to admit she had instigated them, and expressing incredulity at her insistence that she had taken no pleasure or interest in it, but had done it because she feared losing Tom Capano if she said no.

The defense pointed to her lies for investigators and the grand jury and said, she's a liar. The prosecution countered that she'd lied because she was under Capano's control. The defense said that she'd lied about that, too.

Court recessed for the weekend, and on Monday, November 23, Gene Maurer resumed his cross-examination, honing in on the June 28 phone call which Debby MacIntyre had received at 10 A.M. from Tom Capano from Stone Harbor (as he prepared to go to sea to dump the body). Maurer asked if it wasn't true that the defendant had called her to tell her "everything is going fine" with what he was doing. She said no. When she claimed the call had lasted a couple of minutes, Maurer brought in phone records showing that the call had lasted less than a minute.

Maurer brought in the subject of when the witness had first learned of the defendant's affair with Anne Marie Fahey, using it to point the way to the defense's underlying main thesis. "Didn't you find out about Anne Marie Fahey not on July 2, but on June 27 or 28?"

She said tightly, "No, Mr. Maurer, I never heard of Anne Marie Fahey until July second."

"Didn't you go to [ ] Grant Avenue June 27 or 28th with a firearm to visit Tom?"

"Mr. Maurer, I never left my property from the time I returned from the Arden Swim Club until the next morning when I went to Tatnall."

"Didn't you have your firearm at Tom Capano's house on June 28, 1996, when you first learned about him and Anne Marie Fahey?"

"No, I did not."

"You deny that you discharged the firearm?"

"I deny that I discharged that firearm."

"Are you absolutely certain about that?"

"I'm absolutely certain."

"And you deny that your firearm discharged that night in that house, striking her?"

"I don't know what happened to that firearm. I gave that firearm to Tom on May thirteenth."

Finally, the witness was excused, and Debby MacIntyre stepped down. Later that day, asked about his reaction to her testimony, Tom Capano told reporters, "She broke my heart."

Just as her lawyer Thomas Bergstrom and the prosecution had guessed, Debby MacIntyre was the "mystery witness" whose existence had been alleged by the defense, and she was also the author of the "horrible accident" cited by Joe Oteri in his opening statement.

The next witness for the prosecution was Nick Perillo. It was a measure of the Capano trial that admitted thief, scam artist, and drug addict Perillo struck most courtroom observers as a breath of fresh air. On Tuesday, November 24, he took the stand, telling how he'd conned his way into the Gander Hill prison protective custody unit 1F Pod, where he made contact with Tom Capano, communicating with him through the narrow airholes in the bottom of the cell doors. When Capano was punished for violating prison rules, Perillo made calls for him to Kay Capano and tried to reach Debby MacIntyre. Kay Capano put $25 in Perillo's near-empty prison commissary account. He said that Capano had told him that Debby MacIntyre had bought him a gun.

Under questioning by Ferris Wharton, the witness said that Capano had solicited him to arrange for someone on the outside to burglarize Debby MacIntyre's Delaware Avenue house, quoting the defendant as saying it would be "easy pickings" because she was going on a 10-day vacation. Capano had provided him with a diagram and detailed instructions, which included the theft of incriminating adult videotapes, jewelry, and artworks, as well as the nonnegotiable demand that the intruder shatter the full-length mirror in the bedroom, in which she and the defendant had watched themselves having sex.

The prosecution contended that the defendant was trying to intimidate Debby MacIntyre from testifying against him. It went to the larger issue of what Tom Capano was all about, of how dangerous he was in or out of prison, which, if he were found guilty, would have influence during the penalty phase of a death penalty sentence.

The diagram and instructions were in Capano's handwriting. There was no way out of that, so on cross-examination, the defense's John F. O'Donnell hung the monicker "Slick Nick" on the witness and then ripped into his character, his record, and his credibility. He brought out Perillo's addiction to heroin and cocaine, and that he had burglarized the home of his former attorney and ex-wife. O'Donnell accused him of taking advantage of a depressed, drug-befuddled, sensory-deprived, half-out-of-his-mind defendant, luring him into the burglary plot as a way for Perillo to curry favor with prosecutors and plead his way out of the stiff "habitual criminal" sentence facing him for his most recent parole violation.

O'Donnell said, "It never occurred to you that if you set Tom Capano up, you could eat Christmas dinner outside prison?"

"That's ridiculous," Nick Perillo said.

Trial broke for a five-day Thanksgiving Day recess.

On Monday, trial resumed, as the prosecution addressed the questions of Debby MacIntyre's actions and demeanor in the time frame immediately following Anne Marie Fahey's death. Mary Anne White, another administrative employee of the Tatnall School, said that on Friday, June 28, Debby was at work early in the morning, to pick up paychecks. She said Debby "seemed normal, average, the way she always was." But while Debby had said she arrived at work at 6 A.M. and called Capano about 6:45 before returning home briefly, White said Debby didn't arrive at her office until 7 A.M.

Leigh Anne Chesser-Cassidy, who was enrolling her children in Tatnall, said that when she met with Debby there on Friday at about two P.M., Debby "was very pleasant, very professional, and answered questions clearly."

Joan Brady, Debby's former assistant, said she had confided about her affair with Capano. She said that on Thursday, June 27, 1996, she'd been attending a meet at the Arden Swim Club with Debby MacIntyre. The next morning, Debby seemed normal. On July 2, the day Debby said Capano first told of his affair with the missing Anne Marie Fahey, the witness said Debby approached her. "She took me into my office and closed the door and said Tom Capano was the last person seen with Anne Marie Fahey. She was upset."

The prosecution's thrust was that if Debby MacIntyre had been present at Anne Marie Fahey's violent death the night before, she'd hardly have conducted herself at work the next day in an ordinary, normal, unremarked manner, as the witnesses had testified she'd done.

Later, public relations man and Capano friend J. Brian Murphy told of the making of the defendant's unreleased press release expressing his shock and lack of involvement in Anne Marie Fahey's disappearance and his sympathetic concern for her family. The prosecution underscored the fact that Tom Capano had known Fahey was dead and her body buried at sea at the time he'd helped compose the statement. Questioning also brought out the interesting fact that Capano had given Murphy $15,000 for his daughters' tuition at Ursuline Academy, a "loan" that had never been repaid.

December 1, day 18 of the trial began an hour late, on an inauspicious note, when a 45-year-old female juror was dismissed from the case after being arrested during a traffic stop for possessing marijuana. She was replaced by an alternate.

The State then presented yet another female friend of Tom Capano, an attractive blonde named Susan Louth. A former legal secretary at Saul Ewing, she'd dated Capano in November 1995, two months after he'd separated from Kay Capano. When Anne Marie Fahey disappeared, he'd told her that after dinner he'd dropped Fahey off at her apartment. His mother had once referred to the witness as "that slutty little girl," and in one of his letters to her, he'd greeted Louth with the salutation, "Dear slutty little girl." She'd moved to the Virgin Islands, which is where she was living when she and Capano had gotten into a jail-house correspondence, around February 1998, the same time that he was besieging Debby MacIntyre with letters.

In one of those letters, Capano wrote of Debby, "A [cousin] also told me she saw

Debby MacIntyre's picture in the paper and that she looks like a shrew and a backstabber. Pretty perceptive." On March 7, he wrote, urging her to spread the word that the theory that Debby killed Anne Marie Fahey "makes a lot of sense for a lot of reasons." On March 17, he wrote that if she and her friends could get a Debby-did-it buzz going around, "it might get people thinking enough to have an open mind. And that is my jury pool."

Under questioning, she said that in September 1996, he'd moved a heavy dining room table into her town house by himself. To the prosecution, that indicated that at the time of Anne Marie Fahey's death, Capano had been strong and healthy enough to move her body and the bloodstained rug down the stairs.

Louth also said that Capano had offered to pay for flying her in from the islands to testify for him at trial. Now, she was a witness for the prosecution.

At the end of March 1998, Capano asked one of his friends to have sex with Debby MacIntyre. The gentleman in question, Thomas J. Shopa, 49, was a longtime friend of Capano's dating back to Archmere days. He testified that Capano requested that he visit Debby and ask her why she had stopped writing to him and if she still loved him. She told Shopa that prosecutors wouldn't let her contact him. When he later visited Capano at Gander Hill, Capano asked him to have sex with her and retrieve his letters from her house, not necessarily in that order.

"I said no. I refused to and I was shocked and very upset," the witness said.

Detective Robert Donovan was recalled to the stand to read excerpts of a letter Capano wrote from prison to Debby MacIntyre's 16-year-old son, telling him to tell his mother to be "extremely nice" to Shopa. And that he still loved her, even though she had become a witness against him. The letter was introduced into evidence.

The prosecution next moved to the forensic portion of the case against Tom Capano. Linda Harrison, an FBI evidence detection specialist, testified that she found two tiny blood spots in the den of the Grant Avenue house during the search on July 31, 1996. Chris Hancock, a Blood Bank of Delaware donor advocate, told how the sample of Anne Marie Fahey's plasma was retrieved from the Swiss Red Cross.

FBI DNA expert Alan Giusti matched the blood droplet samples with Anne Marie Fahey's plasma sample, stating that only 1 in 11,000 white Americans would have similar DNA. Under cross-examination, he conceded that there was no way of telling when the blood spots had been deposited in the den.

On Wednesday, December 3, Michael Longwill, manager of Air Base Carpet, said that Tom Capano had twice bought rugs from his store, once in 1995 for his Grant Avenue house, and again in 1996, a few days after Anne Marie Fahey's disappearance. Purchase records and credit card receipts were entered in evidence. The same roll from which Capano's 1995 carpet had been taken had also been used to furnish a Wilmington bed and breakfast, whose owner, Steven Marks, testified that he'd given a sample of the carpet to FBI agents. FBI criminalists took the stand, matching the carpet sample to fibers found in Kay Capano's Suburban, bolstering the prosecution's contention that the vehicle had been used to transport the bloodstained rug after the murder.

A credit card receipt from the Sports Authority on Concord Pike, for a 162-quart cooler, dated April 20, 1996 and signed by Tom Capano, was entered into evidence. A manufacturer's representative identified the cooler from its ID numbers. Ronald Smith told how he'd contacted FBI Agent Eric Alpert, the day after Capano's arrest, to tell him that his friend Ken Chubb had landed a like-new cooler while fishing on the July Fourth weekend.

Detective Robert Donovan returned to the stand, saying that he'd driven out to Chubb's trailer, finding the cooler in a shed. One of the clues that police had kept from the public was the fact that Gerry Capano had fired a shotgun into it in an attempt to sink it. Chubb's cooler had bullet holes in it, which he'd epoxied over to make a watertight container. Donovan had taken possession of the evidence.

Donovan also said that after Capano was arrested, and was told Gerry Capano and Louis Capano had become prosecution witnesses, he blurted out, "You believe them?" Told that authorities knew he bought a fishing cooler, Capano admitted he wasn't a fisherman or hunter, but added, "My brothers are." The defendant said he bought the cooler as a gift for Gerry.

Michael W. Ennis, an FBI lab analyst, stated that the holes found in the cooler were probably caused by a single slug or other lead projectile. Red and white fibers were found in the insulation, possibly belonging to Anne Marie Fahey's red-and-white sweatshirt, which her sister Kathleen Fahey-Hosey had reported missing after inventorying her possessions.

During the questioning, the cooler had been under an evidence table. Now, Colm Connolly and Ferris Wharton pulled it into view, picked it up, and laid it down where both the witness and the jury could see it. The wooden handles banged against the cooler, startling some in the courtroom. Ennis identified it as the cooler he'd tested.

The prosecution's last witness was fisherman Ken Chubb, who told how he'd found the cooler while out in his boat. Dumped 60 miles out in the Atlantic Ocean, the cooler had floated back inshore to within 10 miles of land, to be hauled out of the sea as Chubb's lucky catch, later becoming a prime exhibit in the trial of the man charged with murder.

The prosecution rested its case. As per standard trial procedure when the State rests, Charles Oberly rose for the defense with a request to dismiss the charges against the defendant. Rejecting the request, Judge Lee adjourned the court on Wednesday at mid-afternoon, with the trial set to resume on Monday.

Later, after the courtroom had emptied out, the Faheys gathered around the cooler in silent communion.

On Monday, December 7, court reconvened, with the defense scheduled to present its case. But there was a hitch in the proceedings.

Tom Capano was fighting a two-front war, with the prosecution and now, with increasing frequency, his own defense team. The clash had been coming for a long time. Capano considered himself a mastermind, the fifth member of his legal team. He was an inveterate note-taker, spending long periods of court time making voluminous notes on a legal pad. He wasn't shy about giving advice to his lawyers, peppering them with notes during testimony, suggesting lines of questioning for them to follow. Oteri particularly chafed under his client's heavy hand, later saying that maybe 10 out of every 500 suggestions by Capano might have had some small grain of merit.

Capano seemed to conduct himself as if he were part of the defense, not the defendant. He needed the illusion of being in-charge and now his strategy had so far diverged from his defenders that they had come to the breaking point.

There was discord at the defense table, a split between the lawyers and their client. The morning session began with a conference outside the hearing of the jury, as Joe Oteri and the rest of the defense team told Judge Lee that there was a serious strategic dispute between defense and defendant. Capano wanted to fire his lawyers and present his own defense.

On December 7, out of the jury's hearing, Capano addressed the judge, stating that he and his lawyers seemed to have come to a parting of the ways. He was dissatisfied with the defense, feeling that they were holding back, pulling their punches. He expressed the greatest respect for them, especially Joe Oteri, but likened his lawyers' approach to a "scalpel," while he said he favored a kind of "chainsaw" defense, an infelicitous choice of words that drew winces in the courtroom, not the least at the defense table. Using another metaphor, he compared himself to a combat soldier in a foxhole who has ten grenades to use against the enemy, but his lawyers only wanted him to use five. He pointed out that he was fighting for his life and didn't want to find himself three years hence sitting in prison, wishing he had done things that he could do now.

A lengthy period of wrangling followed. Capano was an attorney, but Judge Lee could do nothing but warn him of that old but true legal chestnut, that the lawyer who defends himself has a fool for a client. He pointed out that Capano was paying a lot of money for some very able high-priced legal talent and would do well to follow their advice.

Most of all, the judge was concerned with the threat of a mistrial, which could well result from the defendant's shedding legal counsel midway through the trial. He wanted Capano to know that he would not allow a mistrial.

Capano next suggested a kind of compromise, where he would take the lead in his own defense, with his lawyers acting as backup. That was unsatisfactory both to the bench and to his legal team, who had no intention of sitting back and looking foolish while their client ran his defense into the ground.

At one point, a baffled Judge Lee confessed, "I've been trying to figure out what the hell you want."

By the following day, the breach was mended, with the four lawyers still on the Capano case.

The defense began their case, first calling Michael Hare, a friend of Anne Marie Fahey's. He said that she and Tom Capano had planned to attend a political fund-raiser separately, that she planned to attend it with Michael Scanlan, and that none of them had showed on that night—June 27, 1996.

Al Franke took the stand, saying that Fahey had told him that her relationship with Scanlan wasn't physical and was going nowhere. The defense's point being that Capano hadn't become unhinged because of a hot new love in Fahey's life.

Next came a statement from Capano's secretary at Saul Ewing, who was too ill to testify that day in court. It stated that Anne Marie Fahey called Capano frequently in 1996, and that from what she had observed, the two had a friendly relationship and were on good terms.

Evidence was introduced showing that Capano had bought tickets on June 27, 1996 to an upcoming Jackson Browne concert. If he was planning on killing Anne Marie Fahey that night, why would he buy the concert tickets? A cynic might have remarked that he could always have taken someone else.

A well-worn tactic often used by the defense in federal mob and drug trials was to try to show that the government's witnesses were worse than the defendant. After saying that her relationship with Michael Scanlan wasn't so great, the defense called Robert Donovan as one of their witnesses, to underline Debby MacIntyre's lies to investigators and the grand jury, and her general lack of credibility. On December 9, Nick Perillo came in for similar undermining questioning, as did a couple of

Gander Hill prison inmates who took the stand
to state that Perillo was a slippery snitch, not
to be trusted. He'd had them set up the new
"fish" in the can, Tom Capano, to buy himself
a ticket out of jail. (Later, though, various jurors stated that, as far as this issue was concerned, they had found Perillo credible.)

In the Capano family split, brother Joseph
(Joey) Capano had sided with Tom. Now, he
was called by the defense to testify about the
cooler. He said that in the spring of 1996, Tom
had wanted to buy a gift for Gerry Capano, a
token of appreciation for how well Gerry had
treated Tom's daughters. Joey said that he suggested the idea of the cooler, for hunter and
fisherman Gerry. That would go toward showing that Anne Marie Fahey's death was not
premeditated, if the jurors believed it.

He also told how he'd gotten a new anchor
for Gerry, to replace one which had been lost
on the boat (the anchor which Gerry Capano
and the State had said Tom Capano had used
to weigh down Fahey's body).

Whatever his motivation, Joey Capano's act
of replacing that anchor had led to his inclu-
sion in the civil suit filed by the Faheys against
the four Capano brothers for allegedly conspiring to conceal the murder of Anne Marie Fahey.

Joey Capano stepped down. The next witness called by the defense was Squeaky Saunders, an inmate of Gander Hill prison for the
previous 22 years, ever since being convicted

in 1976 of murder by Tom Capano. It was one of those astonishing second acts that sometimes occur in a lifetime, as the defense now called on him to help Capano beat the rap.

Saunders was part of the effort to tear down Nick Perillo's credibility. He said that, while in Gander Hill, Perillo had sidled over to him to talk about Capano, figuring he would find a sympathetic ear from a man whom Capano had sent to prison for life. Saunders said that Perillo had told him that he had something in mind for the new "fish."

At one point, the witness was reminded by Joe Oteri, "I told you when I talked to you that I was a righteous dude."

Saunders said, "Yeah."

"Did you believe me?"

"No, sir," Saunders said, perhaps mindful that he was under oath.

On cross-examination, the prosecution tried to show that Saunders had a possible motive for testifying. He was still trying to get out of jail on his original murder conviction, and as recently as 1997 had filed a motion to overturn that verdict. The implication was that perhaps if Saunders was helpful to the defense, Capano might discover some reversible error or misconduct in the way he had prosecuted the case, leading to a new trial for Saunders. Saunders denied it.

Still, it was a strange moment in a strange trial, with Squeaky Saunders serving as a kind of bookend marking Capano's rise and fall in the world. More sinister was the thought that perhaps Capano had taken his inspiration for the murder of Anne Marie Fahey from that earlier case. If so, it was another example of Capano's use of templates to structure the crime. There were some striking parallels between both deaths: the headshot and the burial of the body at sea. By that way of thinking, Saunders's flaw was to dump the body in the river, where it was found before it could wash out to sea. No body meant no damning autopsy. Saunders's method of implicating his associates in the crime was repeated with Capano's attempt to rope in Debby MacIntyre for his defense.

Dr. Carol A. Tavani, 52, was a psychiatrist who had treated Capano in prison. She worked at Gander Hill for the Prison Health System, providing inmate medical treatment, and was executive director of Christiana Psychiatric Services. She testified that Tom Capano was severely depressed in March when he asked another inmate to burglarize Debby MacIntyre's house. She said that he suffered from severe depression after 13 months of solitary confinement.

She was the originator of the theory stated by the defense in Oteri's opening statement, that Gerry Capano suffered from "confabulation," a condition afflicting alcohol and drug abusers whereby gaps in the memory are plugged by false memories.

On cross-examination, Ferris Wharton got

Tavani to admit that she'd diagnosed Gerry Capano as a confabulator without ever having met him, when her own methodology said that in-person interviews were vital for an accurate diagnosis. She also conceded that Capano's burglary diagram and instructions were "coherent, lucid."

Now came the main event. With the defense arguing that Anne Marie Fahey's death was no murder, but a "horrible accident," it was perhaps inevitable that Tom Capano would have to take the stand to tell the jury in his own words just exactly what sequence of events had transpired on that Thursday night, June 27, 1996.

But it was risky. Joe Oteri later told *Court TV* that he'd never put a defendant on the stand in a first-degree murder case. This time, though, the defendant had other ideas. On December 16, 1998, at about eleven A.M., Capano told the judge, "I wish to testify," and took the stand.

Oteri had barely begun the friendly questioning when Capano said, "I've been portrayed as a rich, spoiled kid—"

"I object," Colm Connolly said, quickly crossing swords with Capano. Capano glared. He was used to deference and didn't like being interrupted. More important, he didn't like Connolly, and it showed. In fact, he hated his guts, as his letters frequently referred to Connolly as a "snake," "weasel," and "Nazi."

The objection was sustained, and Capano had to rephrase his statement, saying that he came from a blue-collar background that included plenty of manual labor and hard work. With Joe Oteri's gentle leading, Capano related his version of the Capano success story, telling of his posts in city and state government and of his family life. He set the record straight according to his view, first addressing the matter of Gerry Capano.

Gerry, he said, was something of a would-be tough guy. The witness claimed that the loan he'd borrowed from Gerry was to help Anne Marie Fahey get help for her eating disorders, only he hadn't told Gerry the reason, and his younger brother had spun it off into a kind of pulp-fiction fantasy of "extortionists," leading him to offer to arrange to get somebody's legs broken, and then to loan Capano the gun. Tom Capano said he was uncomfortable around guns, didn't really know how to use them, and had returned the gun to Gerry a month later.

He added that Gerry, the "baby" of the family, had suffered from substance abuse problems since high school, lacked the "work ethic" shared by his three older brothers, and used foul language, even in front of their mother.

The next day, December 17, Capano spent some time trashing Debby MacIntyre. According to him, unlike Anne Marie Fahey, MacIntyre was a spoiled rich girl from a privileged background. As far as their affair went, she was the sexual aggressor, not him. He wasn't even all that thrilled by the attention. He said she wasn't the most attractive of the firm's lawyers' wives, and that he could have gotten in trouble for fooling around with her. She'd come chasing him, finding him alone at his house on Memorial Day weekend, 1981, and more or less seducing him.

She had a strong sex drive, as strong as his. It was her idea to get it on with Keith Brady in a threesome. Being with two men at the same time was her fantasy, not his, Capano said. His was to have sex with two women at the same time. Also, it was she who had wanted to make it with her old flame at the high school reunion. He admitted having watched them through the window from outside, but said that he had gone over there only after his wife had gone to sleep. He said, "I'm very liberal, have a very liberal attitude toward sex, and I know Debby felt the same way." He said that after the high school chum left, he went inside and had "different sex" with Debby.

It was because of her sexually voracious appetite and emotional neediness that he'd tried to arrange for his buddy Shopa to have sex with her. MacIntyre had inherited her father's porno collection. She had testified earlier that he had brought x-rated videotapes over to her house on June 30, 1996. They were hers, he said.

Capano also said that buying the gun was her idea, inspired by uneasiness she had felt on a nighttime trip (with him) to high-crime Washington, D.C. She'd shown him the gun and he'd told her to get rid of it. He'd seen it once or twice at her house and then had seen it no more until the night of June 27, 1996.

He detailed his version of the events following his arrest and incarceration at Gander Hill prison, saying that at the time of the arrest, he had planned to marry Debby MacIntyre. Since he'd taken the stand in his own defense, the taped phone conversations he had had with her in late January through early March 1998 were allowed to be entered into evidence. The jurors listened to them through headphones, but their airing was unlikely to soften the image the prosecution had painted of him as a manipulative control freak and schemer.

The day's session was drawing to a close as the questioning came around to Anne Marie Fahey. "The biggest flirt I ever met," Capano said. She'd been after him to go out with her, not the other way around; she'd chased him, even though he hadn't run very hard. They became lovers, occasionally breaking apart, but always coming back together again. He was a confidante, big brother, lover, and sugar daddy all rolled into one.

He said Fahey hadn't told him that she was

dating Michael Scanlan in fall 1995, and that he'd had to find that out for himself, and that it hurt him a little. He'd had Scanlan "checked out," to make sure he was an okay guy.

Capano said that in February 1996, they were closer than ever, and were talking about getting married. Concerned by her eating disorders, he'd borrowed money from Gerry and put in some of his own to make up $25,000 in cash, which he'd offered to her in person, to pay for her stay at some kind of therapeutic clinic. He claimed she threw the cash back in his face.

That ended the day's testimony.

On December 21, Tom Capano began his testimony at the morning session by "apologizing" to the jurors for some things he'd said the week before. Specifically, when he said he'd "checked out" Michael Scanlan, there was nothing sinister in it, he just wanted to make sure that he was a good guy. He apologized for saying Debby MacIntyre was one of the least attractive members of the law firm's social set. He said it must have been the medications he was on that made him misspeak himself. He cleared up the point that his salutation to Susan Louth in one of their letters, "Dear slutty little girl," was endearing and not pejorative. When his mother had once referred to Susan Louth as "that slutty little girl," Capano and Louth had made a private joke of it, that was all.

Capano said that at one time Anne Marie
Fahey said she'd been extremely "promiscuous," and had had herself tested for AIDS.
She'd told him all her secrets and all those of
her family, too. Of course, he would never vio-
late a confidence. That was probably a little
message to the Faheys in court, who were suing him and his brothers. He knew some bad
things about them, which he said had been
told to him by Annie. This brother was an abusive drunk; that one was absent-minded. He
said he knew Kathleen Fahey-Hosey because
she had gone out with a friend of his, that she
was pushy and petty and he didn't have much
use for her.

He spoke of his and Annie's one big trip
together, an August 1995 four-day sojourn at
an exclusive Virginia resort. He thought it was
a success. It was the same trip that Fahey had
later told a friend was the worst time of her
life, a "disaster." It wasn't long after that that
the romance between her and Capano came
apart, as she broke up with him for the first
time. Then came September and his separa-
tion from his wife, Kay. By the winter months
of 1996, Capano and Fahey were together
again, and had resumed a sexual relationship.
The affair was in a state of transition, perhaps
deepening into something more lasting, Capano implied.

Capano said he spent June 27, 1996 closing
a bond deal for the city. At about 6:30 P.M. he
picked up Anne Marie Fahey and drove to

Panorama. He said that during the drive, Fahey expressed her dislike for her psychiatrist, Dr. Neil S. Kaye. He explained that her "somber" mood at the restaurant, noted by waitress Jackie Dansak, was in reality caused by that server's botching an appetizer order, and bringing breaded fried calamari instead of the more special calamari sauteed in garlic. He said that as a former waitress, Fahey resented such carelessness. "She was very upset about that."

They left Panorama about 9:15 P.M. and returned to Wilmington. Upon arriving at her apartment, they decided to watch *ER* together. They decided to go to his house, so she ran upstairs to her apartment to change clothes.

Contrary to most testimony, including that of defense witnesses, he said that Fahey hadn't changed her clothes when she went upstairs, but returned wearing the same floral-print dress which the prosecution had entered into evidence. It wasn't the same, Capano said. Annie had two virtually identical floral-print dresses, and the one in the apartment was the other one.

Ten minutes later she came down to his Jeep, still wearing the same floral-print dress she had worn to dinner. Capano said he figured she was going to change into a T-shirt and men's gym shorts he kept in his house for her. Arriving at his Grant Avenue house, a five-minute drive, they stretched out on the love seat. Fahey kept her dress on, but took off her pantyhose to get comfortable. During the show, she fell asleep. The phone rang about 10:45 P.M. but he didn't answer it. About 11 P.M., Capano said, he went downstairs, checked his phone messages and learned the caller was Debby MacIntyre. He returned the call, telling her not to come over because he had company.

Not long after, he said, he was startled to look up and see Debby entering the den, having apparently used her key to enter his house. He said, "The next thing I know, Debby MacIntyre is in the room. She was pretty ballistic. We didn't even hear her come because of the sound of the air conditioner. She was very upset. She snapped about why I was with another woman. I'm trying to say relax, calm down."

He stated that he said to himself, "Oh boy, is this a situation."

Capano continued. "She pulled out a gun, from a straw handbag-type purse. Annie said, 'Capano, what the hell is this?' "

He said he stood in front of Debby, while Annie pulled her pantyhose back on. She laughed at the strange woman standing there with the gun and he didn't take it all that seriously himself—it was all too utterly fantastic. Debby began sobbing and turned "red from the neck up."

"She said, 'All these years I waited for you. I might as well shoot myself,' " Capano stated.

He said that she put the gun to her head and he grabbed her arm and there was a shot.

Capano held a dramatic pause, head down. "Debby shot Anne Marie. I'm absolutely, positively certain it was accidental. She bought the gun in May and must have had it with her.

"After the shot, we couldn't believe it." Debby said she didn't think that the gun was loaded. Fahey had a wound on the right side of her head, a bullet hole behind her ear. CPR was tried, but to no avail. She was dead. "There was no pulse, no breath. I checked her eyes. Her eyes were open.

"My whole life was flashing before me," he said. "I really and truly didn't believe it. Debby was crying and she's hysterical. I'm trying to calm her down. I always thought I had guts, but I just wanted to protect myself and Debby."

(A possible answer to the question of why Capano maintained, against all the evidence, that Anne Marie Fahey had worn the floral-print dress to his house: Capano's account of her death had Annie being shot while pulling on her pantyhose as Debby waved her gun. Common sense says it's unlikely that Fahey would have bothered to put on pantyhose under those conditions, but it was necessary for Capano's scenario to work. If she'd been clad in a relaxed jogging suit outfit on a hot summer night, it was unlikely she'd be wearing pantyhose underneath.)

Testimony continued, as Capano said that

he got Debby calmed down, telling her that it was his fault because he had never told her about Anne Marie. He then took her to her car outside and told her to go home. "I broke down. I fell apart. I was screaming at myself."

After five minutes, he got it together. He wrapped her body in blankets and put it in the cooler, along with her shoes and, eventually, the gun. He then drove to her apartment, taking some groceries and a gift he had bought her, a Talbot's pantsuit she had wanted.

He said that while he was at her apartment, at 11:52 P.M., as phone records show, he used star-69 to call back the person who had last called her. He said he wanted to make sure it wasn't him. When a man answered, Capano hung up. It was Kenneth Boehl, a top MBNA executive, from whose phone Michael Scanlan had called Annie earlier that evening. Capano turned on the air conditioner and exited.

On Tuesday, December 22, Capano resumed his testimony. Phone records showed that he and Debby MacIntyre had spoken at 12:38 A.M. on June 28. MacIntyre testified she called because they had argued during an earlier phone call. Capano said she called because of the shooting, that she was still upset. He claimed he said, "This is my fault. This is my fault because I love you. You didn't know there was a clip in the gun." He said he told her to come back and help him move the cooler, sofa, and carpet. "I couldn't do it myself."

She returned about 1 A.M. He'd put the gun in the cooler with Fahey. They moved the cooler down the steps to the garage. They rolled up the carpet, dragged it downstairs and rearranged the den's furniture. MacIntyre left between 2 A.M. and 2:30 A.M.

Capano said, "It occurred to me the best way to dispose of the cooler was burial at sea. Selfishly, I had to protect myself and, unselfishly, protect Debby.

"No, I did not fire the gun," he told the jury. "I decided I was going to keep it secret and bury the cooler with Anne Marie in it."

He decided he would need his brother Gerry's boat, moored at Stone Harbor, New Jersey. He arrived at Gerry's Brandywine Hundred home on Friday at 5:45 A.M. They agreed to meet at the defendant's home at 8:30 A.M. He went to Kay Capano's house and borrowed her Chevrolet Suburban, which had a large cargo space. He drove to Tower Hill School, where he took his morning walk at about 7:30. He and Debby MacIntyre met at 8 A.M. at the track as planned, he said, as she drove to her job at nearby Tatnall School. They made plans to spend the night together. He got in the Suburban, met Gerry Capano, and went to Stone Harbor.

He said there was little talk on the way to Stone Harbor. They loaded the boat and headed out to sea, stopping to get gas on the way out. He said that after he weighted down Annie's body with the chain and anchor, he closed his eyes and tipped the cooler over, sinking her. "This was somebody I loved," he said.

After docking in Stone Harbor at 3:30 P.M., the brothers returned to Wilmington, arriving about 5 P.M. They took the bloodstained love seat and carpet to a Dumpster at a Capano worksite operated by the family's development company. He spent Friday night with Debby MacIntyre at her house.

On Saturday morning, he went to Air Base Carpet and bought a replacement rug and some padding. He then went home and spent the night with his daughters, who had come to his house.

At 11:30 P.M., Kim Horstman called, saying that Anne Marie Fahey was missing, and did he know where she was? No, he told her.

After the FBI got involved in the case and raided his home on July 31, 1996, he decided to keep quiet. That continued after his arrest. He said he figured he'd just wait around until the bail hearing, when he was sure to be released. "I was selfish. I was hoping to keep myself from any harm and to protect Debby and Gerry." When the bail hearing came around and his release didn't happen, and MacIntyre "turned" into a government witness and was lying about him, he still kept silent about the truth because, he said, "To this day

I can't believe Debby would be like this. I was out of my mind."

His prison antidepression medication was increased, zonking him out so he couldn't think straight. His thought processes were already scattered from the sensory deprivation of solitary confinement over the months. He was a zombie, not knowing what he was doing, which would explain his abortive schemes to have Debby MacIntyre's house burglarized, and/or have her and Gerry Capano "hit."

He said that there was a high-level conspiracy involving President Clinton and Governor Carper. It was a plot against Tom Capano.

With that, the trial broke for the Christmas recess.

Returning on December 28, trial resumed as the defendant once more took the stand. A shortage of razors at Gander Hill had left him looking scruffily unshaven. He said that there was no way he dominated Debby MacIntyre—why, she had even mocked the idea in one of their letters.

As the direct examination wound down to its conclusion, a weary Oteri asked, "Did you kill Anne Marie Fahey?"

"No, a thousand times no," Capano insisted. "I loved Anne Marie Fahey."

"No further questions, Your Honor," Joe Oteri said.

That ended the friendly questions. Now

came the hostile, as Colm Connolly began his cross-examination. It was an encounter he'd been anticipating with relish for the last two and a half years. This was a showdown. The courtroom was an arena and defendant and prosecutor viewed each other with mutual distaste. During cross-examination, Connolly kept his face blank, but Capano didn't bother to hide his loathing for the prosecutor. Oddly, they'd both attended Archmere, where they'd both been elected student president. Connolly had attended at the same time as Gerry Capano, but they hadn't known each other.

Connolly tagged Tom Capano as a liar, forcing him to concede that he'd asked Louis Capano to lie to a federal grand jury and asked Debby MacIntyre to lie at his bail hearing. Capano agreed, saying, "I never told anyone the truth. I lied to everyone."

As they sparred, Capano tried to break up the other's timing, cross-questioning him (which, being an attorney, he knew was a violation of court procedure), alternately sighing, sneering, and adopting the long-suffering air of a martyr being persecuted by an evil inquisitor. There was one exchange where Capano showed some real rancor. When Connolly brought the questioning around to Capano's daughters. "Don't go there," Capano warned him tightly.

Connolly backed off from that subject for the present. He had time. He brought the questioning around to Anne Marie Fahey's violent death, zeroing in on the story that Debby MacIntyre accidentally shot Fahey during a botched suicide try.

Capano said, "I remember taking the gun from Debby. She said it wasn't loaded. She didn't know how it could have happened."

Connolly recalled Capano's testimony of December 21, when he'd said that he'd picked up the gun from the floor, where Debby had dropped it. Capano couldn't account for the discrepancy.

In a gruesome passage, the defendant told of putting the body in the cooler sideways, tucking her into a fetal position as she lay on her right side. "I had to force her feet in . . . but I didn't break any bones."

Why had he gone back to Anne Marie Fahey's apartment? "It makes no sense," Capano said. "I was out of my mind. I was operating on nothing but panic. It was just something I did."

But it did make sense, according to Connolly, who suggested that Capano had done it for a very good reason, to save his own skin. By making it appear Anne Marie Fahey had returned to her apartment on her own, he hoped to deflect suspicion from himself.

Later, Connolly elicited the revealing observation that the defendant "trusted" the Wilmington State Police, who "played fair," rather than the corrupt federal monolith that was conspiring to railroad him.

Earlier, Capano had spoken of throwing "hand grenades" in his defense. Now Connolly tossed yet another of his own, bringing up the subject of Squeaky Saunders and that long-ago murder that Capano had prosecuted him for. Had Saunders's crime served as a model for the killing of Anne Marie Fahey?

Capano called the idea "nonsense," maintaining that her death had nothing to do with the Squeaky Saunders case. Why, he hadn't really even been involved in it, except on a kind of superficial administrative level. Connolly confronted him with transcripts of the case, quoting from it to show the leading role Capano had played.

That broke up Capano's timing, getting under his skin. He became testy. Later, he shouted an outburst against Connolly for ignoring threats received by Capano's children and putting them in danger.

The judge admonished him. "You will limit your remarks to the appropriate response or I will take the appropriate action." As the day wore on, the increasingly combative tone of the exchanges and Capano's belligerent demeanor prompted the judge to say, "I will not surrender control of this court to the defendant or anyone else."

Later, Connolly asked Capano, "Ever hear of Linda Marandola?"

That prompted a vehement defense objection. They'd heard of her, all right. Court recessed for the day.

The next morning, the judge ruled on the previous day's defense objection, sustaining it and keeping the jury from hearing about how Tom Capano had stalked and schemed against another woman who'd rejected him. But the prosecution was hoping to get it in later, in the penalty phase.

Connolly confronted Capano with e-mails and letters he'd written to Debby MacIntyre and Anne Marie Fahey. He went after the crucial exchange in the prison telephone call where MacIntyre had said that she'd told prosecutors the truth about the gun. Connolly pointed out how Capano's "Do you know what you've done to me?" reaction was inappropriate if, as he'd been saying, the truth was that Debby had really killed Anne Marie Fahey by accident. He should have been overjoyed at being cleared.

Capano said that it was during the second, unrecorded conversation they'd had later that he'd accused her of the killing and of now trying to hang it on him. He blustered, "Don't pretend that second phone call didn't happen! I was a sucker. She took advantage of me."

On that note, court went in recess for the New Year's holiday.

On January 4, 1999, court resumed and Colm Connolly returned to the offensive. He confronted Tom Capano with the fact that the brother who'd stayed loyal to him, Joey Capano, had once been charged with unlawfully imprisoning a former girlfriend and forcing unwanted sexual activity on her. Capano had handled the case, successfully pleading it down to a misdemeanor charge of criminal mischief and assault and defusing a potential conviction and prison term. Connolly was able to get it into the record because while on the stand, Capano had denied it had happened.

Finally, the questioning came around to the subject of Capano's daughters. Ever since the subject had come up in late August 1996, of having his daughters' blood tested so their samples could be tested against the blood droplets found in the den, it had driven Capano into a cold fury.

Connolly pressed hard on an increasingly agitated Capano, once more asking him if he had indeed used his own daughters as part of the murder cover-up.

Now, it was Capano's turn to go ballistic. Enraged, he shouted, "You're a heartless, gutless, soulless disgrace of a human being!"

The master manipulator had blown his cool, shouting, ranting, and raving on the stand. It was scary, a rage so intense that a juror might well be convinced that a man in its grip could put a bullet in the brain of a beautiful young mistress who was trying to get away from him.

Capano calmed down as the bailiff approached to escort him from the stand and out of the courtroom, at the judge's request. That ended the session for the day.

On January 5, at the start of the session, outside the hearing of the jury, Judge Lee laid down the law to a seemingly contrite Tom Capano. The judge told him there would be no more apologies to the jury or the court, that he was instructed merely to answer the questions with no further outbursts, digressions, and diversions, or the court would apply sanctions—"Draconian sanctions,"—to the defendant.

Connolly rose and questioning resumed on the daughter question, with Capano maintaining that he and wife, Kay Capano, had prevented the girls from giving blood samples to protect them from any further "degradation" by prosecutors. He admitted that he'd tried to get his mother to testify against his brother Gerry. He blamed politics and the victim's brother Robert Fahey for much of his current troubles.

Thus ended the cross-examination. On redirect, Joe Oteri made a few half-hearted attempts to rehabilitate his client's shredded image, without making much headway.

More to the point was the defense team's ace-in-the-hole, surprise witness Kim Johnson. A substitute teacher, she lived across the street from Debby MacIntyre. She testified that on a night of June 1996, at about 11:45 P.M., a loud engine noise had caused her to look out her front window, where she saw MacIntyre's car pull up to a screeching halt in her driveway.

She said that she saw MacIntyre get out of the car, stumble, and choke off a wailing sob before disappearing into the house.

She was unsure of the exact date, but thought that it had been somewhere in the last two weeks of June before the Fourth of July. She said that the incident had an eerie quality which had caused it to stick in her mind.

The implication for the defense was that it verified Tom Capano's story of Debby MacIntyre coming to his house on the night in question and precipitating the death of Anne Marie Fahey. Johnson had no ax to grind, so was seemingly an unbiased witness.

The witness also stated that she had never been interviewed or questioned by any detectives involved in the case. The defense made much of that, too, saying it buttressed the concept of the government conspiracy to "get" Tom Capano.

The prosecution tried to minimize the testimony, pointing out that the witness had been some 200 feet away from Debby MacIntyre's house and it had been at night, making it difficult to see what was happening. She might have seen MacIntyre's daughter. Kim Johnson admitted that she had refused to let detectives enter her house the previous night to examine the vantage point, not wanting to disturb her children.

It remained to be seen what effect her testimony would have on the jury, after Gene

Maurer's withering cross-examination of Mac-Intyre.

The defense followed with two Capano relatives, neither of whom appeared to any great effect at this late date. First called was Capano's brother-in-law, Lee Ramunno, who testified to some family dirt on Gerry Capano, saying that he'd thought Capano was keeping silent to protect him. He also claimed that the government's treatment of Marguerite Capano was "harassment," the likes of which he'd never seen in a professional lifetime as a lawyer. His wife, Marian Capano, followed, stating her belief that her brother was incapable of murder.

The defense's last witness was Robert Donovan, recalled to go over yet again the prosecution's strategy of catching Tom Capano by first "taking down his inner circle." After which, the defense rested.

On rebuttal, the prosecution called Robert Gallagher, a handyman who testified that six months after Anne Marie Fahey's death, he'd installed a bright floodlight over the garage in Debby MacIntyre's driveway. Before that, the fixture had been a dimmer, low-wattage bulb. When Kim Johnson testified that she had seen MacIntyre under the pair of shining floodlights, they hadn't yet been installed and wouldn't be for another half-year.

Kim Horstman returned to the stand, to tell of how Capano had lied to Anne Marie Fahey, falsely claiming that his daughter was suffering

from a brain tumor, using it as a ploy to resume contact with her. A representative of the
Beretta gun manufacturer testified that the
weapon's makeup required it to be deliberately
fired to work, and that it had a fail-safe mecha-
nism to prevent it from going off in the event
of such "flinch" shots as the one which Capano claimed had resulted when he grabbed
Debby MacIntyre's arm to thwart her suicide
attempt.

Last on the stand was Annie's brother
Robert Fahey, reading from the letter which
the family had sent to Tom Capano in the
early days of Annie's disappearance, pleading
with him to come forward and tell what he
knew. Less heart-tugging but no less pointed
was the moment when Joe Oteri made the mistake of asking him if he would hire an attorney, then ignore the advice that he gave him?
Eyeing Capano, Robert Fahey said pointedly,
"I believe I've heard that happens sometimes."

The courtroom broke into laughter, causing
the judge to have to strike his gavel for order.

Wednesday, January 13, was reserved for
closing arguments. Prosecutor Colm Connolly
spent a half-day reviewing the evidence, telling
the jury that Tom Capano's version was unten-
able, that he was a liar, manipulator, and cold-
blooded killer who slew Anne Marie Fahey and
dumped her body at sea. He hit hard on Gerry
Capano's testimony, the physical evidence of
the cooler, Debby MacIntyre's gun purchase,
and Capano's demeanor on the day after the

death and also on the stand. The jurors had seen the hidden face of Capano, he argued, and it was the face of a murderer.

He slammed Tom Capano's version of events. Debby MacIntyre wouldn't have come over to his house that night—she knew better, she was under his thumb, well-trained. She wasn't the suicide type, either. Her businesslike demeanor at the Tatnall School on Friday, June 28, testified to in court, showed that she was unaware of the events that had transpired the night before at the Grant Avenue house.

Capano's action in trying to get Nick Perillo to arrange a burglary of Debby MacIntyre's house showed not innocence but guilt. It wasn't credible that Anne Marie Fahey, surprised by a stranger, a disturbed woman with a gun, would have paused to pull on her pantyhose. She would have run out of there and put them on later. It wasn't possible for Anne Marie Fahey to have been shot the way Capano described. It was mechanically impossible for the gun to have fired under those circumstances and the trajectory of the fatal slug after Capano had supposedly grabbed MacIntyre's gun hand didn't jibe with the known facts.

If the slaying was an accident, why did Capano get rid of the body? He would have known that an autopsy would prove whether it was an accident or not. This was no accident, it was murder.

What's more, he used his lovers, his brothers, and his daughters to try to help get him off the hook. His story didn't add up because it was a lie.

"Now is the time for justice," Colm Connolly concluded. "The only verdict consistent with all the evidence is a vote of guilty."

Then it was defense's turn. Joe Oteri rose, wearing the lucky cowboy boots which Capano had forbidden him from wearing during the rest of the trial for fear of alienating the staid Wilmington jurors. Connolly had pounded the facts, now Oteri would pound the prosecution's witnesses. He began his closing.

He said that Tom Capano was no saint, to be sure, and that some of his behavior was indeed reprehensible, but the question before the jury wasn't if he was a nice guy or not, it was whether or not it was proved beyond a reasonable doubt that he'd killed Anne Marie Fahey.

How could there be anything but reasonable doubt, he asked, with witnesses like Gerry Capano, with his booze-and-drug-riddled brain confabulating wiseguy scenarios that never were? Or, worse, Debby MacIntyre? He slammed her as a foul-mouthed, sex-freak pervert, a liar, and a shameless "devil of deceit."

Surely Kim Johnson's powerful testimony had introduced irrefutable evidence pointing toward reasonable doubt regarding the defendant's guilt. And Louis Capano and Gerry Capano were a pair of false liars who'd set their hands against their brother.

"In the jury room, you walk in the valley of decision. The agony of decision is upon you," he concluded. His closing had taken almost exactly as long as Connolly's had, over three and a half hours each.

Ferris Wharton delivered the final summation, saying that whatever and whenever Kim Johnson saw what she thought she saw, it wasn't believable here in the courtroom. Capano hadn't done what he had done for the last two and a half years because of a tragic "accident." Wharton suggested that the jurors try a little experiment by pretending to hold a gun to their head as Capano claimed MacIntyre had and then see if it was plausible or even possible for someone else to knock the gun away before the trigger was pulled. Tom Capano was a sociopathic plotter who almost got away with murder, he said. Don't let him get away with murder.

Closings ended, and at 9:30 P.M. the judge began charging the jury.

Jury deliberations took 21 hours over three days. During that time, among other things, every juror tried out Ferris Wharton's suggested experiment of holding a make-believe gun to their heads, and no one was ever able to duplicate Capano's alleged feat of knocking the gun hand away faster than a trigger pull. At another point, a female juror got into the cooler, to see how Anne Marie Fahey would have fit.

On the morning of January 17, as court was

called in session, the jurors returned, filing into the jury box with their verdict: "We find the defendant guilty as charged."

When the crowds gathered outside the courthouse heard the verdict, they cheered.

At the penalty hearing on January 20, 1998, the jurors heard testimony from Linda Marandola, whose name had been teased during Colm Connolly's cross-examination of Capano, but which was not allowed into evidence until now. She told her story of being sexually involved with Tom Capano and how he had stalked, persecuted, plotted, and eventually run her out of the state.

Next, Anne Marie Fahey's family members took the stand, telling of the traumatic emotional devastation wrought by her mysterious disappearance and the revelations of her violent death.

Testimony was also placed in evidence regarding Capano's intractability as a prisoner, and his continuing efforts to circumvent the rules and extend his reach beyond his cell into the outside world, including other prisoners as go-betweens and agents. Even behind bars, he was a dangerous individual, vengeful and unregenerate.

The defense countered with Capano's family members, pleading for his life. Even his ex-wife, Kay Capano, and his in-disgrace brothers Gerry Capano and Louis Capano begged that he be spared the death penalty. Daughters

Christy and Jenny took the stand, saying that they loved their father and wanted him to live.

The prosecution called its last witness, convict Henry Fusco, a convicted pedophile and current resident of Gander Hill prison who'd been delegated by Capano to be one of his go-betweens to the outside world. He said Capano had asked him to phone his daughters periodically to check up on them, and had used him as a middleman to get letters to them.

For the defense, an aged priest, a longtime family friend and confidante, spoke out for Capano's life to be spared. So did Marguerite Capano, his mother.

After closing arguments, the jury retired to their deliberations and voted ten to two to recommend that Capano receive the death penalty, which in the State of Delaware is administered via lethal injection.

Official sentencing was on March 16, 1999. Judge William Swain Lee was not bound by the jury's recommendation, and had the option of handing down a sentence of life without parole.

Judge Lee described the defendant as a ruthless, remorseless killer, a malignant force from whom no one who had crossed him could ever be secure, even if he was incarcerated for life. Then he sentenced Tom Capano to death.